# CHALLENGES FOR WORK AND FAMILY IN THE TWENTY-FIRST CENTURY

## SOCIAL INSTITUTIONS AND SOCIAL CHANGE

*An Aldine de Gruyter Series of Texts and Monographs*

EDITED BY

James D. Wright

Vern L. Bengtson and W. Andrew Achenbaum, **The Changing Contract Across Generations**

Thomas G. Blomberg and Stanley Cohen (eds.), **Punishment and Social Control: Essays in Honor of Sheldon L. Messinger**

Remi Clignet, **Death, Deeds, and Descendants: Inheritance in Modern America**

Rand D. Conger and Glen H. Elder, Jr., **Families in Troubled Times: Adapting to Change in Rural America**

Joel A. Devine and James D. Wright, **The Greatest of Evils: Urban Poverty and the American Underclass**

G. William Domhoff, **The Power Elite and the State: How Policy is Made in America**

G. William Domhoff, **State Autonomy or Class Dominance? Case Studies on Policy Making in America**

Paula S. England, **Comparable Worth: Theories and Evidence**

Paula S. England, **Theory on Gender/Feminism on Theory**

George Farkas, **Human Capital or Cultural Capital? Ethnicity and Poverty Groups in an Urban School District**

Davita Silfen Glasberg and Dan Skidmore, **Corporate Welfare Policy and the Welfare State: Bank Deregulation and the Savings and Loan Bailout**

Ronald F. Inglehart, Neil Nevitte, Miguel Basañez, **The North American Trajectory: Cultural, Economic, and Political Ties among the United States, Canada, and Mexico**

Gary Kleck, **Point Blank: Guns and Violence in America**

Gary Kleck, **Targeting Guns: Firearms and Their Control** (paperback)

James R. Kluegel, David S. Mason, and Bernd Wegener (eds.), **Social Justice and Political Change: Public Opinion in Capitalist and Post-Communist States**

Thomas S. Moore, **The Disposable Work Force: Worker Displacement and Employment Instability in America**

Clark McPhail, **The Myth of the Madding Crowd**

**Talcott Parsons on National Socialism** (*Edited and with an Introduction by Uta Gerhardt*)

James T. Richardson, Joel Best, and David G. Bromley (eds.), **The Satanism Scare**

Peter H. Rossi and Richard A. Berk, **Just Punishments: Federal Guidelines and Public Views Compared**

Alice S. Rossi and Peter H. Rossi, **Of Human Bonding: Parent-Child Relations Across the Life Course**

Joseph F. Sheley and James D. Wright: **In the Line of Fire: Youth, Guns, and Violence in Urban America**

David G. Smith, **Paying for Medicare: The Politics of Reform**

Dana Vannoy and Paula J. Dubeck (eds.) **Challenges for Work and Family in the Twenty-First Century**

James D. Wright, **Address Unknown: The Homeless in America**

James D. Wright and Peter H. Rossi, **Armed and Considered Dangerous: A Survey of Felons and Their Firearms, (Expanded Edition)**

James D. Wright, Peter H. Rossi, and Kathleen Daly, **Under the Gun: Weapons, Crime, and Violence in America**

James D. Wright, Beth A. Rubin, and Joel A. Devine, **Beside the Golden Door: Policy, Politics, and the Homeless**

Mary Zey, **Banking on Fraud: Drexel, Junk Bonds, and Buyouts**

# CHALLENGES FOR WORK AND FAMILY IN THE TWENTY-FIRST CENTURY

Dana Vannoy and Paula J. Dubeck
*Editors*

ALDINE DE GRUYTER
New York

## About the Editors

**Dana Vannoy** is Professor of Sociology at the University of Cincinnati.

**Paula J. Dubeck** is Associate Professor and Head of the Department of Sociology at the University of Cincinnati.



ALDINE DE GRUYTER
A division of Walter de Gruyter, Inc.
200 Saw Mill River Road
Hawthorne, New York 10532

This publication is printed on acid free paper ♾

**Library of Congress Cataloging-in-Publication Data**
Challenges for work and family in the Twenty-First century / Dana Vannoy and Paula Dubeck, editors.
p. cm. — (Social institutions & social change)
Includes bibliographical references and index.
ISBN 0-202-30567-8 (alk. paper). — ISBN 0-202-30568-6 (pbk. : alk. paper)
1. Work and family—United States—Forecasting. 2. Women—Employment—United States—Forecasting. 3. Twenty-first century—Forecasts. I. Vannoy, Dana, 1940– . II. Dubeck, Paula, 1944– . III. Series: Social institutions and social change.
HD4904.25.C447 1998
306.3′6′0973—dc21 98-11940
CIP

Manufactured in the United States of America

10 9 8 7 6 5 4 3 2 1

## Contents

## Contributors to the Volume

"The Need and Challenge to Better Integrate Work and Family Life in the Twenty-First Century"

***Paula Dubeck*** is associate professor and head of the Department of Sociology at the University of Cincinnati, where she has served as head since 1983. Professor Dubeck's research interests focus upon work, namely, the organization of occupations and professions. Her special interest is women working in traditionally male-dominated professions. Recent work includes the book, *Women and Work: A Handbook* (1996, coedited with K. Borman).

"Gender and the Future of the Family: Implications for the Postindustrial Workplace"

***Kathleen Gerson*** is professor of sociology at New York University, where she teaches courses on gender, work, family, and social change. She is the author of several books including *No Man's Land: Men's Changing Commitments to Family and Work* (1993) and *Hard Choices: How Women Decide About Work, Career, and Motherhood* (1985). She has been awarded numerous research grants, and she is now examining work-family conflicts in the modern workplace and how children growing up in diverse types of families have responded to the gender revolution at home and at the workplace.

"Downsizing the American Dream: Work and Family at Century's End"

***Michael Wallace*** is professor of sociology at Indiana University. His research has centered on the organization of work, technological change in the workplace, and the consequences of workplace change for workers. He is currently investigating the political economy of industrial restructuring as it is reflected in state economic development policy and outcomes. He has served as editor of *Research in Social Stratification and Mobility* and has coauthored a book with Y. Bradshaw, entitled *Global Inequalities* (1996).

"Toward a Twenty-Four-Hour Economy: The U.S. Experience and Implications for the Family"

***Harriet Presser*** is professor of sociology and director of the Center on Population, Gender, and Social Inequality at the University of Maryland, College Park. Professor Presser is a past president of the Population Association of America, and she was named George Washington University's Distinguished Alumni Scholar in 1992–1993. Her recent research interests focus on the high prevalence of nonstandard work schedules among employed

Americans, both its causes and consequences. She is also writing on international population policy issues from a gender perspective.

"Race and the Family Values Debate"

***Maxine Baca-Zinn*** is professor of sociology and senior research associate at the Julian Samora Research Institute at Michigan State University. As a specialist in race relations, gender, and the sociology of the family, she has written extensively about the family lives of women and men in Latino communities. Among other books, she is the coauthor with D. S. Eitzen of *Diversity in Families* (1996) and coeditor with P. Hondagneu-Sotelo and M. A. Messner of *Through the Prism of Difference: A Sex and Gender Reader* (1997).

"Dominant and Minority Couples: An Exploratory Analysis of Strategies for Family Economic Well-Being"

***Marilyn Fernandez*** is assistant professor in the Department of Anthropology and Sociology at Santa Clara University. Her research interests lie in the areas of economic, social, and cultural adaptation of Asian-Americans, cross-cultural issues in domestic violence, and adolescent childbearing. She and Professor Kwang Chung Kim have coauthored two papers published in the *International Migration Review* on the self-employment of Asian-Americans. ***Kwang Chung Kim*** is professor of sociology at Western Illinois University and has conducted extensive research on immigrant life in America and the Asian-American experience. Recently, he was a visiting scholar affiliated with the Center for the Study of Urban Inequality of the University of Chicago. He has edited a book entitled *Korean and African American Conflict: An Inter-City Comparison.* Currently, he is conducting a nationwide survey of three hundred second-generation Korean-Americans regarding their life experience, with an emphasis on ethnic identity formation.

"Being a Part-Time Manager: One Way to Combine Family and Career"

***Phyllis Hutton Raabe*** is professor of sociology at the University of New Orleans, where she teaches and researches on work-family trends and policies. She is particularly interested in viable, alternative work arrangements and career paths in work organizations. Recent publications include "Constructing Pluralistic Work and Career Arrangements" in *The Work Family Challenge: Rethinking Employment* (1996, edited by S. Lewis and J. Lewis, and "Work-Family Policies for Faculty: How Career and Family Friendly Is Academe?" in *Academic Couples* (1997, edited by M. Ferber and J. Loeb).

"Economic Transition in a Company Town: The Politics of Work and Possibility in Post-Industrial Rochester"

***Andrew J. Perrin*** is presently a doctoral candidate at the University of California, Berkeley. His research focuses upon the links among work organizations, community, and politics. He is presently conducting follow-up research about these interconnections in Rochester, New York.

"Negotiating Parental Involvement: Finding Time for Children"

***Kerry Daly*** is associate professor in the Department of Family Studies at the University of Guelph, Ontario, Canada. His research interests focus on the social meaning of time, the social construction of fatherhood, and the nature of adoptive relationships. He is author of *Families and Time: Keeping Pace in a Hurried Culture,* coeditor of *Qualitative Methods in Family Research* (1992), and coauthor of *Adoption in Canada* (1993). ***Anna Dienhart*** is assistant professor at the University of Guelph. Her research is broadly located in questions of gender relations in the family. Publications from her recent research include articles on how family therapy practices may effectively engage men in family change. Anna is also an active couple and family therapist, and she uses narrative family therapy to engage fathers in responsible parenting of their children.

"Working Mothers, Welfare Mothers: Implications for Children in the Twenty-First Century"

***Toby Parcel*** is professor of sociology and associate dean, College of Social and Behavioral Sciences, at The Ohio State University. With E. Menaghan, she is coauthor of *Parents' Jobs and Children's Lives* (1994, the winner of the American Sociological Association Family Section 1996 Goode Book Award). She recently edited a special issue of the journal *Work and Occupations* (1996), entitled "Work and Family: Research Informing Policy." Her current research interests concern welfare receipt and child well-being, and the effects of neighborhood and school characteristics on child outcomes.

"All Children Can Read at Grade-Level by the End of Third Grade. Is It Possible?"

***George Farkas*** is professor of sociology and political economy at the University of Texas, Dallas. He is also the founding director of the Center for Education and Social Policy at the university, where he initiated the program Reading One-to-One, with M. Warren. The chapter in this volume was used as the basis for President Clinton's "America Reads Program." Recent publications include the book, *Human Capital or Cultural Capital? Ethnicity and Poverty Groups in an Urban School District* (1996); and "Cognitive Skill, Skill Demands of Jobs, and Earnings among Young European Americans, African Americans, and Mexican American Workers," with P. England, K. Vicknair, and B. Kilbourne in *Social Forces* (1997). ***Keven Vicknair*** is at the University of Texas-Dallas and administers the Reading One-to-One Program. ***Jim Fischer*** and ***Ralph Dosher*** are retired employees of Texas Instruments Corporation who have been actively involved in assisting public education in Dallas.

"Occupational Constraints on Women's Entry into Management"

***David J. Maume, Jr.*** is associate professor of sociology and present director of the Kunz Center for the Study of Work & Family at the University of Cincinnati. He teaches and researches on the sociology of work, poverty, social inequality, and the U.S. welfare state. Recently published articles include "Reconsidering the Declining Significance of Race: Racial Differences in Early Career Wages," "Cognitive Skills and Racial Wage Inequality: Reply to Farkas and Vicknair," with S. Cancio and T. D. Evans, both in the *American Sociological Review* (1996). Presently he is engaged in research on the impact of occupational segregation on career mobility, and the effect of alternative work arrangements on men's participation in household work.

"Employee-Paid Health Insurance in a Changing Economy"

***Lisa A. Cubbins*** is assistant professor of sociology at the University of Cincinnati. She has worked as a research associate at Battelle Research Center in Seattle studying various health issues in the United States. Recent publications include "Gender Race, Class and Self-Reported STD Incidence," with T. Koray and J. Billy, *Family Planning Perspectives* (1995), and "Coital Frequency among Never-Married Women in the U.S.," with T. Koray, *Journal of Sex Research* (1992). Professor Cubbins's interests are labor market processes, gender inequalities, and health concerns, and she is now studying the effects of family and work upon alcohol use.

"The Impact of Family Care-Giving to the Elderly on the American Workplace"

***Judy Singleton*** has an M.A. in Social Work and is a doctoral candidate in the Department of Sociology at the University of Cincinnati. She is also an adjunct instructor at Antioch University and in the School of Social Work at Raymond Walters College of the University of Cincinnati. She has directed community-based care programs for the elderly, and she has presented numerous workshops and seminars for social work and long-term care professionals.

"Problems and Prospects for More Effective Integration of Work and Family in the Twenty-First Century"

***Dana Vannoy*** is professor of sociology at the University of Cincinnati, where her teaching and research interests are family, work, gender, and identity development. During her career she has served as the founding director of Women's Studies and director of the Kunz Center for the Study of Work & Family at the University. She has published several articles and the book

*Equal Partners* (1989) with W. Philliber on the effects of high achievements of women for marriage relationships. Presently she is completing a study of Russian families: *A Window to Russian Private Life: Russian Couples in 1996,* which will appear in 1998.

# Introduction to the Volume

# I

# The Need and Challenge to Better Integrate Work and Family Life in the Twenty-First Century 1

Paula J. Dubeck

As the 1990s have progressed, increasing attention has been given to the unprecedented changes that have transformed the nation's social landscape over the past three decades and that hold profound implications for twenty-first-century America: the decline in high-paying manufacturing jobs, the emergence of a service economy, women's taking advantage of higher education opportunities, the rapid entry and continuous full-time participation of married women with children in the labor force, corporate "downsizing," escalating divorce rates, changing perspectives on the welfare system, and "the squeeze" for middle-aged women between child care and eldercare. In this context, the long-standing assumption that work (economy) and family are distinct spheres has been challenged, as these competing forces disrupt and question the legitimacy of what was perceived to be the "normal" or "usual" ways of doing things.

Among the many societal changes, the dramatic increase in women's employment has had pivotal effects. Not only have women entered the labor force in unprecedented numbers, they also have *stayed* there. With increases in educational attainment combined with legal changes and the enforcement of new laws, women have sought and attained positions that have been unavailable to them in the past. Further, gender-based barriers to opportunities have been challenged as the labor force experience of women has increased while positions associated with such experience have not appeared to open up. Other characteristics have distinguished the more recent pattern of women's employment from the past. For example, having young children has not resulted in women abandoning employment. Indeed, in 1990, nearly 59 percent of married women with children under the age of six were employed, compared to only 19 percent in 1960; similarly, nearly 74 percent of married women with school-age children were employed in 1990, compared to 39 percent in 1960 (Mandelson 1996).

The changing patterns of women's labor force participation have been central in drawing attention to institutional arrangements as a focus of research. Our social institutions, as Bellah and colleagues note in *The Good Society* (1991), give meaning and place to the individual. They link individuals to the larger society and provide the framework for interpreting how individual actions combine to serve the broader social good or need. Yet with the changing patterns of employment for women, traditional institutional arrangements are proving unworkable. The rules and norms that governed traditional family arrangements often appear not to "make sense." As Bellah et al. (1991) repeatedly point out, the narrow specifications of roles can not respond to the complexity of issues that have emerged within the new social context.

Equally important, in the 1990s it has become clear that the institutional patterns that characterize the changing economy are playing an increasing role in framing the issues families face. As a result, scholarly inquiry, which traditionally has posed questions that imply separation of these two spheres, is recast in terms of the *explicit interdependence* between work and family.

Finally, scholars are being challenged to examine a number of work and family issues through a lens that incorporates the intersection of gender, race, and class. These analyses bring to the forefront the complexity of our current society and the context in which emerging institutional arrangements must respond in the future. Not only are "traditional family visions" no longer effectively meeting the needs of individuals and families in society, but their "idealization" also hinders a careful examination of the alternative forms of family life that have emerged in response to the needs of various subgroups. To the extent that these forms are responses to competing work and family pressures, they serve as possible ways for restructuring institutional arrangements in society. An investigation into and discussion about their functioning is essential for understanding the needs of a complex and changing society.

It was with these issues in mind that the Kunz Center for the Study of Work and Family organized the conference, Agenda for the 21st Century Labor Force, held in Cincinnati, Ohio, in November 1996. There were a number of premises underlying the focus of the conference. First, *we, as a society, cannot "go back"* to embrace the family arrangements of the past, but neither do we have an effective set of institutional arrangements that will serve us well in the future. Second, there is *a need for a shift in the frameworks* we use to address current issues relating to work and family. Third, it is not just the family that must respond to change; rather, the economy—in this case, *employers—must be cognizant that significant labor force changes,* particularly the role of women and the work and family interface, *will affect their fortunes* as they define their place in a global economy. Finally, *policymakers in government and corporations have a responsibility to grapple with these issues* in order to develop informed policy affecting work and family.

A number of distinguished authors were invited to participate in the conference to address issues that emerged from changes mentioned above and to set the stage for a discussion of what we as a society must consider from this point forward. Others presented research on alternative strategies that seek to respond to the changing relationship between work and family. Except for the piece by Daly and Dienhart, all of the chapters included in this volume were selected from presentations at that conference.

## ORGANIZATION OF THE VOLUME

We have organized the chapters in this volume into three parts. In Part II, *Present Realities: Setting the Stage,* authors provide an overview of the current context in which a dialogue about the family, work, and their interdependence take place. Chapter 2, by Kathleen Gerson, provides an overview of the current state and future prospects for family structure and gender relations. She argues that the lack of change in structures in work and other public institutions has created difficult dilemmas for both men and women and that solutions to these personal dilemmas will require fundamental changes in the structure of the twenty-first-century work place.

In Chapter 3, Michael Wallace grapples with issues associated with corporate "downsizing," including constraints on the corporation and costs imposed upon the worker. In discussing job creation he examines the contingent labor force and the changing value of a college degree. In looking toward the future, he discusses "growth" occupations over the next decade in terms of the working conditions and standard of living they are likely to provide American workers.

Drawing on a similar theme, Harriet Presser, in Chapter 4, discusses the demand for nonstandard work schedules that can be expected at the turn of the century. Pressures for this demand include the growth of the service economy, the employment of women, and the aging of the population. Presser then addresses the implications of nonstandard work schedules for family life.

In the final chapter in this section, Maxine Baca-Zinn critiques the family values debate. She asserts that in ignoring the changing economic and social conditions that today's families encounter, the "traditional family values" approach also limits our understanding of the structure of today's family. Using three current perspectives—feminist, political economy, and family demography—Baca-Zinn incorporates elements of each to bring a better understanding of the structure of today's family. The Latino family serves as an example to illustrate the issues that emerge in the family today.

*Part III, Work and Family Adaptations in a Changing Context,* explores approaches to work and family that reflect the complexity of today's society. In Chapter 6, Marilyn Fernandez and Kwang Chung Kim analyze employment and income for minority and white dual-earner couples. In documenting different patterns in employment and earnings for different minority groups, they argue the need to broaden the scope of discussion about minorities in American society beyond the traditional biracial (black/white) framework. Rather, a multiracial framework is needed so that attention can be paid to the variations in minority family adaptation in the current economy.

A different form of adaptation is discussed in Chapter 7 by Phyllis H. Raabe in her research on part-time managers as a strategy to combine family and career. Her research on part-time managers in the Federal Civil Service examines both the advantages and costs, which represent competing "tugs" of career and family experienced by persons in such positions. The need for a supportive supervisor underscores the social dynamic needed to provide the underpinnings of a successful structural change.

A different approach to the changing nature of the economy is provided in Chapter 8, Andrew Perrin's study of the social impact of downsizing for a community. While the number of jobs lost is regularly reported in accounts of downsizing, a neglected concern is the loss of "social capital" for a community. Perrin elaborates on the loss of social capital in terms of community leadership, the emotional costs on workers, and the narrowing perceptions of "political possibility" for change.

Chapter 9 presents the complexity of work and family changes by exploring the social and contingent nature of fathers' involvement with children. Kerry Daly and Anna Dienhart extend the framework for examining father involvement in parenting to one that is co-constructed with mother involvement. Further, time emerges as the medium through which parenting is constructed and negotiated. In approaching father involvement with children as a negotiated phenomenon, the authors lay ground for a framework that incorporates the internal dynamics and external constraints on parenting.

In Part IV, the final section of the book, *New Considerations for the Twenty-First Century,* authors examine timely issues that have important implications for employment and family well-being in the coming decade. In Chapter 10, Toby Parcel explores the implications of the new (1997) welfare reform for women and families. By carefully examining the transition from welfare to work for women over time, she highlights the complexity of both the transition and the implications for child well-being. In addition, she recommends steps states might take to assist families in making the transition from welfare to work.

Chapter 11, by George Farkas and colleagues, focuses on the preparation of future members of the work force. Examining the essential need for the *ability to read* for someone to become a productive member of society, Farkas et al. present the challenge of bringing elementary school students to grade-level reading by third grade. The authors discuss the present four elements that add incrementally to bringing students up to grade-level reading by the third grade.

A different work force issue—women's entry into management and promotion opportunities—is addressed by David Maume in Chapter 12. Using the Panel Study of Income Dynamics (PSID), Maume examines the promotion opportunities for college-educated women. He is exploring factors that could account for the "glass ceiling" effect in management. His findings suggest that women managers in traditionally female jobs have appreciably fewer chances to move up in the organization, compared to those in traditionally male jobs, and that women have not benefited from employment in the public sector. The results provide thought-provoking considerations for career choices by women in managerial ranks.

A related issue, availability of employee health benefits, is examined in Chapter 13 by Lisa Cubbins. In particular, Cubbins examines how women and minorities have fared given changes in labor market conditions that affect employer-paid health insurance. Both race and gender have significant effects on the receipt of such benefits. Further, the same effects are found in 1989 and 1995, suggesting stable patterns of difference in employer-paid health insurance for men and women, and for whites and for minorities.

The final chapter in Part IV, Chapter 14 by Judy Singleton, focuses on an increasingly urgent issue for middle-aged adults: the need to care for dependent elderly family members. Singleton summarizes a number of the job-related problems of employed caregivers, as well as the related strains and conflicts that are felt at home. The situation poses a significant issue for employers because of their need to retain an experienced work force. In light of this increasing need, policies and services that are present today or needed in the future are reviewed.

In Part V, Dana Vannoy offers some thoughtful conclusions related to the chapters included here and challenges us to search for new institutional arrangements promoting good family relationships as well as high productivity.

## A FINAL COMMENT

The Agenda for the 21st Century Labor Force Conference proved to be a fertile ground for the exchange of information and ideas concerning the work and family interface in the coming decades. The premises associated with the need for new institutional arrangements for and between work and family provided a stimulating and challenging format from which to start the discussion. It is our hope that the selections included in this book provide the reader with information and ideas to help in the process of rethinking and reinventing the institutional arrangements which embody work, family, and their interdependence.

## REFERENCES

Bellah, Robert N., Richard Madsen, William M. Sullivan, Ann Swidler, and Steven M. Tipton (1991). *The Good Society*. Alfred A. Knopf: New York.

Mandelson, Dayle A. (1996). "Women's Changing Labor-Force Participation in the U.S." Pp. 3–7 in *Women and Work: A Handbook*, edited by Paula J. Dubeck and Kathryn Borman. New York: Garland.

# Present Realities: Setting the Stage

# II

# Gender and the Future of the Family: Implications for the Postindustrial Workplace 2

Kathleen Gerson

## INTRODUCTION: AN OVERVIEW OF FAMILY AND GENDER CHANGE

Before we can even begin to imagine the future, much less predict it, we need to have a clear picture of the present. The prospects for the future of work and family life depend on how well we are able to assess the choices we face and the limits on those choices. As we approach a new century, we need first to understand where we have been and where we are now.

The closing decades of the twentieth century have witnessed changes in family life and the position of women so vast that they constitute a genuine revolution. These changes have rearranged the foundations of our society and affected every level of social life and almost every member of our society. They are also irreversible. For reasons that will become clear, no politician, social critic, or government policy can make them go away. The broad contours of recent family and gender change are here to stay.

This revolution may be irreversible, but it is also incomplete. While families are irrevocably changed, the workplace has not changed to an equal degree. One consequence is that upheavals in the lives of women, men, and children have created both new opportunities and new dangers. If we hope to take advantage of the opportunities and avoid the dangers, we would do well to heed Reinhold Neibuhr's famous creed, which admonishes us to accept the things we cannot change, change the things we can, and, most of all, to recognize the difference between the two. In this essay, I will try to clarify the differences between what we need to accept and what we are capable of changing. More specifically, I will explain how basic and irreversible changes in family life and gender relationships require equally fundamental changes in the organization of work and child rearing.

## THE CURRENT STATE AND FUTURE PROSPECTS OF AMERICAN FAMILIES

As the twentieth century draws to a close, married couples with a breadwinning husband and homemaking wife account for less than 15 percent of all American households, down from almost 60 percent in 1950. Nontraditional families, including dual-earner couples, single-parent households, and single adults, make up over 85 percent of American households. No one family form predominates today. Instead, we have many family types. As important, American society is experiencing increasing confusion and disagreement about which family forms are better suited to provide for the needs of adults and children.

Why has considerable family diversity replaced the homemaker-breadwinner family? There are several reasons, and they are all rooted in fundamental social and economic changes that are intrinsic to modern societies and over which no one person or group can exercise control. First, and perhaps foremost, are changes in the economic and social fortunes of women. Women have experienced both the expansion of opportunities for outside employment and the foreclosing of opportunities to stay home. While modern women still face glass ceilings, employment discrimination, and wage inequities, they have made unprecedented advances into the labor force and more significantly into male-dominated jobs and professions. In addition to the pull of job opportunities, factors such as divorce, declining male wages, and the general devaluation of homemaking as a life pursuit have pushed most women to build their lives around paid work—whether or not they are married and whether or not they have children.

The most dramatic changes have occurred among younger generations of women and among mothers of young children. Over two-thirds of married women with preschool children, including children under the age of one, are in the paid labor force. In addition, women's earnings are not mere "extras." In the United States today, over half of working women bring home at least half the household income and that includes many women who support their families on their own. Among two-paycheck couples, nearly one in four wives earns as much or more than her husband. In short, most women are now committed to paid work, and most families depend on their earnings.

A second and related change has occurred in the economic and social fortunes of men. In general, male earnings have stagnated and many men now face declining economic fortunes. While highly educated men are doing well economically, most men are not able to earn a "family" wage that pays enough to support a whole family. In this situation, men can either choose to share breadwinning with a partner, or they can choose to avoid making commitments that imply economic responsibilities. But what most men can no longer do is provide enough income to be the sole support for wives and children.

A third, highly important change has occurred in the structure of marriage. Higher rates of divorce, postponed marriage, and permanent singlehood have produced a situation of fluid sexual partnerships. Marriage remains popular, to be sure, and the vast majority of Americans continue to marry. Moreover, those who divorce express a strong desire to remarry, and most of them do. But people are more likely to postpone marriage, to divorce or separate, to remarry, and to stay single than they were forty years ago. The institution of marriage is not dead, but it no longer represents a permanent commitment to another partner for life.

Americans may feel uneasy about the rise of nonpermanent and diverse sexual partnerships, but they are even more uncomfortable with the prospect of adopting laws that would force people to get married or stay married against their will. Most now see marriage as an emotional commitment that need not—and perhaps should not—be sustained if the emotions change. In sum, marriage has been redefined as a fluid institution—one where people can, and often do, change partners more frequently and less predictably.

Finally, in a fourth and related development, the growth in changeable and more voluntary sexual partnerships has produced a growing separation between marriage and parenthood. The birthrate has stabilized at a low, but steady level, but the circumstances under which people bear and rear children have changed dramatically. Women have more choice about whether, when, and under what circumstances to become a parent. And since parenthood is less tied to being married or staying married, men have more freedom to avoid the responsibilities of parenthood. As a result, a rising proportion of children are spending at least some portion of their childhood with a single parent, usually a mother, or a stepparent.

These changes in the nature of marriage, the labor market, and the economy have created both new opportunities and new dilemmas for women and men. Women have new opportunities to seek personal and social independence outside the domestic sphere. Yet with divorce rates stabilized at about 50 percent, women can no longer look to marriage as a lifetime guarantee of economic support. And mothers face a "damned if you do and damned if you don't" set of choices, in which they are expected to bring home income but are admonished for leaving their children in the care of others.

In a similar manner, men face new options and new pressures. They have more freedom to avoid the pressures of supporting a wife and children. But they also find it harder to live up to the breadwinning ethic that defines manhood in terms of successful breadwinning. Moreover, men have become dependent on the earnings of wives and find themselves having to compete with women at the workplace. They face new pressures to give up power and control in the home and at work.

ges in the lives of women and men have reverberated into the en. The well-being of children was once largely tied to their mic position. Today their economic fate depends more on their umstances. A child whose mother is married or has a good job enjoys some measure of economic security. But a child whose mother is not married and cannot find a good job is economically vulnerable. And since the economic situation of women is readily subject to unexpected change, children's circumstances are also less predictable and more vulnerable. Given children's dependence on women's earnings, which on average remain well below that of men, it is no mystery why children are the largest group living in poverty in the United States today.

For better or worse, these trends are highly interrelated, deeply anchored, and mutually reinforcing. And while Americans tend to think of them as unique to the United States, the other advanced, industrial societies are experiencing similar changes. The fact that these economic and social changes are both international in scope and highly interrelated suggests that they are also irreversible. No government policy, no matter how well-intentioned, can turn back the clock to an earlier period (when Ozzie and Harriet dominated our national consciousness).

Although these trends have eroded the prevalence of the homemaker-breadwinner family, they have not produced a new predominant pattern. To the contrary, we have diverse family forms competing with each other for social and political support. We can expect the men and women of the twenty-first century to follow diverse and uncertain paths as they create new family patterns with limited support and few previous models.

## RESISTANCE TO CHANGE IN THE WORKPLACE

It is fair to ask at this point why these changes, if they are so widespread, have caused so much political upheaval and personal consternation. Why do we continue to give homemaker-breadwinner families a moral authority that dual-earner, single-parent, and single-adult households cannot yet claim? Why do we continue to feel nostalgic for the "fifties' family" of Ozzie and Harriet even though the fifties were an atypical period? We continue to label this family form "traditional," even though it was never as widespread or idyllic as many imagine. Indeed, the drawbacks of that period's "feminine mystique" spawned the movement for women's equality that followed. And, images notwithstanding, even Harriet Nelson was a working mother.

So why is there so much resistance to accepting family and gender change and making the necessary adjustments in other spheres of society? To a large extent, nostalgia for the past persists because of a lack of change in other American institutions. The persistence of economic, work, and community arrangements based on the assumption of a "traditional family" has made it difficult to create viable alternatives.

In the United States, intransigent employers, ambivalent policymakers, and a socially divided citizenry have made it difficult to create new institutions to support new family forms. Most notably, the gender and family revolution has "stalled" at the door of the workplace, where children's needs remain largely invisible and parenting desires—whether felt by a man or a woman—are often penalized and frowned upon.

The lack of a supportive and consistent response on the part of employers or government agencies has created dilemmas and cross-pressures for parents and workers of both sexes. For example, even though employers no longer routinely pay enough to support a nonworking parent at home, they have not rearranged the workplace to accommodate the family needs of either female or male workers. Even though most families depend on either two earners or one parent, the rigid "forty-hour-plus" work week, based on the notion of a male career and a woman at home, remains the model. So does the lack of child care programs, making it difficult for employed parents of either sex to combine work and child rearing.

In a similar way, even though divorce and out-of-wedlock childbearing are leaving a growing proportion of children dependent on the earnings of mothers, women still face a gender gap in earnings and work opportunities. In this context, workers with the greatest responsibility for children's welfare have access to the fewest resources to meet them.

In the case of dual-earning couples, the structure of work and the economy continue to make it difficult for couples to share domestic burdens equally. The culture of the workplace penalizes anyone for taking time off to be with children, but the notion of "mommy tracks" reinforces the idea that women, not men, should be the ones to pay the price. And since men still tend to earn more than women, husbands (and wives) face incentives to recreate domestic inequality even if both parents work. The persistence of traditional work arrangements, predicated on the homemaker-breadwinner family, has created new personal dilemmas about how to balance work and family responsibilities, new social uncertainties over who will care for our children, and deepening political conflict about the proper roles of women and men.

In my research on how men and women are choosing between work and family, I found that the lack of genuinely satisfactory avenues to resolve the conflicts between parenting and work has left everyone facing dilemmas and cross-pressures. However, different groups are responding to these dilemmas in different ways. A significant minority of women and men are trying to hold onto a modified homemaker-breadwinner pattern despite the changes taking place around them. Women in these situations continue to see themselves as domestic and to place home and family first even when they work outside the home. Traditionalist men continue to see themselves as the breadwinner and main family provider even when their wife works outside the home.

For these men and women, eroding male incomes and women's entry into the workplace have not changed their outlook on gender and family. They maintain an unequal division of labor at home despite the need for a wife's income. As a result, the women feel overburdened, and the men feel under siege because their incomes are eroding and they are losing control. In an effort to shore up declining support for their life-style, these traditionalists tend to oppose family change as well as social policies that appear to support new family forms or to help women workers.

But most women and men do not fall in this "traditionalist" category. They are striving to create new ways of living and new relationships between the sexes. Nontraditional women place work commitment on a par with family commitment and recognize that work will play a central role throughout their lives. These women do not distinguish between choice and necessity. Most work both because they want to *and* because they have to. They need the income their earnings provide, but they also derive personal satisfaction from earning money, participating in the public sphere, and pointing to personal achievements beyond marriage and motherhood.

These women face difficult choices about how to make room for motherhood within the context of committed work. One strategy for coping with this difficulty is to have fewer children. Some women are even deciding to have none at all. It appears, for example, that about 15 to 20 percent of baby-boom women will not have any children at all, and another 10 to 15 percent will have only one child. Most women, however, wish to combine committed work and motherhood, despite the difficulties. These working mothers express great pride in their accomplishments and, in general, do not express the feelings of guilt that journalists ascribe to them. Unlike the media image of the "guilty working mother," these work-committed women feel proud but exhausted and, most of all, frustrated about the lack of support at work and elsewhere.

Among "nontraditional" men, the choices are just as confusing. The bad news is that many men are responding to the decline of breadwinning by avoiding parental involvement. Some have decided never to marry or have children. Although it is difficult to measure childbearing patterns for men, there are probably about as many men as women who will not have children. However, those men who have children but do not care for them are of far greater concern. These "estranged fathers" or "deadbeat dads" find themselves avoiding responsibility for their children in the wake of divorce or an out-of-wedlock birth. A growing but still small number of men are retaining some sort of custody after a breakup, but most divorced and unmarried fathers spend little time with their children and contribute less financially.

The news, however, is not all bad. A substantial group of men are becoming "involved fathers," who participate extensively in caring for their children. About a third of the men I studied, for example, either were or wished to be intimately involved in child rearing and were willing to make work and financial sacrifices to do so. These men found themselves facing the same conflicts and cross-pressures that confront working mothers. A hostile workplace culture and the lack of formal family-related policies made it hard for them to act on their desires for family involvement.

The outgoing secretary of labor, Robert Reich, recently lamented in the *New York Times* that the difficulties of balancing challenging work with child rearing had led him to resign from "the best job I ever had or will have." Sadly, instead of proposing needed changes in the organization of work, he concluded that "you can't have your cake and eat it, too." But, unlike Robert Reich, most working parents don't have a choice. They have to work, and they need viable ways of being good parents and committed workers at the same time.

## WHERE ARE THESE TRENDS LEADING?

What conclusions can we draw from these findings and trends? First, only a minority of twenty-first-century families will have the option and the desire to recreate the homemaker-breadwinner family. Those who do are likely to feel threatened by the erosion of their way of life and will likely oppose further change. Their opposition will no doubt fuel continuing political controversy over "family values." This opposition to social policies that support women's equality or family diversity can make change more difficult, but it cannot prevent family change from occurring.

We cannot go backwards because most men and women are not able to do so and would not choose to do so if they could. Most men are no longer able or willing to support their families alone. Most women are not able or willing to go solely back into the home. They shoulder too many economic responsibilities and derive too much satisfaction from the independence and sense of accomplishment that paid work provides. In fact, the demise of welfare for poor women shows how little support remains for the idea that mothers should stay home. And finally, there is little support for public policies that would force people to marry and stay together for life no matter how bad the circumstances or how much their feelings change.

Some sort of family and gender role change is inevitable, but the specific paths are far less clear. Put simply and boldly, things can get better, and they can get worse. As more women join the labor force, gender inequality can decrease or it can find a new form in the public sphere. As men offer less financial support to families, they can become more involved parents, or they can become more estranged from family life. As nontraditional families continue to grow, the workplace can respond to new family needs, or it can leave workers facing increased work-family conflicts. And as children become increasingly dependent on either two-earners or a single parent, we can develop new ways of caring for them, or we can leave them to fend for themselves.

Whether things get better or worse depends on how we respond to inescapable but still uncertain change. Our responses depend, in turn, on how well we are able to clarify the choices we face and the things we can do to make the twenty-first century a time of expanding opportunities rather than diminishing hope.

## POSSIBILITIES FOR THE TWENTY-FIRST-CENTURY WORKPLACE

If incomplete change, and not change itself, has caused our current impasse, then genuine resolutions to the dilemmas of twenty-first-century families depend on our ability to accept the inevitability of change and make it more complete. We need to stop resisting change and focus instead on making it more equitable and more comprehensive. Specifically, this means fashioning workplace and social policies that accept the family change and make the necessary adjustments in the workplace. This means building social policy around the twin goals of gender equity and work-family integration. Neither, taken alone, is sufficient.

In the absence of gender equity, "family-friendly" workplaces will simply recreate old forms of inequality in a new way. The notion of a "mommy track," for example, leaves women who want children at a disadvantage and leaves men without the option to be involved in child care. In the absence of family-friendly policies, gender equity can mean the equal right to sacrifice family needs in favor of overwork. Both women and men will have to choose between involved parenthood and success at work. A recent study found, for example, that very few of the companies known for their family-friendly policies had good records for promoting women. Similarly, companies with a larger number of women at the higher levels of management did not support family involvement.

In order to move beyond the conflict that forces workers to choose between work success and family involvement, we need both equal opportunity for women workers and workplace support for parents of either sex. This will require change on a variety of fronts.

First, we need to reorganize the structure of work and careers, replacing the ubiquitous and rigid forty-plus hours a week, eight-plus hours a day, with a more flexible and responsive structure. Workers need more flexibility in establishing the boundaries between home and work and the scheduling of work and family activities over the day, the week, the year, and the work career. Flexible work scheduling recognizes that both work and family demands are likely to ebb and flow over time, and gives workers more discretion over how to balance the two without sacrificing the quality of their accomplishments. With the rise of the service sector and decline of manufacturing, this trend has already begun. It is time to institutionalize work and career flexibility in such a way that it helps workers and parents as well as their employers.

Second, we need to establish parental rights at the workplace, including supports and incentives for fathers as well as mothers. In a world where employers no longer routinely subsidize an unpaid partner at home, they have a practical as well as moral obligation to help workers meet their family needs. If family-support policies are confined to women, however, such policies (like "mommy tracks") will become a new form of sex segregation at work. Therefore, formal policies must be supported by changes in the culture of the workplace that do not penalize parents of either sex for having and taking care of children and that encourage and expect men to be involved at home. When formal policy is not enforced and embedded in workplace culture, it will not protect the rights of workers or parents.

Third, we need to ensure that women enjoy genuinely equal work and economic opportunities. Twenty-first-century families will depend on the earnings of women, and equal economic opportunity is the best way to ensure that children do not suffer. In a related manner, one way to get men more involved in child care is to raise the earnings of women. If women earn more, men will face more pressure and have more options to share caring for their children. On the other hand, if men are absent, then well-paying jobs and good child care options for mothers are the best ways to support their children.

In concert with equal opportunity, we thus need to create community, work, and domestic supports for children. In other words, we need to restructure child rearing in a world where mothers cannot do it all. This means establishing child care supports that extend beyond the nuclear family and the individual mother. We need local community as well as workplace options for child care. And we also need to hold fathers equally responsible for the care and nurturance of their children.

## HOW DO WE GET THERE FROM HERE?

To be sure, these goals sound utopian. If these goals seem unreachable, it is useful to remember that fundamental change always seems elusive before it is accomplished. There was a time when the forty-hour work week and the minimum wage seemed out of reach. Yet now that these rights have been won, we take them for granted. Moreover, many of the changes suggested here are already under way, albeit in a haphazard fashion.

Equally important, widespread gender role and family changes have created the social and political constituencies for these initiatives. Today, a growing group of women face strong incentives to push for change and vote for social policies that support working women and family diversity. The large percentage of women voting for candidates who support "women's issues" is not likely to disappear as family change proceeds apace. Though like-minded men may form a smaller group, as the electoral gender gap seems to indicate, there are strong indications that a growing group of egalitarian men, who want to be involved fathers, are prepared to join with working women to support equal rights and workplace change.

Employers also face good reasons to implement these changes. First, they have a practical and moral obligation to offer new ways of supporting families, since most no longer pay enough to allow for a wife to stay home. Second, employers are increasingly dependent on the work of women and men with family responsibilities. They will benefit from workers who are happy and sane. Most studies show that family-friendly policies save more money then they cost and enhance worker productivity. And finally, businesses and corporations rely on a well-functioning society. They, too, have a stake in providing for the well-being of children, who will ultimately become the next generation of workers. During this period of economic transformation, work organizations would do well to recognize that change will find them if they do not seek it.

As we approach the twenty-first century, gender role and family changes pose a number of challenges and difficulties, but they also provide an unprecedented opportunity to achieve greater equality between women and men, to expand personal options for integrating and sharing work and family responsibilities, and to secure the well-being of our children. Reaching these goals means working on a variety of fronts at the same time—at work, in our communities, in politics, and at home. Yet if we continue to decry and resist family and gender change, we will simply increase the dilemmas it has spawned.

## CONCLUSION

Sociologists usually focus on "what is" rather than "what could be." Yet most of us also believe in the power of human thought and action to channel social forces that would otherwise control our destiny. The future may not be entirely open to our whims, but it is also not completely determined. It depends on the political and personal choices we make today in the face of new circumstances and constraints. Fifty years from now, let us hope that those looking back on this period in our history will conclude that this was a time when people grasped the significance of the changes they were living through and had the courage and foresight to make the transition to a world where men and women share equally in the joys and burdens of family and work. For that to happen, we must first accept the fact that family diversity and the need for gender equality are here to stay. The fate of the next generation and the twenty-first century depend on our responses.

# Downsizing the American Dream: Work and Family at Century's End

# 3

Michael Wallace

## INTRODUCTION

Welcome to the wonderful, whacked-out world of downsizing! It's a curious world indeed. It's a world where the productivity of U.S. workers has increased by 37 percent since 1970, but where their real wages have declined by 14 percent. It's a world where the average corporate CEO in America makes 120 times the wages of the typical factory worker (Calhoun, Light, and Keller 1997:428). It's a world where AT&T lays off 40,000 workers and is rewarded by an immediate $6 billion increase in its value on the stock market; and where AT&T CEO Robert Allen pockets a $12 million increase in his stock option for doing the dirty deed. It's a world where 11 percent of college-educated male workers—mostly managers and professionals—lost their jobs between 1991 and 1993, ostensibly years of economic expansion. And it's a world where the largest private employer in Mexico is General Motors and the largest private employer in the United States is Manpower Temporary Services (*New York Times* 1996).

There's something very wrong with this picture. The comfortable job security of your father's generation is a thing of the past. In the 1990s, downsizing and job *in*security have become an unfortunate way of life for millions of workers as American corporations undergo the wrenching transformation toward an information-driven global economy. The numbers do not lie, or do they? While the numbers reflected in low unemployment, low inflation, a booming stock market, and soaring corporate profits suggest a buoyant economy, the convulsing undercurrents of merger mania, corporate retrenchment, and technological dislocation bespeak a different story. Millions of American workers live a "duck and dodge" existence as they shadow box with an economic system they can neither vanquish nor fully comprehend. In jeopardy is a middle-class way of life that has been the hallmark of the American worker since the end of World War II.

## THE SCOPE OF THE DOWNSIZING CRISIS

"Downsizing" has become the fashionable term to describe the complicated combination of threats to the job security of the American worker in the 1990s. It captures simultaneously the constraints imposed on the corporation and the costs imposed upon the worker, and perhaps for that reason, has a more sanitized, neutral ring to it than clumsier euphemisms of a previous era such as "deindustrialization," "corporate restructuring," "reductions in force," "outsourcing," "technological displacement," or simply "layoff." *Downsizing* first crept into the corporate lexicon when the deindustrialization of the blue-collar workers in the 1970s began to have repercussions for white-collar, middle-management, and professional positions in the 1980s. It has now become a term that applies with equanimity to all times and places where the news is bad for workers: We hear of downsizing of blue-collar workers, white-collar workers, government workers, academics, and even welfare recipients.

How pervasive is downsizing? Consider that according to statistics from the U.S. Bureau of Labor Statistics, the U.S. economy has lost nearly 43 million jobs since 1979; but it has created 27 million more jobs than it has lost in that same time. But here's the catch: most of the new jobs pay much less than the jobs they replaced and offer less potential for rewarding careers. As a result the American family of the 1990s is running faster to stay in the same place: after controlling for inflation, median family income has increased from about $35,407 in 1970 to about $38,782 in 1994 (both figures in 1994 dollars), but this modest increase has occurred only because more households have second and third earners, who work longer hours or work at multiple jobs. In 1995, the fourth year of an economic expansion, U.S. corporations laid off almost a half million workers. Some of the biggest corporate downsizers in the 1990s are shown in Table 1.

The pain of downsizing has touched millions of families. A national survey carried out by the *New York Times* in December 1995 sought to discover the extent of downsizing. The *Times* survey deliberately defined "job layoffs" as layoffs that are not temporary or seasonal in nature, but due to "employer downsizing, reductions in force, corporate restructuring, permanent plant closings, jobs moving overseas, or jobs just permanently disappearing." By this definition, about one-third of all households have a member who has been laid off at least once since 1980 and another 40 percent know of a friend, relative, or neighbor who has lost a job. Of those who had lost a job, 48 percent had been laid off more than once. Downsizing has very traumatic consequences for careers, families, and self-esteem. Of those who were downsized, 29 percent said that it created a major crisis in their lives and 47 percent said that it caused a minor crisis. Forty-three percent of those who were downsized took six months or more to find new work and 29 percent

*Table 1.* A Partial List of Major Corporate Downsizings (10,000 or More Laid Off) in the 1990s

| *Company Name* | *Year* | *No. of Layoffs* |
|---|---|---|
| McDonnell Douglas | 1990 | 17,000 |
| General Motors | 1991 | 74,000 |
| Boeing | 1993 | 28,000 |
| Sears Roebuck | 1993 | 50,000 |
| IBM | 1993 | 63,000 |
| Philip Morris | 1993 | 14,000 |
| Xerox | | 10,000 |
| Eastman Kodak | | 16,800 |
| Delta | 1994 | 15,000 |
| GTE | 1994 | 17,000 |
| Digital Equipment | 1994 | 20,000 |
| Nynex | 1994 | 16,800 |
| Lockheed-Martin Marietta merger | 1995 | 30,000 |
| Tenneco | since 1990 | 11,000 |
| United Technologies | since 1990 | 33,000 |
| AT&T | 1990–1995 | 83,000 |
| AT&T | 1996 | 40,000 |

exhausted unemployment benefits. Thirty percent were unable to find a permanent job to replace the one they had lost.

Perhaps one of the most debilitating things about downsizing in the current economy is that the constantly changing mix of jobs in the economy causes lasting disruptions in careers. It seems that not only people, but the very jobs that the new economy is churning out are being "downsized." Old, skilled jobs go away and the new jobs either require less skill or they require skills that downsized workers do not have. The result is a vicious cycle of downward mobility for many workers. The *New York Times* survey found that only about 24 percent of downsized workers were able to find reemployment in the same line of work and about 42 percent who found new jobs had to take jobs that paid less than their old jobs. Studies have shown that the income loss for many downsized workers is permanent: they never catch up with their colleagues in the industry who kept their jobs (Jacobsen 1978).

Rene Brown's story is an all too familiar portrait of downsizing and downward mobility. In the past fifteen years, she has been downsized out of three jobs, each time slipping further down the income ladder: an $8.50 an hour job in a meatpacking plant, a $7.25 an hour job in a bank mailroom, and a $4.75 an hour job loading newspapers. Now in her forties, she's making $4.25 an hour cleaning office buildings and sees little prospects for improvement with only a high-school diploma (*New York Times* 1996:14).

Education is a buffer against downsizing, but no guarantee. Male college graduates showed a modest 5 percent increase in real earnings between

1979 and 1992, while female college graduates gained 19 percent. However, unlike previous decades, more than half of downsized workers in the 1990s have at least some college education. In the topsy-turvy world of downsizing, *not* having a college degree is sometimes a plus. Robby Smith, a thirty-four-year-old engineer with an oil and gas consulting firm, is a few hours shy of a college engineering degree. His firm has already done some downsizing, but he figures his job is safe for now because the firm will reap greater savings by laying off colleagues who are higher-paid college graduates (*New York Times* 1996:31).

Another indication of the diminishing power of the college degree is reflected in some revealing statistics about future occupational growth from the Department of Labor. Table 2 shows the ten occupations that are projected to account for the largest number of new jobs between 1992 and 2005. Most of the occupations on the list are menial, low-wage jobs that require little college education—hardly the kind of jobs from which one launches lucrative careers.

Two exceptions—registered nurses and computer systems analysts—typically require a college degree. Only three—nurses, systems analysts, and truck drivers—provide an annual income level about $20,000 (in 1995 dollars). Cumulatively, the 6.3 million *new* jobs these ten large-growth occupations will generate for the twenty-first-century U.S. economy will average

*Table 2.* Where Will the Jobs Be? Top Ten Large-Growth Occupations, 1992–2005 (Employment Figures in Thousands)

| *Occupations* | *1992* | *2005* | *Number of New Jobs* | *Avg. Weekly Earnings* |
|---|---|---|---|---|
| Retail salespersons | 3660 | 4446 | 786 | $252 |
| Registered nurses | 1835 | 2601 | 766 | $643 |
| Cashiers | 2747 | 3417 | 670 | $195 |
| General office clerks | 2688 | 3342 | 654 | $333 |
| Truck drivers | 2391 | 3039 | 648 | $489 |
| Waiters and waitresses | 1756 | 2394 | 638 | $262 |
| Nursing aides, orderlies, and attendants | 1308 | 1903 | 595 | $275 |
| Janitors and cleaners | 2862 | 3410 | 548 | $263 |
| Food preparation workers | 1223 | 1748 | 525 | $181 |
| Systems analysts | 455 | 956 | 501 | $931 |
| Total new jobs created: 6,331,000 | | | | |
| Avg. yearly income: $19,649 (in 1995 dollars) | | | | |

*Source: Statistical Abstract of the United States* and *Current Population Survey.*

less than $20,000 per job (in 1995 dollars), not quite three-quarters the $27,000 mean income for *all jobs* in the 1995 economy.[1] This alarming evidence provides little solace for the downsized worker and suggests that education alone is no panacea for the reemployment of laid-off workers.

How are we to explain what some have called the greatest workplace upheaval in the twentieth century? And what are the consequences for workers and their families as we approach the end of the century? I address each of these topics in the remainder of the chapter.

## SPATIALIZATION AND THE SHIFT TO A DOWNSIZED ECONOMY

Schumpeter (1939) has noted that the capitalist economy is characterized by "a perennial gale of creative destruction" whereby the system constantly recreates itself out of the remnants of an earlier system. U.S. workers who have lived through the unprecedented workplace revolution of the last two decades can attest to the creative destruction taking place all around them. In this section, I outline a theoretical approach that situates the current downsizing problem in the broader political economy of U.S. capitalism, specifically the spatial restructuring of the labor process that began in the 1970s.

But first some background. In other research (Wallace 1996a) I have argued that the current configuration of workplace arrangements must be understood by analyzing the dynamics of capitalist economy in historical perspective. I build upon the framework developed by Gordon, Edwards, and Reich (1992) in which they argue that workplace organization in any particular period of capitalist development is an outgrowth of *social structures of accumulation* (SSA), which are historically specific institutional environments that facilitate the accumulation of profits. Social structures of accumulation undergo successive cycles of exploration, consolidation, and decay that last about fifty years. Inevitably, crises of accumulation press the limits of the prevailing SSA, creating the impetus for a transition to a new system. A period of *decay* in one SSA is simultaneously a period of *exploration* of new systems that will *consolidate* into the SSA of the next stage of capitalist development.

Gordon, Edwards, and Reich identify three major social structures of accumulation beginning in the 1820s, each associated with a major transformation in workplace organization and a dominant system of labor control exercised by capitalists over workers. First, the SSA of *proletarianization,* roughly from the 1820s to the 1890s, forged a wage-labor market out of a collection of farmers, artisans, women and children, and immigrants. These wage laborers submitted to a *simple control system* in which entrepreneurs or trusted supervisors exercised autocratic control over all aspects of work organization, often eliciting heroic efforts from workers on the basis of either loyalty or threats of dismissal. The proletarianization phases of capitalist development encountered two obstacles that it could not overcome: the control over the work process by skilled craftsmen and the burgeoning size of the capitalist firm, which rendered the face-to-face basis of simple control ineffectual.

The crisis in the proletarianization phase was answered with the mechanization of the labor process, which simultaneously reduced the skill levels required to perform the work and linked the firm's workers together in a vast, pulsating, interconnected system of production. Gordon, Edwards, and Reich refer to this period, which lasted from the 1870s to the 1940s, as the *homogenization* phase of capitalist development because of the manner in which technological changes leveled the skill requirements of workers in many industries. The dominant control system of this period was *technical control,* epitomized by the automobile assembly line, in which the pacing and control of work activities were embedded in machinery. The crisis of homogenization and technical control, evidenced in the labor unrest of the Great Depression of the 1930s, was that they galvanized a more solidary workers' movement that threatened, for a time, the continuation of capitalism.

Another deficiency of technical control was that it was not effective for reining in the expanding white-collar work force of the post-World War II period. So capitalists turned to a new SSA of *segmentation,* in which the labor market was divided into separate primary and secondary labor markets governed by different rules of work organization and skill acquisition. Racial and gender divisions further reinforced the occupational segmentation in the labor market. The dominant control system in this era was *bureaucratic control,* in which control of labor was encoded into bureaucratic rules and procedures of the organization. A key aspect of the era of bureaucratic control was a tacit *social contract* between workers and employers in which employers agreed to share the benefits of postwar prosperity in exchange for a promise of labor peace by organized labor. This social contract provided the promise of the good life for American workers who played by the rules—a good job with good wages, good fringe benefits, and long-term job security—the kind of jobs with which families could pursue their American dream. Indicative of the benefits of the social contract, real hourly wages increased by 51 percent between 1950 and 1970.

But the contract began to unravel in the 1970s. First, there was a slowdown in economic growth, which meant that companies had a tougher time holding up their end of the social contract. In the 1950s, corporate profit margins (profits as a percentage of sales) had averaged about 17 percent, but by the 1980s had fallen to about 9 percent (Samuelson 1996). If the pie was not expanding, companies would be increasingly hard-pressed to guarantee job security and fringe benefits like health care, pension plans, and paid vacations. Second, the oil crisis of the 1970s created spiraling inflation, which challenged families' ability to make ends meet. Inflation also strengthened the dollar in foreign trade, cheapening the cost of foreign goods, and opening the U.S. market to an influx of foreign consumer goods like automobiles and electronics, which threatened U.S. producers. Inflation also cheapened the cost of foreign labor for American firms, creating incentives for U.S. business to move domestic production overseas. Ready or not, the United States was entering the global marketplace on a grand scale.

Increasing globalization of the U.S. economy marked the onset of a new SSA, which I call *spatialization* (Wallace 1996a). Spatialization refers to the spatial restructuring of the labor process whereby employers are no longer constrained by spatial constraints in the organization of their businesses. No longer bound by conventional constraints on business location, employers may use the threat or actuality of relocation to achieve more desirable terms with their labor force. The emerging control system in this era is *technocratic control,* which hinges on technical expertise wielded by knowledge workers coupled with electronic technologies such as computers and microprocessors. A key component of technocratic control is "technoscience," which is radically restructuring every aspect of work to accommodate the forces shaping the global economy (Aronowitz and DeFazio 1994).

The first evidence of the new SSA of spatialization was the "deindustrialization of America," which began in the 1970s, in which millions of blue-collar workers lost their jobs as plants closed, moving their operations overseas or consolidating them into more streamlined operations domestically (Bluestone and Harrison 1979; see also Wallace and Rothschild 1988). Bluestone and Harrison document a loss of 38 million jobs in the 1970s, counterbalanced by the creation of about 37 million new jobs—primarily in the low-wage sector—during the same time. While blue-collar workers bore the brunt of the job losses, deindustrialization also hit managers and white-collar workers hard. Flaim and Sehgal (1987) show that by 1984, 51 percent of displaced experienced workers were from nonmanufacturing industries; 14 percent were managers and professionals; and 28 percent were from technical, sales, service, and administrative support occupations.

Bluestone and Harrison (1979) attribute deindustrialization to the "hypermobility" of capital, which allowed major corporations to set up, coordinate, and control multiple operations in far-flung corners of the world. Several factors contributed to this hypermobility: technological advancements in the transportation of raw materials and finished goods, and sophisticated communications technologies, which allowed U.S. companies to monitor their global operations on a daily basis from the comfort of their U.S. headquarters. In addition, technological advances in the labor process, coupled with the allure of huge, low-wage labor pools in Third World countries, spurred the migration of jobs beyond the U.S. border. The end of the cold war in 1988 helped make the world safe for capitalism, and U.S. business began reaching out to Eastern Europe, China, and Latin America (Bradshaw and Wallace 1996).

In the United States, workers who were fortunate enough to keep their jobs faced the prospects of accepting deep wage concessions and fringe benefit givebacks in the 1980s. Bitter labor struggles at companies like Hormel and Caterpillar frequently ended in futility as workers either buckled under or lost their jobs. During the heyday of the wage concession movement, average wage increases among unionized manufacturing workers plummeted from 10.2 percent in 1980 to 1.5 percent in 1986. Workers in nonunionized settings fared better in some cases but generally followed the pattern set by unionized workers. The long-term effect was to seriously depress the wage structure for middle-class workers and send a sobering message to workers who stepped out of line.

Piore and Sabel (1984) argued that the U.S. mass production economy was in crisis, too unwieldy to respond to changes in a rapidly changing global economy, and that we needed to create a new system of flexible specialization in order to compete on a global scale. The 1980s witnessed a historic rate of corporate mergers and reorganizations ostensibly designed to achieve this goal. But many of the mergers of the 1980s were acts of "paper entrepreneurialism" (Reich 1983), designed more to manipulate corporate assets on paper and appease stockholders' concerns about the bottom line than to produce any real improvement in productivity. The merger mania of the 1980s consolidated operations among many of the country's megacorporations, forcing the elimination of redundant positions in clerical, sales, middle-management, and professional jobs as well as more blue-collar jobs (Harrison and Bluestone 1988). Deregulation spawned labor strife and painful downsizing in airlines, communications, and, recently, utilities (Brown 1987; Walsh 1994). AT&T, the telecommunications giant, has eliminated about 154,000 jobs since 1985. All the while, technological innovation has eliminated, transformed, and created jobs with unprecedented rapidity in every sector of the economy.

Part of the lean and mean look of the new U.S. corporation is the unprecedented rise of contingent labor. The basic strategy is for corporations to reduce their permanent labor force to essential personnel who have demonstrated skills and expertise that the companies need and to farm out less essential or intermittent work to temporary workers on a contingency basis. Contingent workers are typically subject to lower pay than regular employees and are not eligible for fringe benefits.

The beleaguered American unions have been struggling against many of the precursors of the contingent labor movement for almost two decades: *whipsawing* (pitting two unionized plants in the same company against each other in order to force concessions), *two-tiered wage structures* (offering new employees lower wages and benefits than long-time employees), *outsourcing* (having workers in lower-paying, nonunionized plants do part of the work formerly assigned to unionized employees), and *industrial homework* (a special type of outsourcing where work is hired out on a contingency basis to individual workers in their homes). An especially pernicious form of contingent labor is the rise of *child labor,* in which U.S. corporations in industries like apparel and toys hire children in Third World countries to work in deplorable conditions for contemptibly paltry wages.

The contingent labor movement is moving ahead at full speed. Temporary employment firms such as Kelly and Manpower (the latter employs 767,000 workers as temps) offer employers contingent workers in data entry, clerical, word processing, general labor, light industrial, and warehouse work. Recently, "temping of America" has even begun to infiltrate professional, technical, and managerial occupations. Between 1982 and 1992, temporary employment grew three to ten times faster than overall employment, and two-thirds of all new employment in the private sector in 1992 was temporary jobs (Ansberry 1993). Another variant of the contingent labor movement is the use of independent contractors whom employers hire to work on short-term projects that were previously done in-house (Christensen 1989). According to the U.S. General Accounting Office (1991), there were about 9.5 million independent contractors in 1988, many of them without health insurance and other benefits. As a sign of the times, Aetna Life & Casualty laid off 2600 workers in 1992, then rehired them as independent contractors to do the same work for less pay and no fringe benefits (Zachary and Ortega 1993; Reskin and Padavic 1994). Other corporations such as Marriot, McDonald's, J.C. Penny, and Aramark make up part of the new "low-wage vanguard" of the new economy, a breed of employers who prosper by hiring younger, less educated, minority, or immigrant workers who are willing to work at jobs with low wages that offer little potential for advancement. The cumulative impact of contingent labor practices on wages has not gone unnoticed. According to the Economic Policy Institute, 30 percent of U.S. employees today are employed for under $7.28 an hour compared to 23.5 percent in 1973 (cited in Yang, Palmer, Browder, and Cuneo 1996).

Downsizing is simply an extension of processes that have been under way for two decades in the American labor force. It has many faces—deindustrialization, outsourcing, wage concessions, contingent labor, and layoffs—but its central tenet is the undermining of job security that prevailed among American workers in the 1950s and 1960s. The social contract that buoyed the middle-class American dream since World War II has been supplanted by a new insecurity about employment, careers, educating one's children, health care, and old-age security. More sanguine observers argue that these trends portend the "end of the job," a new, halcyon era in which work will no longer be packaged into "jobs" in single firms, but will consist of teams that are pulled together for specific projects and then disbanded (Bridges 1994). Workers in all occupations will be freelance entrepreneurs, the quintessential contingent workers, marketing their individual skills with employers and hopping from project to project. These new independent contractors, not their employers, will craft their own pension and health insurance plans, plan their own vacations between projects, and take charge of their own careers. Aronowitz and DeFazio's (1994) portrayal of the "jobless future" argues for a similar result but points, more pessimistically, to the continual subordination and displacement of both manual and intellectual labor due to "technoscience." From either perspective, downsizing is going to be with us for awhile.

## DOWNSIZING THE AMERICAN DREAM?

What implications does downsizing have for the quality of life for Americans? Does the downsizing of American jobs mean the downsizing of the American dream? In this section, I review some of the implications of downsizing for the American way of life.

One of the great transformations in American society during its ascendance as an industrial power was the emergence of a broad middle class. Under the social contract of the 1950s and 1960s, both blue- and white-collar workers could aspire to own and furnish a home, purchase an automobile or two, provide education and opportunity for their children, and take care of their families' needs during sickness and old age. There is mounting evidence that downsizing is taking its toll on the American family: that the middle-class way of life is slipping away for more and more Americans.

Robert Kuttner (1983) first advanced the thesis of "the declining middle class" in the mid-1980s to describe the impact of transformations at work and in the economy on family well-being. The downward mobility of the middle-class American family has been the subject of much subsequent research (Newman 1988, 1991, 1994; Rubin 1994). A central cause for the "declining middle class" thesis is the low-wage character of the "American job machine" in the 1980s (Bluestone and Harrison 1986) and the reversal of fortunes that this created for many American workers, what Harrison and Bluestone (1988) call the "Great U-Turn." About 85 percent of the jobs created by the "American job machine" during the 1980s were in low-wage occupations like retail trade and personal, business, and health services (Newman 1991), a trend that we saw from Table 2 is likely to continue. Kuttner and others have argued that this is leading to a two-tiered occupational structure in many corporations as well as society as a whole that has ramifications for overall class inequality.

After two decades of progress toward decreasing inequality, the gap between the rich and the poor began to widen again in the 1970s. Between 1977 and 1992, the poorest fifth of the American population saw their share of family income *decrease* by 17 percent while the richest fifth of the population saw theirs *increase* by 28 percent (the richest 1 percent of the population increased their share by 91 percent!) (Boroughs 1996; see also Samuelson 1996; *New York Times* 1996). The percentage of those people squarely in the middle class (with family incomes between $25,000 and $50,000 in real 1994 dollars) decreased from 32.8 to 32.3 percent (Boroughs 1996), palpable evidence of a declining middle class. As the middle class depleted their savings to make ends meet, wealth inequality also widened. Whereas the richest 1 percent owned about 20 percent of all family wealth in the mid-1970s, they own about 42 percent today (Boroughs 1996). The gap between corporate CEOs and their employees widened considerably, in no small part due to the bonuses CEOs reap every time they tweak Wall Street with a mass layoff. The ratio of CEO salaries in the ten largest U.S. companies compared to wages of the average worker soared from 41:1 in the early 1970s to 225:1 in the early 1990s (the ratio in German firms is about 20:1) (Boroughs 1996).

As I noted earlier, middle-class families are running faster to stay in the same place. Married women have almost doubled their labor force participation rates since 1960 and, despite the rise in the divorce rate, the percentage of dual earner households rose from about 20 percent in 1950 to about 42 percent in 1992. During the same period, families with employed husbands and stay-at-home wives plummeted from 64 to 18 percent (Reskin and Padavic 1994). Women are entering the labor force in larger numbers than ever, are having fewer children, are returning to work sooner after bearing children, and are having longer careers in the labor force. Thus, the widening gap between rich and poor in family income and other indicators is all the more remarkable given women's growing economic contribution to family well-being.

A bellwether indicator of the middle-class dream is the capacity to own one's own home. By all indications, the prospect of becoming a homeowner is diminishing. In the early 1980s, Kuttner (1983) showed that rates of home ownership had declined to the point that about 75 percent of all households could not afford to buy a new home. More recent statistics paint a similar picture. Between 1970 and 1994, median household income (in real dollars) increased by about 9.5 percent, but the median cost of a single-family home has increased by 44 percent. The impact has been hardest for the "thirty-something" cohort: between 1973 and 1990, home ownership rates slipped from 60 to 52 percent for 30- to 34-year-olds and from 69 to 63 percent for 35- to 39-year-olds (Newman 1994). Moreover, home mortgage foreclosure rates have tripled since 1970 and consumer credit has taken an ever larger bite out of families' disposable income (U.S. Department of Commerce 1996).

Education and the payoffs to a college degree are equally imperiled. Between 1970 and 1994, the percentage of Americans with college degrees increased from 11 to 23 percent, but starting salaries of new college graduates *decreased* by 26 percent. But having a college degree was certainly better than the alternative: between 1979 and 1992 male college graduates realized only a 5 percent increase in real earnings, but all other males lost ground (males without a high school degree lost 27 percent). Female college graduates gained 19 percent, however, while females without high school diplomas lost 7 percent (Boroughs 1996). All the while, the United States made no real progress in creating new training or apprenticeship programs for youths pursuing careers in technical trades.

If the harsh economics portrayed in these statistics were not enough, national surveys indicate workers' sense of anxiety and concern about their well-being at work. The *New York Times* (1996) survey referred to earlier found that only 15 percent of the respondents thought the economy was getting better, only 20 percent said they were getting ahead financially in the past couple years, and only 44 percent were as well off financially as they expected to be at this point in their life. Of the survey respondents who identified as "middle class," 36 percent felt they were in danger of falling out of it. Another axiomatic assumption of the middle-class dream is that each generation has a better life than the generation before. But the *Times* survey respondents were pessimistic about the prospects of the future generation: only 49 percent believed that it was likely that today's youth would be better off. Youth themselves are more pessimistic. A recent survey found that only 24 percent feel they will be better off than their parents and that their concerns about coping in the adult world have created unprecedented levels of stress, alienation, and thoughts about suicide.

The publicity about downsizing has created heightened concerns about the problem among workers. In the recent Indiana Quality of Employment Survey, only 39 percent of the respondents agreed with the statement, "It is OK for companies to downsize employees in order to increase their profits." As shown in Table 3, workers who occupied more vulnerable positions in the labor force expressed stronger opposition to downsizing (as evidenced by *lower* rates of agreement with the statement): the less educated, the lower paid, nonwhites, women, working- and lower-class respondents, lower-status occupations, and those who worked fewer hours. In addition, unionized workers, middle-aged workers, those with spouses who worked, and those who came from households with three or more workers expressed greater opposition to downsizing (Wallace 1996b).

Downsizing and the demise of the social contract between employers and workers is also apparent in feelings workers have about their employers and even the economic system as a whole. Among *New York Times* survey respondents, 75 percent felt that companies were less loyal to their employees than they were 10 years ago and 64 percent felt that employees were less loyal to their companies. When asked how much they blamed the economic system in the country for loss of jobs, 60 percent of those touched by layoffs

*Table 3.* Variations in Support for Downsizing: Indiana Quality of Employment Survey [a]

| | | | |
|---|---|---|---|
| **Gender** | | **Occupational Status** | |
| Men | 45.6 | Low | 34.7 |
| Women | 31.6 | Medium | 32.6 |
| | | High | 50.2 |
| **Race** | | **Union Status** | |
| Whites | 41.1 | Belong to union | 22.5 |
| Nonwhites | 21.3 | Don't belong | 42.1 |
| **Education (years)** | | **Spouse's Employment** | |
| 0–12 | 32.4 | Spouse has a job | 38.0 |
| 13–15 | 36.1 | Spouse has no job | 47.4 |
| 16+ | 52.8 | | |
| **Age** | | **Hours Worked** | |
| 18–30 | 40.2 | 20–39 | 32.7 |
| 31.40 | 37.5 | 40 | 36.7 |
| 41–50 | 35.2 | 41+ | 44.5 |
| 51+ | 44.4 | | |
| **Social Class** | | **Years with Employer** | |
| Lower/working | 34.5 | 1 or less | 36.7 |
| Middle/upper middle | 42.0 | 1–9 | 41.7 |
| | | 10+ | 38.8 |
| **Income** | | **Number of Workers in Household** | |
| 0–$19,999 | 33.1 | 1 | 41.7 |
| $20,000–39,999 | 41.2 | 2 | 38.1 |
| $40,000+ | 47.5 | 3+ | 32.0 |

[a] Percentage agreeing with statement: "It is OK for companies to downsize employees in order to increase their profits." (Total agreement = 39.0%, *N* = 705.)

said "a lot" and 26 percent of their colleagues who had been untouched by layoffs concurred.

The pall of downsizing lingers over those who continue to work as they worry, "Will my job be next?" Workers become distrustful of both their bosses and coworkers, become less productive and less valuable employees, and are anxious about their prospects for reemployment. When asked if they cooperate or compete more with their employees than they used to, 70 percent of the *New York Times* survey respondents said they compete more, and 53 percent said there was an angrier mood at work than there used to be. Only 29 percent felt more secure and confident that they could continue in their job as long as they wanted and 78 percent said that it would be hard for someone in their community to find a good job with good wages.

As a result, those who remain employed are more likely to make sacrifices to keep their jobs. Although 54 percent in the *Times* survey said that household members had to work more hours than normal in the past three years—a pattern consistent with Schor's (1992) thesis of the "overworked American"—82 percent said that they would work still longer hours to keep their jobs. In addition, 44 percent said that they would accept a smaller wage, 71 percent said they would accept fewer vacation days, 53 percent said they would accept fewer benefits, 93 percent would get more training or education, and 49 percent would challenge the boss less often. As might be expected, each of these figures was higher for workers in households that had been touched by a layoff.

The overall picture is not a bright one. Workers are mad as hell and . . . well, they're going to continue to take it for awhile. The scenario of downsizing is likely to continue in the foreseeable future. The restructuring of the global economy has unleashed a tremendous torrent of technological and organizational changes that are leaving in their wake broken careers, disheveled families, and shattered dreams. The affluent society is being divided into winners and losers, haves and have-nots, the jobbed and the dejobbed. And the American job machine keeps on cranking them out.

## NOTE

1. These income figures were calculated as follows. The number of new jobs in each occupation was multiplied by the average weekly income in each occupation; this product was summed across the ten occupations; this sum was then divided by the total number of new jobs for all ten occupations to get an average weekly income for all ten occupations; this figure was then multiplied by 52 (for 52 weeks) to get an annual income figure for the ten occupations ($19,649). The same procedure was used to calculate the mean income for all occupations. These calculations assume, of course, that workers in these jobs will work year-round, an assumption that might be called into question, but *not* one that will likely bias the conclusions I draw with these figures since the top ten jobs are probably *more likely* than other jobs in the economy to experience less than full-time employment.

## REFERENCES

Ansberry, Claire. 1993. "Workers Are Forced to Take More Jobs with Few Benefits." *Wall Street Journal* (March 11):A1.

Aronowitz, Stanley and William DeFazio. 1994. *The Jobless Future*. Minneapolis: University of Minnesota Press.

Bluestone, Barry and Bennett Harrison. 1979. *The Deindustrialization of America: Plant Closings, Community Abandonment, and the Dismantling of Basic Industry*. New York: Basic Books.

Bluestone, Barry and Bennett Harrison. 1986. "The Great American Job Machine: The Proliferation of Low-Wage Employment in the U.S. Economy." Study prepared for the Joint Economic Committee of the U.S. Congress.

———. 1996. "Winter of Discontent." *U.S. News and World Report* (January 22):47–54.

Bradshaw, York and Michael Wallace. 1996. *Global Inequalities.* Thousand Oaks, CA: Pine Forge.

Bridges, William. 1994. "The End of the Job." *Fortune* (September 19):62–74.

Brown, Anthony. 1987. *The Politics of Airline Deregulation.* Knoxville: University of Tennessee Press.

Calhoun, Craig, Donald Light, and Suzanne Keller. 1997. *Sociology,* 7th ed. New York: McGraw-Hill.

Christensen, Kathleen. 1989. "Flexible Staffing and Scheduling in U.S. Corporations." Research Bulletin No. 240. The Conference Board, New York.

Flaim, Paul O. and Ellen Sehgal. 1987. "Reemployment and Earnings." Pp. 101–30 in *Deindustrialization and Plant Closure,* edited by Paul D. Staudohar and Holly E. Brown. Lexington, MA: Lexington.

Gordon, David M., Richard Edwards, and Michael Reich. 1992. *Segmented Work, Divided Workers: The Historical Transformation of Labor in the United States.* New York: Cambridge University Press.

Harrison, Bennett and Barry Bluestone. 1988. *The Great U-Turn: Corporate Restructuring and the Polarizing of America.* New York: Basic Books.

Jacobsen, Louis S. 1978. "Earnings Losses of Workers Displaced from Manufacturing Cities." In *The Impact of International Trade and Investment on Employment,* edited by William G. DeWald. Washington, DC: U.S. Government Printing Office.

Kuttner, Bob. 1983. "The Declining Middle." *Atlantic* (July):60–72.

*New York Times.* 1996. *The Downsizing of America.* New York: Times Books.

Newman, Katherine. 1988. *Falling from Grace: the Experience of Downward Mobility in the American Middle Class.* New York: Random House.

———. 1991. "Uncertain Seas: Cultural Turmoil and the Domestic Economy." Pp. 112–30 in *America at Century's End,* edited by Alan Wolfe. Berkeley: University of California Press.

———. 1994. *Declining Fortunes: The Withering of the American Dream.* New York: Basic Books.

Piore, Michael J. and Charles F. Sabel. 1984. *The Second Industrial Divide: Prospects for Prosperity.* New York: Basic Books.

Reich, Robert B. 1983. *The Next American Frontier.* New York: Penguin.

Reskin, Barbara and Irene Padavic. 1994. *Women and Men at Work.* Thousand Oaks, CA: Pine Forge.

Rubin, Lillian B. 1994. *Families on the Fault Line: America's Working Class Speaks about the Family, the Economy, Race, and Ethnicity.* New York: Harper Collins.

Samuelson, Robert. 1996. *The Good Life and Its Discontents: The American Dream in the Age of Entitlement, 1945–1995.* New York: Times Books.

Schor, Juliet B. 1992. *The Overworked American: The Unexpected Decline of Leisure.* New York: Basic Books.

Schumpeter, Joseph. 1939. *Business Cycles: A Theoretical, Historical, and Statistical Analysis of the Capitalist Process.* New York: McGraw-Hill.

U.S. Department of Commerce. 1996. *Statistical Abstract of the United States,* 115th ed. Lanham, MD: Bernan.

U.S. General Accounting Office. 1991. *Workers at Risk: Increased Number in Contingent Employment Lack Insurance, Other Benefits.* GAO Report No. HRD-91-56. Washington, DC: U.S. Government Printing Office.

Wallace, Michael. 1996a. "The Next Long Wave: Globalization and the Spatial Restructuring of Work in the U.S. Economy." Unpublished manuscript. Indiana University, Bloomington.

———. 1996b. *The Indiana Quality of Employment Survey.* Bloomington: Center for Survey Research, Indiana University.

Wallace, Michael and Joyce Rothschild. 1988. "Plant Closings, Capital Flight, and Worker Dislocation: The Long Shadow of Deindustrialization." Pp. 1–35 in *Research in Politics and Society,* Vol. 3: *Deindustrialization and the Restructuring of American Industry,* edited by Michael Wallace and Joyce Rothschild. Greenwich, CT: JAI.

Walsh, David J. 1994. *On Different Planes: An Organizational Analysis of Cooperation and Conflict Among Airline Unions.* Ithaca, NY: ILR.

Yang, Catherine, Ann Therese Palmer, Seanna Browder, and Alice Cuneo. 1996. "Low-Wage Lessons." *Business Week* (November 11):108–16).

Zachary, G. Pascal and Bob Ortega. 1993. "Workplace Revolution Boosts Productivity at Cost of Job Security." *Wall Street Journal* (March 10):A1.

# Toward a 24 Hour Economy: The U.S. Experience and Implications for the Family 4

Harriet B. Presser

As we approach the twenty-first century, we are witnessing an important yet often overlooked trend: the movement toward a twenty-four-hour, seven-days-a-week economy. Increasingly, there is a demand for people to work evenings, nights, and weekends. Labor force scholars have long studied *how many* hours and days people are employed, but they have typically neglected to consider *which* hours or days they work—and why this matters.

First, I shall present some basic parameters of nonstandard work schedule behavior in the United States—that is, nondaytime and weekend employment—and what we can expect around the turn of the century. Next, I shall discuss some explanations as to why there is the increasing demand for employment during nonstandard hours and days—and why people are willing to meet this demand. Finally, I shall discuss the implications of the growth of the twenty-four-hour economy for family life.

## BASIC PARAMETERS

Before presenting some basic parameters, I would like to briefly review the definitions of nonstandard work schedules I am using.

First, let us consider the definitions of *work shifts*, which categorize hours of employment in a broad way. The specific definitions of each shift are as follows:

Fixed day: at least half the hours worked most days last week fell between 8 A.M. and 4 P.M.

Fixed evening: at least half the hours worked most days last week fell between 4 P.M. and midnight.

Fixed night: at least half the hours worked most days last week fell between midnight and 8 A.M.

Rotating: schedules that change periodically from days to evenings or nights.

When I refer to standard hours of employment, I mean fixed days; nonstandard shifts refer to nondaytime employment: fixed evenings, nights, and rotating shifts. These are conservative definitions, producing minimal estimates of the percentage working nonstandard hours, since at least half of one's hours of employment need to be before 8 A.M. or after 4 P.M., or rotating. Also, I would like to make clear than when I speak of nonstandard work shifts, I am not referring to flexitime, in which employees can set the time they begin and end work within a few hours of the core schedule for personal reasons. Nonstandard work shifts, in contrast, are set by employers to meet their needs, not those of their employees.

By working nonstandard *days,* I am referring to weekends: Saturday and/or Sunday.

Nonstandard work *schedules,* accordingly, refer to nonstandard hours and/or nonstandard days.

With these clarifications in mind, let us look at some basic facts. The source of these data is the May 1991 *Current Population Survey* (known as the CPS)—a survey of about 55,000 households in the United States. This is our best and most recent source of nationally representative data on the wok schedules of employed Americans. I have limited the sample to those employed aged eighteen and over. Here are some of the basic parameters on the prevalence of nonstandard hours and days in 1991, as reported in my earlier research (Presser 1995):

- One in five employed Americans works evenings, nights, or rotating schedules.
- One in four employed Americans works Saturday and/or Sunday.
- Only 31.5 percent of employed Americans work during the daytime, 5 days a week, Monday through Friday, 35–40 hours a week: the "standard" work schedule.
- When dropping the restriction of 35–40 hours above, the percentage with such a work schedule is 55.1, a bare majority.
- Women are as likely as men to work late or rotating schedules and on weekends, although men are more likely to work nights vs. evenings and Sundays vs. Saturdays.
- Unmarried people are more likely to work nonstandard schedules than married people.
- The presence of children, for both married and unmarried parents, increases their likelihood of working nonstandard schedules.

Research that I have done specifically on "dual earners" (Presser 1988, 1989a)—that is, for married couples with both spouses employed—reveals that one in four are "split-shift" couples: one spouse works during the daytime and the other evenings, nights, or on a rotating schedule (hours changing from days to evenings to nights, or the reverse). And for dual-earner couples *with preschool-aged children,* the ratio is one in three. Moreover, for *young* dual-earner couples with young children—that is, those with at least one spouse aged nineteen to twenty-seven, who typically are recently married and the most economically vulnerable—the ratio increases further to one in two; that is, one-half of young dual-earner American couples with preschool-aged children are split-shift couples. (This latter figure is based on the 1984 National Longitudinal Survey of Youth, the NLSY; the other data are based on the 1991 CPS.)

I shall come back to these figures when I talk about possible consequences for the presumably "intact" family.

It is not just the married who experience a high prevalence of nonstandard work schedules; indeed, single people are more likely to have nonstandard work schedules than married people, and single mothers with young children more so than their married counterparts. Further, the more children, the more likely the nonstandard schedule. But the phenomenon is widely experienced by all subgroups within American society—both married and unmarried; those with and without children; blacks, whites, and Hispanics; the better and less educated, etc.—even though there are differences in prevalence among these subgroups.

What is driving the growing demand for employment during the evening, night, and weekends, and why do Americans accommodate to this growing demand? Is it due mostly to an increasing lack of daytime job opportunities, or to people's preference for working odd hours to accommodate their personal or family needs?

## DEMAND

My thesis concerning demand is that the growth of the service economy, linked to the increasing employment of women and the aging of the population, is intensifying the demand for nonstandard work schedules. As more and more women are employed during the *daytime,* the demand for nondaytime and weekend services increases, because women are less available to shop during the daytime and on weekdays. Increasingly, family members are eating out and purchasing other homemaking services that previously would have been performed by full-time housewives. Moreover, the rise in families' real income due to the growth of dual-earner couples has heightened the demand for recreation and entertainment during evenings, nights, and weekends. Further, the aging of the population has increased the demand for medical services over a twenty-four-hour day, seven days a week.

Technological changes are also moving us to a global economy. The ability to be "on call" at all hours of the day and night to others around the world generates a need to do so. For example, the rise of multinational corporations, along with the use of computers, faxes, etc., increases the demand that branch offices operate at the same time that corporate headquarters are open. Similarly, international financial markets are expanding their hours of operation.

The future trend in the United States will undoubtedly be toward greater diversity in work schedules, particularly among employed women. Table 1 demonstrates this. This table lists the ten occupations that are projected to grow the most between 1992 and 2005 (on the basis of moderate projections), as well as the distributions of work schedules and the percent female for these occupations as of May 1991. We see that in most of these occupations, unusually high percentages work nonstandard hours and/or days. Future growth in nonstandard hours and days of employment should be especially evident among women because seven of these ten growth occupations are disproportionately female and account for 18.5 percent of the overall projected growth in employment in this period. Thus I would expect further increases not only in the employment of women, but more of them—including mothers with young children—will be working nonstandard hours and days. Moreover, the feedback between women's daytime and nondaytime employment is sure to continue, along with the aging of the population and the resulting demand for continuous twenty-four-hour medical care.

## SUPPLY

Turning to the supply side, why do Americans agree to work nonstandard hours? The limited data we have suggest it is more because it is a job requirement than for family or personal reasons—or, as the U.S. Bureau of Labor Statistics puts it, for "involuntary" rather than "voluntary reasons." Even though women are much more likely than men to report family reasons, for both men and women, most report involuntary reasons—even women with preschool-aged children. This can be seen in Table 2, which reports the main reasons given by those who work nonstandard shifts.

It is particularly notable that less than 5 percent of employed Americans who work evenings, nights, or rotating schedules indicate they do so for better pay (a voluntary personal reason). The pay differentials in the United States, when they exist, are generally not substantial.

An approach I have taken to indirectly assess gender differences in the importance of family characteristics for working nonstandard schedules is a multivariate analysis of the 1991 CPS data (Presser 1995). This analysis controlled for job and background characteristics. It showed that being married reduces women's but not men's likelihood of employment during nonstandard hours. Moreover, the presence of children affects women's but not

*Table 1.* Occupations in 1992 with the Largest Projected U.S. Job Growth (Moderate Estimates) for 2005, the Percentage in These Occupations Who Work Nonstandard Schedules in May 1991, and the Percentage Female in These Occupations in May 1991

| | *Employment (in 1000s)* | | *% Work Nonstandard Schedules: May 1991* | | | |
|---|---|---|---|---|---|---|
| *Job Growth Rank/Occupation* | *1992 (Actual)* | *2005 (Projected)* | *% Nonday or Rotating Hours* | *% Weekend Variable Days* | *% Nondays + Weekends or Variable Days* | *% Female May 1991* |
| 1. Salespersons | 3,660 | 4,446 | 24.7 | 73.6 | 75.2 | 55.5 |
| 2. Registered nurses | 1,835 | 2,601 | 40.1 | 63.2 | 67.4 | 96.7 |
| 3. Cashiers | 2,747 | 3,417 | 43.4 | 74.9 | 80.2 | 80.2 |
| 4. General office clerks | 2,688 | 3,342 | 7.4 | 14.0 | 17.5 | 80.5 |
| 5. Truck drivers, light and heavy | 2,391 | 3,039 | 16.2 | 36.8 | 42.8 | 3.6 |
| 6. Waiters and waitresses | 1,756 | 2,394 | 58.6 | 83.0 | 90.0 | 84.1 |
| 7. Nursing aids, orderlies, and attendants | 1,308 | 1,903 | 40.7 | 68.9 | 75.9 | 89.0 |
| 8. Janitors and cleaners, including maids and housekeeping cleaners | 2,862 | 3,410 | 29.6 | 38.0 | 56.2 | 41.2 |
| 9. Food counter, fountain, and related workers | 1,223 | 1,748 | 48.5 | 76.2 | 86.5 | 71.7 |
| 10. Computer scientists and systems analysts | 455 | 956 | 3.6 | 11.8 | 14.4 | 33.6 |

*Source:* Presser (1995) and *Statistical Abstract of the United States.*

*Table 2.* Percentage of Distribution of Main Reason Reported for Working Nondays (Including Rotators), by Gender and Age of Youngest Child: May 1994

| | | *Male* | | | | *Female* | | | |
|---|---|---|---|---|---|---|---|---|---|
| *Main Reason* | *Total* | *Total Male* | *No Child* | *Child <5* | *Child 5–13* | *Total Female* | *No Child <5* | *Child <5* | *Child 5–13* |
| Voluntary reasons | 36.1 | 29.5 | 30.8 | 24.4 | 29.0 | 44.7 | 40.7 | 56.7 | 46.7 |
| Better pay | 4.9 | 4.8 | 4.3 | 4.9 | 7.2 | 4.9 | 5.6 | 2.8 | 5.1 |
| Better child care arrangements | 5.1 | 1.5 | .1 | 5.3 | 4.2 | 9.9 | 0.8 | 32.4 | 19.9 |
| Better arrangements for care of other family members | 3.5 | 1.7 | 1.0 | 3.1 | 3.9 | 5.8 | 2.6 | 12.7 | 11.0 |
| Allows time for school | 9.9 | 8.6 | 11.5 | 2.3 | .6 | 11.6 | 16.0 | 3.2 | 3.3 |
| Other voluntary | 12.7 | 12.9 | 13.9 | 8.8 | 13.1 | 12.5 | 15.7 | 5.6 | 7.4 |
| Involuntary reasons | 58.7 | 65.4 | 63.9 | 71.1 | 66.8 | 49.8 | 54.6 | 36.3 | 46.5 |
| Requirement of the job | 52.4 | 58.9 | 57.2 | 64.8 | 60.7 | 43.7 | 48.3 | 31.2 | 40.4 |
| Could not get any other job | 4.9 | 5.0 | 5.4 | 4.1 | 4.1 | 4.8 | 5.1 | 4.5 | 3.8 |
| Other involuntary | 1.4 | 1.5 | 1.3 | 2.0 | 2.0 | 1.3 | 1.2 | 0.6 | 2.3 |
| No response/don't know | 5.2 | 5.1 | 5.3 | 4.6 | 4.2 | 5.5 | 4.7 | 7.0 | 6.8 |
| Total % | 100.0 | 100.0 | 100.0 | 100.0 | 100.0 | 100.0 | 100.0 | 100.0 | 100.0 |
| No. of cases (*N*) | (7930) | (4372) | (3045) | (757) | (570) | (3558) | (2333) | (713) | (512) |

*Note:* Percentages are weighted; *N* are unweighted. Percentages for underlined reasons indicate the sum for all responses in that group.
Source: Presser (1995).

men's hours of employment. Interestingly, having preschool-aged children *increases* the likelihood of women working nonstandard hours but having school-aged *decreases* the likelihood women will work such hours. Insofar as school substitutes for child care, this difference suggests that the full-time child care demands of preschoolers are an important inducement for some women to work nonstandard hours—even though they may not be a primary reason for most.

This analysis also showed that nonstandard work schedules are pervasive throughout the occupational hierarchy, but men and women employed in service occupations, particularly in personal services, and in service industries such as eating and drinking places, are most likely to work these schedules, net of family and background factors.

## CONSEQUENCES

So much for what we know about the causes or determinants—which is not that much. What about the consequences? Here, too, our knowledge is limited.

We know that, biologically, working nights and rotating schedules alters one's circadian rhythms, often leading to sleep disturbances, gastrointestinal disorders and chronic malaise. Such negative health and psychological consequences are extensively documented (see, for example, U.S. Congress 1991), although there are problems in the design of many of these studies (small samples, lack of control groups, etc.).

Putting aside these important considerations of health and psychological consequences, I wish to address here the implications of nonstandard work schedules for family life, including marital formation and dissolution, the timing and number of children, and child rearing. I say "implications," as we have very little empirical data on this topic.

Clearly, working nonstandard schedules typically puts one's availability for family interaction and leisure out of sync with others. I have argued that the "at-home" structure of family life is changing dramatically in the United States because of the growth of the twenty-four-hour economy (Presser 1989a); for example, among presumably "intact" families, dinner time—in my view, the most cohesive daily activity for families—has many absent fathers and mothers as a consequence of shift work.[1] A national U.S. study showed that working late or rotating hours was associated with greater difficulty in scheduling family activities and more time spent on housework; also, working weekends or variable days was linked with less time in family roles and with higher levels of work/family conflict and family adjustment (Staines and Pleck 1983). Another national U.S. study (White and Keith 1990) found a modest negative effect of shift work on marital quality and significantly increased the likelihood of divorce over a three-year period. (This is the only longitudinal analysis of work schedules that I am aware of, although I am in the process of conducting such an analysis with the first and second waves of the U.S. National Survey of Families and Households.)

Earlier work I have done on the relationship between work schedules and child care showed that, among dual-earner American couples who work different shifts and have preschool-aged children, virtually all fathers who are at home when mothers are employed care for their children during this time (Presser 1988). Thus, although couples may not have chosen different work hours because of child care, their work schedule behavior facilitates the sharing of child care when both are employed. Similarly, many single as well as married employed mothers in the United States rely on grandmothers who are also employed to share child care with them, and this is possible because they work different hours (Presser 1989b). Thus, what may be stressful for the marriage or for intergenerational relations may be good for children: more fathering or grandparenting rather than substitute care. I have also shown that nonstandard work schedules among dual earners cause an increase in men's share of household tasks (Presser 1994), although one may question whether this is the best route to gender equality in this regard.

As for the issue of work schedules and fertility behavior, there have been no studies to date on this, in the United States or elsewhere. Yet one might expect that nonstandard work schedules decrease the frequency of sexual behavior, postpone the timing of births, and decrease overall family size desires.

## CONCLUSIONS AND IMPLICATIONS

To conclude, there is clear evidence that nonstandard work schedules are pervasive in the United States, they are most evident in service occupations and industries, and although employed men and women are equally engaged in such schedules, future growth will be disproportionately female. Whereas family considerations are not the predominant reason for working nonstandard schedules, the consequences of such employment may be profound in both negative and positive ways. On the negative side, such employment radically alters the at-home structure of family life, perhaps increasing marital instability; on the positive side—at least from the child's perspective—it increases men's and grandmother's participation in child care; and from women's perspective, it increases men's participation in household tasks.

Clearly, there are other potential consequences that merit investigation that have not been studied. I find this an especially interesting research area because it addresses the linkage between changes in the economy and changes in the family—that is, how macro changes alter the nature of the family at the micro level. I believe research in this area tends to be neglected because there is no clear policy directive. We have not yet been able to adequately cope with *day* care problems: who wants to deal with night care problems? And if split shifts among couples are shown to increase the risk of divorce, should we discourage such employment—and could we, when this is where much of the job growth lies?

To conclude, it is clear to me that the twenty-four-hour, seven-days-a-week economy is increasingly becoming a reality, and we need to pay more attention to what this means for the quality of family life and the health and well-being of individual family members.

## NOTE

1. Based on my preliminary analysis of the data from the 1986–1987 National Study of Families and Households, for all married couples—regardless of employment status—only 71.0 percent of mothers and 51.0 percent of fathers ate dinner with their children all seven days of the prior week, and both parents were present all seven days for only 40.8 percent. More interesting is the fact that 10.2 percent of the mothers and 24.2 percent of fathers did not eat dinner with their children at least five days in the prior week (although rarely were both missing more than two days).

## REFERENCES

Presser, Harriet B. 1988. "Shift Work and Child Care among Young Dual-Earner American Parents." *Journal of Marriage and the Family* 50:133–48.

———. 1989a. "Can We Make Time for Children?: The Economy, Work Schedules, and Child Care." *Demography* 26:523–43.

———. 1989b. "Some Economic Complexities of Child Care Provided by Grandmothers." *Journal of Marriage and the Family* 51:581–91.

———. 1994. "Employment Schedules among Dual-Earner Spouses and the Division of Household Labor by Gender." *American Sociological Review* 59(June): 348–64.

———. 1995. "Job, Family, and Gender: Determinants of Nonstandard Work Schedules among Employed Americans: 1991." *Demography* 32:577–98.

Staines, Graham L. and Joseph H. Pleck. 1983. *The Impact of Work Schedules on the Family.* Ann Arbor: Institute for Social Research, The University of Michigan.

U.S. Congress. 1991. *Biological Rhythms: Implications for the Worker,* OTA-BA-463. Washington, DC: Office of Technological Assessment.

White, Lynn and Bruce Keith. 1990. "The Effect of Shift Work on the Quality and Stability of Marital Relations." *Journal of Marriage and the Family* 52:453–62.

# Race and the Family Values Debate 5

Maxine Baca Zinn

The national tempest over family values shows no signs of subsiding. One side of the divide argues that current family changes are symptoms of moral decline and social decay. The other side calls on substantial bodies of theory and research to demonstrate that changes in family life are taking place throughout the world. The critique of family values offers compelling evidence that shifting social and economic conditions are more important than declining moral standards in the creation and perpetuation of current family problems. Yet the critique is hampered by how it "sees" race.

In this essay, I examine racial matters that lie at the heart of the national debate. My goal is to extend the progressive challenge by building multiplicity into the dialogue. This requires incorporating two features into this discussion. The first is the inclusion of the racial hierarchy as a key part of the structural matrix affecting family formation. The second is the inclusion of different racial groups in an increasingly diverse society. First, I identify dominant themes in the conservative and progressive arguments. Three strands of profamily critiques—feminist perspectives, political economy perspectives, and family demography perspectives—reveal race-sensitive understandings. However, a structural analysis of race eludes each strand of the progressive critique. I suggest that careful attention to racialized patterns of family formation would sharpen our understanding of structured inequalities. Finally, I draw on family dynamics among Latinos to provide a distinctive vantage point on race and the family values debate.

## IDEOLOGICAL FAULT LINES

Definitions of the family are hotly contested in the contemporary political arena, in the academy, and in the cultural conflict over the definition of America. Debates surrounding family life have become a site of struggle over such pressing political and social issues as access to and funding for abortion and birth control, single pregnancy, gay and lesbian rights, disability rights, discrimination against women in the work force, welfare funding, homelessness, divorce, substance abuse, and urban violence. Depending on the speaker's location in this dialogue, the family is alternatively mythologized, blamed, glorified, reclaimed and/or redefined. Within each of these positions there are distinctive ideas about what constitutes a family and about the relationship between family and society.

## CONSERVATIVE PERSPECTIVES

The conservatives, or, as they are sometimes called, the "profamily" forces, believe that the family is the basic building block of society. The family is where members' basic needs are met, where children learn their most important lessons, and where individuals are loved unconditionally. According to Barbara Dafoe Whitehead, "The social arrangement that has proved most successful in ensuring the physical survival and promoting the social development of the child is the family unit of the biological mother and father" (1993:48), a claim presumed to hold true "across time and across cultures" (ibid.). [For the intellectual foundations of the cultural position see, for example, Murray (1984), Wilson (1993), Whitehead (1993).]

Conservatives are alarmed and appalled by the breakdown of the traditional family as represented in high divorce rates, rising levels of female households, out-of-wedlock childbearing, fatherlessness, and nonparental child care due to the high proportion of mothers in the workplace. The principal causes of family decline in the past three decades or so are said to be cultural and political. The primary reason is the decline of family values, which has led to the moral decay of society's members. People are making selfish decisions (e.g., women having to work full-time in the labor force rather than having husbands who provide for themselves and their families) or behaving immorally (e.g., premarital sex, abortion, and homosexuality). Conservatives are also incensed at government policies that have furthered the decline of the traditional family such as no-fault divorce, legalized abortion, birth control counseling, compulsory sex education, legal decisions said to encourage homosexuality, and welfare policies (Baca Zinn and Eitzen 1996:418).

Conservatives are particularly anxious about family life in minority communities. Their alarmist treatment of teen pregnancies and female-headed families is part of a long history of blaming families for structural failures. In the sixties Daniel Patrick Moynihan (1965) held black families responsible for deteriorating communities. But long before that, in the origins of family studies, minority families came under attack for not maintaining their families in the same form as families of the dominant society. In much popular thought, the "breakdown of the black family in inner city neighborhoods in the past . . . generations shows in particularly stark form the societal consequences of a loss of certain cultural values" (Fukuyama 1993:28). In reality, family values is a way to distinguish the two-parent family from all other family arrangements and to make families a scapegoat for society's problems. Fatherless families are said to be the root cause of all social decline. This line of thought led former vice-president Dan Quayle to denounce television character Murphy Brown for having a baby without a husband. Declaring that unwed motherhood was having harmful effects on the nation, Quayle blamed the 1992 Los Angeles riots on family breakdown. Increasingly, conservatives are sounding the alarm that Latino immigrants are a threat to family values and other core American cultural characteristics. Indeed, much immigrant sentiment rests on the public perception of Latinos as the bearers of undesirable families.

## PROGRESSIVE POSITIONS

For progressives, the traditional family is *not* a given. Rather, family forms are socially and historically constructed, not uniform arrangements that exist for all times and places. One critical difference between the conservatives and progressives is causation: What is the cause of family changes over the past thirty years or so? Conservatives believe a shift in values accompanied by government policies has weakened the family. For progressives, this view is wrong. Instead, a variety of social and economic forces have contributed to changes in families.

Three strands of thinking figure prominently in this critique of family values. While they often overlap, the first emphasizes gender, the second emphasizes class, and the third emphasizes family structure.

### *Mainstream Feminist Perspectives*

Although there is no single feminist perspective on families, it is fair to say that feminism has been at the forefront of efforts to clarify our understanding of family life. Feminists have long worked for the recognition of diverse forms of family and household arrangements, demonstrating that family forms are socially and historically constructed, not monolithic universals that exist across all times and all people, and that the social and legal arrangements governing family life are not the result of unambiguous differences between women and men. Feminists have drawn attention to the disparities between idealized and real patterns of family life, to the myths that romanticize "traditional" families in defense of male privilege, and to the fact that only a small minority of families and households have ever resembled the sentimentalized form. In challenging the dichotomy between public and private spheres, feminists have deepened our understanding of the social conditions surrounding women's family experiences (Dill, Baca Zinn, and Patton 1993).

An important conclusion from the vast feminist literature on changing families is that family forms once thought to be natural and immutable are declining throughout the industrial world. Conditions of postindustrial capitalism are contributing to the demise not of *"the family"* but an arrangement that Judith Stacey calls "the *modern* family"—an intact nuclear household composed of a male breadwinner, his full-time homemaker wife, and their dependent children (Stacey 1996). This model is being replaced by rising levels of female-headed households and growing impoverishment of women and their children. According to Stacey, marital instability and women-centered household arrangements are becoming endemic facts of life all around the world. She calls these new family forms "postmodern" because they do not fit the criteria for a "modern family."

### *Political Economy Perspectives*

Progressive economists have contributed another strong challenge to family values rhetoric. Less concerned with gender relations in family life and more concerned with market forces and class formation, this work is a variant of feminist thought that directs attention to the close connections between family life and global economic developments. These thinkers call on macrostructural economic changes to explain why families are far different from what they used to be. Agreeing that families are more diverse, that they are more easily fractured, that family members spend less time together, and that parents have less influence over their children, many political economists reason that "the current economic system is no longer congruent with traditional nuclear family values" (Thurow 1997). Economic realities including men's declining wages and the pressures on women to work outside the home mean that the family is an institution both in flux and under pressure.

As the need for certain kinds of labor diminishes, more and more working- and middle-class families are the victims of economic dislocations. Families are profoundly affected when their resources are reduced, when they face economic and social marginalization, and when family members are unemployed or underemployed. As Lester Thurow explains, the traditional family is being destroyed by a modern economic system. Families are under attack:

> not by government programs that discourage family formation (although there are some) and not by media presentations that disparage families (although there are some), but by the economic system itself. It simply won't allow families to exist in the old-fashioned way, with a father who generates most of the

> earnings and a mother who does most of the nurturing. The one-earner middle class family is extinct. (ibid.)

The argument that changes in the economy and the class structure undermine family stability is widespread within the social sciences and family studies. William Wilson's contention that supportive forces in the larger society have undergone major shifts and undermined family stability is the exemplar, but "there is no shortage of evidence of the impact of economic hardship on the family" (Skolnick and Rosencrantz 1994:64). Though this position rests on growing structural inequalities rather than individuals, families, or their moral standards, this analysis does not discount the roles of values in producing family change. "Values follow economic realities" (Thurow 1997). Or as economist David Gordon put it "values matter, but jobs matter, at least as much if not more" (1996:16).

### *Family Demography Perspectives*

Conservatives believe that declining family values threaten the collective good. Yet when they say "family values," they often mean "family structure," or more precisely *nuclear* family structure. The question, What difference does family structure make? is posed by sociologists and demographers, often quantitative social scientists. Although they do not usually engage in ideological debates about the relationship between values, single-parent households, and social problems, these scholars provide powerful evidence that social conditions are the shapers of family arrangements. This body of work empirically challenges the preoccupation with family structure as the cause of social pathologies.

By disentangling family structure from socioeconomic background, education, race, and other variables, research in this vein reveals that family structure is paramount in determining the life-chances of children. Furthermore, there is a relationship between family structure and poverty (O'Hare 1996:347). Still, despite the correlations between family structure and family resources, we cannot conclude that single-parent households are the "root cause of poverty" (McLanahan and Sandefur 1994:3).

This research finds that family structure is an increasingly important axis of racial inequality, especially between black and white children (Lichter and Landale 1995:347). Yet it also shows that child poverty cannot be reduced to family structure for either blacks or Latinos. In the words of Sara McLanahan and Gary Sandefur, "If there were no single parents, Black children would still have much higher poverty rates" (1994:85). To put it more precisely, for African-Americans, "emulating the White family structure would close only about one-half of the income gap" (Hacker 1996:309). If Puerto Rican children lived in nuclear families, their poverty would be reduced from 41 to 24 percent (in other words, half is due to family structure). But poverty rates would be reduced only slightly if Mexicans and Cubans had the nuclear family structures of non-Latinos (Lichter and Landale 1996:347).

For feminists, progressive economists, and family demographers alike, a variety of social and economic forces have contributed to the decline of traditional family arrangements. Feminists such as Judith Stacey (1996) and Iris Marion Young (1994) have drawn from all three clusters of thought to reveal two overarching flaws in the family values position. First, it reverses the relationship between family and society by treating the family as the building block of society rather than as a reflection of social conditions. Second, it ignores the structural reasons for family breakdown.

### *Racial Themes in the Progressive Critique*

The works of mainstream feminists, progressive political economics, and family demographers offer an extensive critique of the conservative family values rhetoric. Each stream of work moves in a different direction. Still, the critiques are similar in that they all show the link between larger economic forces and family patterns. All three argue that family life is being reconfigured more by severe structural problems than by a shift in values. Moreover, progressive scholars have been major voices in exposing the racial scapegoating that lies at the heart of conservative thought.

Of particular importance to many progressive scholars are the racial images in the national discussion. Each body of literature recognizes that "family breakdown" is often a thinly-veiled attack on the black urban underclass and that single motherhood is "often a codeword for Black single mother" (McLanahan and Sandefur 1994). For example, Ruth Sidel confronts the myth that most poor, single childbearing women are black (Sidel 1996:29), and Judith Stacey notes that racial anxiety about family structure is as old as the United States itself:

> Racial anxiety predates Moynihan's incendiary 1965 report. It reaches back a century to xenophobic fears about high fertility rates among Eastern and Southern European immigrants . . . [and] it reaches back much further into the history of colonial settler fears of diverse sexual and kinship practices of indigenous cultures (1990:72).

Progressive critics of family values are especially successful in unmasking the color-evasive language of family moralists who long for a return to a mythical time when normal values of normal Americans were sacrosanct and the law of the land (Sidel 1996:29). Stacey interprets former vice-president Dan Quayle's interpretation of Murphy Brown as an ill-fated attempt to play the Willie Horton card in whiteface. "Without resorting to overtly racist rhetoric, the image conjured up frightening hoards of African American welfare 'queens' rearing infant fodder to sex, drugs, and videotaped uprisings, such as had just erupted in Los Angeles" (Stacey 1996:72). The message engages an enemy and the effect is to construct shadowy immoral "others" who are slipping their moral aberrations into the cultural mainstream (Marone 1996:34).

Progressive scholarship has not been silent about race. Nevertheless, despite all the attention given to racial scapegoating, the treatment of race is unsatisfactory. Two limitations prevent the progressive critique from fully exposing the racial dimensions within the profamily position. The first limitation is theoretical. The progressive framework does not reflect current conceptualizations of race as a macrostructural force that situates families differently and produces, indeed *requires* different arrangements. Progressives contend that the conservative view of social reality is wrong. It is steeped in racial prejudice, which becomes a "kind of family Darwinism" (Polakow 1993:39) that is blind to larger economic forces. Such exposure of the racial bias in profamily positions is crucial, but it does not go far enough in addressing the importance of race in shaping family life.

The second limitation has theoretical as well as empirical features. These rest on a black/white treatment of race. Progressive discourses on family values devote almost exclusive attention to African-Americans. Except in some small clusters of scholarship by family demographers, Latinos are ignored. Their invisibility in the national discussion is surprising since Latinos are rapidly approaching the epicenter of the current family crisis. Latinos now have the highest poverty rate in the United States. In addition, Latinos now make up the largest category of minority children in the country. These economic and demographic changes are introducing new complications into the family values debate, yet they are invisible in most progressive literature. Even Judith Stacey's brilliant and searing critique of family values remains within a biracial framework. In order to ground my argument that the progressive challenge requires a more inclusive treatment of race, I will briefly consider these matters. This is not meant to deny the value of progressive perspectives but to enhance them with insights from more recently developed positions.

## RACE AS SOCIAL STRUCTURE

Over the past decade, a considerable amount of attention has been devoted to race as a primary axis of inequality for situating families differently (Baca Zinn 1990, 1994; Dill 1988, 1994; Hill Collins 1990, 1997; Glenn 1992). Instead of focusing on economic conditions alone, this emergent framework for studying families argues that racial inequality is also part of the larger structure in which families are embedded. Along with class and gender, race is a hierarchical structure of opportunity and oppression that has profound material consequences for family formation. The long-standing diversity of family forms by race is produced, in part, by an unequal distribution of social opportunities in U.S. society.

Some of the most influential work linking family formation with racial patterns of social relations is found in a conceptual framework called *multiracial feminism.* Grounded in multiple, interlocking hierarchies, what Patricia Hill Collins (1990) calls the matrix of domination, this perspective underscores the pervasive nature of race in shaping the experiences of women and men throughout society. At the same time, this framework acknowledges how race is shaped by a variety of other social relations, especially class and gender (Baca Zinn and Dill 1996).

This perspective offers a useful set of analytic premises for thinking about and theorizing family life. It views families in relation to a racially organized social structure that provides and denies opportunities and therefore influences the way families in different social locations organize themselves to survive. One of the crucial lessons of multiracial feminism is that "race has always been a fundamental criterion in providing the kind of work people do, the wages they receive, and the kind of legal, economic, political and social support provided for their families" (Dill 1994:166). "Groups subordinated in the racial hierarchy are often deprived of access to social institutions that offer supports for family life" (Baca Zinn 1990:74). As Hill Collins contends, "actual families all live somewhere, and that somewhere in the United States is typically segregated" (Hill Collins 1997:18).

When we examine how families are positioned within intersecting inequalities, we have a better grasp of family diversity. People experience the family differently depending on their social, class, race, ethnicity, age, and sexual orientation, and from their experiences they construct different definitions of what families are. Multiracial feminism has furthered our understanding of the racialized connections between normative family structure and social support. The family that conservative writers uphold as "legitimate" is a product of socially structured opportunities. It emerged as a result of social and economic conditions that are no longer operative for most Americans, and that never were operative for many poor Americans and people of color. From the original settlement of the American colonies through the mid–twentieth century, families of European descent often received economic and social supports to establish and maintain families (Dill 1988). Following World War II, as Stephanie Coontz (1992) points out, the GI Bill, the National Defense Education Act, the expansion of the Federal Housing Authority and Veterans Administration loan subsidy programs, and government funding of new highways provided the means though which middle-class whites were able to achieve the stable suburban family lives that became the idea against which all other families were judged. These kinds of support have rarely been available for people of color, and until quite recently were actively denied them through various forms of housing and job discrimination. A careful reading of family history makes it clear that family structure is the result of far more than economic transformations (Dill et al. 1993).

Today's economically based reorganization of U.S. society is reshaping family structure through distinctive racial patterns. Families mainly headed by women have become permanent in all racial categories with the disproportionate effects of change most visible among nonwhite ethnic groups. While the chief cause of the increase in female-headed households among whites is the greater economic independence of white women, the longer delay of first marriage and the low rate of remarriage among black women reflects the labor force problems of black men (Wilson and Neckerman 1986:265). Thus race and gender create different routes to female headship, but whites, blacks, and Latinos are all increasingly likely to end up in this family form (Baca Zinn 1990:129).

### *Bringing In Latinos*

Attention to African-Americans alone is insufficient to sort out the flaws in the conservative family values campaign. Bringing in Latinos remains a challenge, a necessary next step in making the discussion more representative of demographic realities in U.S. society. Certainly there is some risk in making generalizations about this very diverse category that includes Mexican-Americans or Chicanos, Puerto Ricans, Cubans, and Central and South Americans. Hispanics are found in many legal and social statuses from fifth generation to new immigrants. Such diversity means that there is no "Hispanic" population (Massey 1993:11). Saying that someone is Hispanic or Latino reveals little about attitudes, beliefs, class, or family characteristics. Nevertheless, the label Hispanic or Latino is useful in describing the changing demography of race and beginning to think more systematically about different family realities in a multiracial society.

Family solidarity is commonly thought to be a defining feature of the Latino population. In both the popular images (Estrada 1989) and social science literature (Vega 1995), Latinos are regarded as "traditional" in their family convictions and behaviors. Even though research shows that Latinos are not monolithically familistic, nor are their family relations uniformly traditional, "current literature is characterized by a redundancy in accounts of Latinos familism" (ibid.:9). A distinctive style of Latino family solidarity presumably makes it distinct from the family orientations of other family-centered ethnic groups.

The traditional Latino family archetype has always been controversial. In the earliest research on Mexican-origin families, structural functionalism and its variant cultural determinism attributed negative outcomes to strong family values. Mexicans were *criticized* for the strength of their family ties. Their lack of social progress was blamed on a way of life that kept them tied to family rather than economic advancement. During the 1960s and 1970s, many scholars vigorously refuted cultural deficiency explanations of Mexican families by showing that family life was not deviant, deficient, or disorganized. Instead, what were once viewed as culturally deficient Mexican family lifestyles reflected adaptive response to the hardships of poverty and minority status (Baca Zinn 1995:180).

A new twist on the "social adaptation" approach has emerged in response to the family values debate. Several scholars have expressed the view that familism facilitates adaptation in difficult social settings and that strong family orientations serve Mexican immigrants in ways little understood by social scientists and policymakers. For example, David Hayes Bautista and his colleagues found that Mexican immigrants arrive in the United States imbued with rich family values, high rates of family formation, and high labor force participation (Hayes-Bautista 1989). According to these researchers, "since Latinos have large families they are quite committed to fulfilling their parental roles and assuming familial obligations" (cited in Zavella 1996:369).

Other scholars have asserted that not only do strong family values facilitate immigrant adaptation, but that Latinos are *better* able than other groups to withstand economic hardship. Large webs of close-knit kin, strong propensity to marry and raise large families, and above all "strong" family values are said to be *cultural* strengths that are now absent in black communities. For example in finding that poor Mexicans in Chicago often work at two jobs, one researcher concluded that they had an intense commitment to the marital bond and to work, whereas blacks did not, presumably because of cultural differences between the two populations (cited in Zavella 1996:363–64).

Such interpretations about Latinos having "strong family values" and "better family demographics" are meant, no doubt, to challenge conservative assumptions that "Latinos as a whole have joined inner city blacks to form one vast, threatening underclass" (Fukuyama 1993:29). However, they perpetuate racial stereotypes. In their zeal to refute the negative outcomes of culture for Latinos, they use the logic of cultural determinism to "imply that Blacks and other groups do not have strong family values or a work ethic, and ironically they ultimately reinforce the model itself" (Zavella 1996:370).

A better line of attack is to use the Latino experience to show that we cannot blame the family for social inequality. Two developments belie conservative assumptions about family. The first brings a new perspective to the discussion about the two-parent family and the impact of family structure on family well-being. The second reveals that social and economic conditions are reconfiguring living arrangements even among groups with strong commitments to family life.

Whether Latinos (or some Latino groups) have stronger family values and live in close-knit family arrangements is a question for further research. But the fact remains that the family convictions and behaviors attributed to Latinos have not prevented them from becoming the poorest racial category in the United States. As Daniel T. Lichter and Nancy S. Landale conclude, "although Latino families typically 'play by the rules,' they often remain poor" (1995:347). These researchers found that while substantial variation exists across Latino groups, parental work patterns are more important then family structure in accounting for poverty among Latino children:

> The vast majority of Latino children live in two-parent families and almost one-half of all poor Latino children live in married couple families, compared with 17 percent of poor African American children. (ibid.)

The conventional wisdom about the association between family structure and poverty does not hold up for Latinos. Hence policies designed to "strengthen the family" will not be enough to alleviate poverty among Latinos.

Another paradox of the Latino presence in the United States underscores the importance of social and material conditions in shaping attitudes, behaviors, and family patterns. Despite high official rates of intact family characteristics upon their arrival in the United States, these characteristics are weakened in successive generations. Through the 1980s and 1990s Latinos' rates of female-headed households have risen. Furthermore, research shows that life in the United States exposes immigrants (even those with strong family values) to the current social context, which gives rise to high rates of single parenthood and divorce. Although marriage is idealized in many Latin American countries, and there is a stigma to being divorced (Turner 1996), the U.S. social context produces family patterns that are part of a worldwide trend toward greater maritally disrupted family structures. This generational trend is true for all immigrant groups (Rumbaut 1997).

### *Anti-Immigration Sentiment and Family Values*

With rare exceptions, little connection is made between immigration and family values. Yet the link reveals a distinctive form of racism embedded in conservative profamily rhetoric, where there is said to be "too much of the former and too little of the latter" (Rumbaut 1997:1). Such thinking rests on enormous contradictions insofar as family matters are concerned. Latino immigrants are perceived as a threat to core American characteristics even though they embody what conservatives purport to cherish most: strong families. Indeed, "most Latin American immigrants may be a source of strength with regard to family values, and not a liability" (Fukuyama 1993:28). The discord is driven by fears of cultural invasion. In the same breath, anti-immigrant rhetoric can bemoan family breakdown and its attendant social disruptions and "worry whether the 'brown hoards' of Mexicans and Central Americans, with their high fertility rates will soon deplete American jobs and social services" (Zavella 1996:366).

When it comes to Latino immigrants, conservatives pathologize the values they champion and recast strong families as a menace to society. Anti-immigrant campaigns rest on a racist and misogynist *family* imagery. Immigration scholar Pierrette Hondagneu-Sotelo describes how stereotypes of Latina immigrants as breeders of large families were used in California's 1994 campaign to pass Proposition 187:

> The protagonists . . . were poor, pregnant immigrant women who were drawn to the U.S. [to] give birth in publicly financed county hospitals, allowing their children to be born as U.S. citizens and subsequent recipients of taxpayer-supported medical care, public assistance and education. In this scenario, immigrant families constitute a rapidly expanding underclass draining education and medical resources in the United States. (Hondagneu-Sotelo 1995:173)

Hondagneu-Sotelo explains that the villain in this caricaturelike rendition is a newly racialized *family* image. Proposition 197 was an antifamily campaign, targeting the use of public resources immigrant families need to sustain their daily lives.

Including Latinos in the national discussion can uncover some of the myriad connections between family, race, and social inequality. The current Latino experience strengthens the progressive critique by documenting that family values and family structure matter far less than conservatives claim. As Latinos become an ever larger share of the U.S. population, their presence shapes the conservative agenda in complex and contradictory ways. Recent developments reveal that family can become a powerful symbol of otherness. Furthermore, *any family form* can be deployed to exclude unwanted racial groups. A multiracial analysis poses empirical and intellectual challenges and points to the need for new directions in understanding.

## REFERENCES

Baca Zinn, Maxine. 1990. "Family, Feminism, and Race in America." *Gender & Society* 4(1):68–82.

———. 1994. "Feminist Rethinking from Racial-Ethnic Families." Pp. 303–14 in *Women of Color in U.S. Society,* edited by Maxine Baca Zinn and Bonnie Thornton Dill. Philadelphia: Temple University Press.

———. 1995. "Social Science Theorizing for Latino Families in the Age of Diversity." Pp. 177–87 in *Understanding Latino Families: Scholarship, Policy, and Practice,* edited by Ruth E. Zambrana. Thousand Oaks, CA: Sage.

Baca Zinn, Maxine and Bonnie Thornton Dill. 1996. "Theorizing Difference from Multiracial Feminism." *Feminist Studies* 22(Summer):321–31.

Baca Zinn, Maxine and D. Stanley Eitzen. 1996. *Diversity in Families,* 4th ed. New York: Harper Collins.

Coontz, Stephanie. 1992. *The Way We Never Were: American Families and the Nostalgia Trap.* New York: Harper Collins.

Dill, Bonnie Thornton. 1988. "Our Mothers' Grief: Racial Ethnic Women and the Maintenance of Families." *Journal of Family History* 13:415–31.

———. 1994. "Fictive Kin, Paper Sons, and Compadrazgo: Women of Color and the Struggle for Survival." Pp. 149–70 in *Women of Color in U.S. Society,* edited by Maxine Baca Zinn and Bonnie Thornton Dill. Philadelphia: Temple University Press.

Dill, Bonnie Thornton, Maxine Baca Zinn, and Sandra Patton. 1993. "Feminism, Race, and the Politics of Family Values." *Philosophy and Public Policy* 13(3):13–18.

Estrada, Richard. 1989. "Myths of Hispanic Families' Wellness." *Kansas City Star* (September 10):5-I.

Fukuyama, Francis. 1993. "Immigrants and Family Values." *Commentary* (May): 26–32.

Glenn, Evelyn Nakano. 1992. "From Servitude to Service Work: Historical Continuities in the Racial Division of Paid Reproductive Labor." *Signs: Journal of Women in Culture and Society* 18(1):1–43.

Gordon, David. 1996. "Values That Work." *Nation* (June 17):16–22.

Hacker, Andrew. 1996. "The Racial Income Gap." Pp. 308–14 in *The Meaning of Difference,* edited by Karen E. Rosenblum and Toni-Michelle C. Travis. New York: McGraw Hill.

Hayes-Bautista, David. 1989. "Latino Adolescents, Families, Work, and the Economy: Building upon Strength or Creating a Weakness?" Paper prepared for the Carnegie Commission on Adolescent Development, Washington, DC.

Hill Collins, Patricia. 1990. *Black Feminist Thought: Knowledge, Consciousness, and the Politics of Empowerment.* Boston: Unwin Hyman.

———. 1997. "African-American Women and Economic Justice: A Preliminary Analysis of Wealth, Family, and Black Social Class." Unpublished paper, Department of African American Studies, University of Cincinnati.

Hondagneu-Sotelo, Pierrette. 1995. "Women and Children First: New Directions in Anti-immigrant Politics." *Socialist Review* 25(1):169–90.

Lichter, Daniel T. and Nancy S. Landale. 1995. "Parental Work, Family Structure, and Poverty among Latino Children." *Journal of Marriage and the Family* 57(May):346–54.

Marone, James A. 1996. "The Corrosive Politics of Virtue." *American Prospect* 26(May–June):30–39.

Massey, Douglas A. 1993. "Latino Poverty Research: An Agenda for the 1990s." *Items—The Social Science Research Council* 47(March):7–11.
McLanahan, Sara and Gary Sandefur. 1994. *Growing Up with a Single Parent.* Cambridge, MA: Harvard University Press.
Moynihan, Daniel P. 1965. *The Negro Family: The Case for National Action.* Washington, DC: Office of Policy Planning and Research, U.S. Department of Labor.
Murray, Charles. 1984. *Losing Ground.* New York: Basic Books.
O'Hare, William P. 1996. "A New Look at Poverty in America." *Population Bulletin* 51(2, September):entire issue.
Polakow, Valarie. 1993. *Lives on the Edge: Single Mothers and Their Children in the Other America.* Chicago: University of Chicago Press.
Rumbaut, Ruben G. 1997. "Ties That Bind: Immigration and Immigrant Families in the United States." Pp. 3–46 in *Immigration and the Family,* edited by Alan Booth, Ann C. Crouter, and Nancy Landale. Hillsdale, NJ: Erlbaum Associates.
Sidel, Ruth. 1996. *Keeping Women and Children Last.* New York: Penguin.
Skolnick, Arlene and Stacey Rosencrantz. 1994. "The New Crusade for the Old Family." *American Prospect* 18(Summer):59–65.
Stacey, Judith. 1990. *Brave New Families: Stories of Domestic Upheaval in Late Twentieth-Century America.* New York: Basic Books.
———. 1996. *In the Name of The Family: Rethinking Family Values in the Postmodern Age.* Boston: Beacon.
Thurow, Lester C. 1997. "Changes in Capitalism Render One-Earner Families Extinct." *USA Today* (Monday, January 27):17A.
Turner, Scott. 1996. "Single Parenthood Hurts Immigrants' Economic Gains." *Population Today* (May):4–5.
Vega, William A. 1990. "Hispanic Families in the 1980s: A Decade of Research." *Journal of Marriage and the Family* 52:1015–24.
———. 1995. "The Study of Latino Families: A Point of Departure." Pp. 31–17 in *Understanding Latino Families: Scholarship, Policy, and Practice,* edited by Ruth E. Zambrana. Thousand Oaks, CA: Sage.
Whitehead, Barbara Dafoe. 1993. "Dan Quayle Was Right." *Atlantic Monthly* 271(April):47–84.
Wilson, James Q. 1993. "The Family Values Debate." *Commentary* 95(April):24–31.
Wilson, William and Katheryn Neckerman. 1986. "Poverty and Family Structure: The Widening Gap between Evidence and Public Policy Issues." Pp. 232–59 in *Fighting Poverty,* edited by Sheldon H. Danziger and Danil Weinberg. Cambridge, MA: Harvard University Press.
Young, Iris Marion. 1994. "Making Single Motherhood Normal." *Dissent* 41(Winter):88–93.
Zavella, Patricia. 1996. "Living on the Edge: Everyday Lives of Poor Chicano/Mexicano Families." Pp. 362–86 in *Mapping Multiculturalism,* edited by Avery F. Gordon and Christopher Newfield. Minneapolis: University of Minnesota Press.

# III

# Work and Family Adaptations in a Changing Context

# Dominant and Minority Couples: An Analysis of Family Economic Well-Being 6

Marilyn Fernandez and Kwang Chung Kim

## INTRODUCTION

Many scholars of race and ethnic relations in the United States have documented the gradual transformation of the United States from a biracial to a multiracial and multiethnic society (Farley 1995; Feagin and Feagin 1996; Schaefer 1996). Largely as a result of the 1965 revision of the U.S. immigration law, the immigration flow into the country has been dominated by people from Latin America and Asia (Barringer, Gardner, and Levin 1993; U.S. Commission on Civil Rights 1988, 1992).

However, as Yinger (1994) points out, much of the current sociological research on race/ethnic relations in the United States continues to use a biracial framework with a focus on white and African-American relationships. In order to capture better the changing reality of American ethnic relations, a multiracial and multiethnic focus is necessary. The dominant and minority group relationship perspective (Farley and Allen 1987; Feagin and Feagin 1996; Schaefer 1996), within which are embedded the relationships among minority groups, offers a useful framework for such an analysis. Currently in the United States, U.S.-born non-Hispanic whites are considered the dominant group; the minority groups include African-Americans, native Americans, Hispanics, and Asian-Americans. A multirace/multiethnic focus requires not only a dominant-minority group comparison but comparisons among minority groups as well.

The extent of and success in the incorporation of multiple ethnic groups in a society can be studied at many different levels. Their economic and family lives, the nature of linkages between the two, and their implications for the individual and society are some important dimensions (Voydanoff 1984). While much of the research on economic adaptation of ethnic groups generally focuses on individuals, a case can be made to shift the unit of analysis to the family or the couple. The family is a primary institution within which most individuals' lives, including their economic lives, are organized (Queen, Habenstein, and Quadagno 1985). For example, many immigrants are known to pool their resources with immediate and extended family members to ease their transition into the host society (Bonacich and Modell 1980; Light and Bonacich 1988). As a first step in this analytical approach, this chapter will focus on married couples and describe the strategies couples use to maintain their family's economic well-being. More specifically, race/ethnic differences in the labor force participation of couples and the economic contributions that couples make to their families will be examined.

The 1990 5 percent Public Use Micro Sample (PUMS) data from the U.S. Census are used to examine differences among the major ethnic groups in the United States, namely, non-Hispanic whites, the six largest Asian American groups (Chinese, Japanese, Filipinos, Asian Indians, Koreans, and Vietnamese), Hispanics, and African-Americans. Nativity differences are examined for select Asian-Americans—Japanese, Chinese, and Filipino—who have sizable U.S.-born populations as well as for Hispanics.[1]

## COMPARATIVE RACE/ETHNIC FRAMEWORK OF STRATEGIES

The strategies used by couples to maintain their family's economic well-being can be influenced by at least two sets of interrelated factors: (1) the human capital resources available to minority groups, which are largely a product of (2) the historical and current nature of race/ethnic relations in the United States.

African-Americans have not only historically experienced discrimination in the form of residential segregation and occupational discrimination, they also have been most impacted by the deindustrialization and deinvestment in major American cities (Massey and Denton 1993; Wilson 1987). The many generations of discriminatory experiences have depleted the individual and collective resources of inner-city African-Americans. Combined with the limited job opportunities available to inner-city residents, these factors also appear to have discouraged many from actively seeking jobs and developing a stable work pattern (Wilson 1987).

Hispanic-Americans are an ethnically diverse group. Yet 60 percent are Mexican Americans and more than 10 percent are Puerto Ricans (Feagin and Feagin 1996; Marger 1991; Schaefer 1996). They have experienced severe handicaps in their limited educational and occupational opportunities, racial stereotyping, language and institutionalized discrimination, industrial restructuring, and internal colonialism (Farley 1995; Feagin and Feagin 1996; Yinger 1994). They also have limited human capital resources (for example, lower education) compared to the dominant white group (Feagin and Feagin 1996). Although their educational attainment is gradually improving, the low levels of education are considered a product of decades of limited opportunities. In addition, the circular migration (between the

United States and country of origin) pattern that characterizes Mexican-Americans and Puerto Ricans has strengthened their ethnic identity and attachment to their home culture and language. These factors appear to create adjustment problems for Hispanic children in American schools (Marger 1991).

Immigrant Asian-Americans have higher levels of human capital resources (for example, education) than the white dominant group (Barringer et al. 1993; U.S. Commission on Civil Rights 1998, 1992). The preimmigration middle-class status of a large proportion of Asian immigrants indicates relatively rich personal human capital as well as collective family and community resources. Using these resources, Asian immigrants with transferable skills (such as doctors and engineers) have been able to secure jobs commensurate with their training. However, many Asian-Americans work in jobs that have a short supply of workers partly because they are avoided by native workers. They also work in jobs that require low skills, pay low wages, and/or have unfavorable working conditions (U.S. Commission on Civil Rights 1988, 1992). Growing numbers create their own jobs and become self-employed (Fernandez and Kim 1995).

Asian-Americans also occupy a unique position in the dominant-minority ethnic hierarchy in the United States. The majority of all Asian groups, with the exception of the Japanese, entered the United States after the 1965 immigration reform either as immigrants or refugees. When Asian immigration gained momentum in the 1970s and 1980s, Asian immigrants did not experience significant hostility from the dominant white group, either because the host society was indifferent to or ignorant of their arrival. Yet, over time, Asian-Americans, both U.S.-born and immigrants, have been subjected to various forms of subtle discrimination in the labor market as evident in the glass ceiling (Tang 1993) and concentration in the secondary labor market (U.S. Commission on Civil Rights 1988, 1992). Such discrimination is partly attributed to their racial and cultural distinctiveness (Hurh and Kim 1989).

Further, Asian-Americans, because of their relatively rich human capital resources, have been found to cope with the economic challenges and discrimination they face in their new home society by mobilizing all available resources, including that of the wife and children (Barringer et al. 1993). Thus, in many Asian-American families, the wife, children, and other relatives participate in the labor market and contribute to the family's economic well-being. This is despite the traditional norms of Asian cultures, which are often reflected in traditional gender roles in the family, where the husband is expected to be the main breadwinner while the wife takes care of the children and the home (Kim and Hurh 1991). Nevertheless, husbands continue to be the main providers.

In short, given the different historical and current experiences of the minority groups in the dominant-minority hierarchy and their human capital resources, the strategies they use to maintain their family's economic well-being can be expected to vary. Human capital resources and the resulting labor market opportunities are expected to shape couples' economic contribution to the families.

## DATA

Data for this chapter are derived from the 5 percent Public Use Microdata Sample of the 1990 U.S. census (Bureau of the Census 1992a). Because the focus of the chapter is on the strategies couples use to maintain their family's economic well-being, only households with both husband and wife present are selected to create the couple file.[2,3] Ethnicity and nativity (that is, whether they are foreign or U.S.-born) of the couple presented in the tables are identified by that of the husband.

A family's *economic well-being* or status is operationalized by the family's total income, which represents the sum of the incomes of all members who are 15 years old and over in a family.[4] Strategies used by the couple are defined by the labor force participation characteristics of the husband and wife, the couple's combined work status, and their contribution to the family's income. *Labor force participation* is operationalized by the husband and wife's occupational prestige scores (Stevens and Cho 1985) as well as by the number of weeks and hours per week worked in 1989. The *couple's combined work status* refers to whether they are a dual-worker couple or not. The husband and wife's contribution to the family income is measured as the proportion of the total family income from two sources:[5] (1) each of their work-related earnings in 1989 (from wages or salaries from employment or income from self-employment) and (2) each of their incomes from all sources. The balance in the family income (after the husband and wife's contributions through their income from all sources are subtracted) is the contribution of other family members. Human capital resources are measured by age and years of schooling completed.

## PROFILE OF MARRIED-COUPLE HOUSEHOLDS

There are 48,765,934 married couples that meet the selection criteria. A great majority or 84 percent (41,172,352) of the couples in the analyses are U.S.-born non-Hispanic white (referred to as whites from here on). About 7 percent (3,201,282) are African-American and 7 percent (3,304,377) are Hispanic couples. Couples of the six major Asian-American categories comprise 2 percent (1,087,923).

Panels 1 and 2 of Tables 1 and 2 present the mean human capital characteristics of husband and wives in the thirteen ethnic groups.[6] The average age of husbands in all race/ethnic groups is around 40 (Panel 1 of Table 1), with the exception of U.S.-born Japanese husbands. Foreign-born husbands tend to be younger than U.S.-born husbands. Wives are somewhat younger than their husbands (Panel 1 of Table 2). Wives range in age from a low of 37 among foreign-born Vietnamese to a high of 45 among whites. On balance, both husbands and wives in all groups are in peak wage earning age groups.

Asian-American husbands and wives (with the exception of foreign-born Vietnamese) have higher educational levels than whites, African-Americans, and Hispanics (Panels 2 of Tables 1 and 2). Hispanic husbands have lower levels of education than their white counterparts. A similar pattern is found in Table 2 for Hispanic wives when compared to white wives.

African-American husbands and wives generally have either equal or lower human capital resources when compared with Hispanic husbands and wives, respectively. African-American husbands are equal to U.S.-born Hispanics in their education (9.6), but their education is higher than that of immigrant Hispanic husbands (7.8). In contrast, African-American wives have higher educational levels (10.1 in Table 2) than both foreign (7.9) and U.S.-born Hispanic wives (9.4).

Data presented in Tables 1 and 2 suggest that Asian-American couples have the highest levels of human capital resources, followed by white couples, and then by Hispanic and African-American couples. Hispanic and African-American couples appear similar in their human capital.

## LABOR FORCE PARTICIPATION AND WORK STATUS

The high labor force participation of Asian-American husbands and wives found in Panels 3–5 of Tables 1 and 2 is commensurate with their high levels of human capital. Among all the groups considered in this analysis, Asian-American husbands have the highest occupational prestige scores (with the exception of Vietnamese and Filipino husbands), and work the most weeks and hours per week in 1989 (U.S.-born Japanese and Vietnamese are exceptions).

Hispanic husbands work more hours and weeks in 1989 than white husbands. Yet, Hispanic husbands work in jobs that are of lower occupational prestige (U.S.-born Hispanics = 32.7; foreign-born Hispanics = 28) than their white counterparts (39.5). Similar patterns are found in the labor force participation of Asian-American and Hispanic wives when compared to white wives (Table 2).

African-American husbands have the lowest labor force participation levels of all groups. They work in jobs that have, on average, lower occupational

*Table 1.* Mean Human Capital Resources of Husbands by Race/Ethnicity of Households[a]: 1990 U.S. Census 5% PUMS Data[b]

| | (1) Age | (2) Education | (3) Occupational Prestige | (4) Weeks Workedin 1989 | (5) Hours Worked per Week in 1989 | (6) (N) |
|---|---|---|---|---|---|---|
| U.S.-born non-Hispanic whites | 47.9 | 10.9 | 39.5 | 39.1 | 36.2 | 41,172,352 |
| U.S.-born African-Americans | 46.7 | 9.6 | 31.1 | 37.1 | 33.2 | 3,201,282 |
| Hispanics | | | | | | |
| U.S.-born | 42.2 | 9.6 | 32.7 | 40.6 | 37.3 | 1,405,504 |
| Foreign-born | 41.8 | 7.8 | 28.0 | 40.4 | 37.8 | 1,898,873 |
| Chinese | | | | | | |
| U.S.-born | 46.3 | 12.7 | 51.5 | 42.6 | 38.2 | 44,645 |
| Foreign-born | 45.9 | 11.4 | 44.3 | 40.6 | 37.8 | 277,797 |
| Japanese | | | | | | |
| U.S.-born | 52.6 | 11.6 | 44.3 | 38.0 | 33.5 | 117,683 |
| Foreign-born | 41.5 | 12.9 | 50.1 | 45.6 | 44.3 | 51,844 |
| Filipinos | | | | | | |
| U.S.-born | 41.1 | 11.1 | 37.6 | 44.5 | 39.5 | 25,605 |
| Foreign-born | 46.4 | 11.9 | 39.2 | 42.3 | 37.4 | 186,311 |
| Foreign-born Asian Indians | 41.8 | 13.5 | 53.4 | 46.5 | 43.0 | 170,054 |
| Foreign-born Koreans | 43.5 | 12.3 | 42.5 | 42.6 | 43.1 | 125,729 |
| Foreign-born Vietnamese | 41.0 | 10.2 | 36.1 | 40.2 | 35.6 | 81,683 |

[a] Race/Ethnicity of household is identified by the race/ethnicity of husband.
[b] The numbers are weighted back to the total population: (a) percentage of husband's contribution to the family income; (b) percentage of married couple's contribution to family income.

*Table 2.* Mean Human Capital Resources of Wives by Race/Ethnicity of Households:[a] 1990 U.S. Census 5% PUMS Data[b]

| | (1) Age | (2) Education | (3) Occupational Prestige | (4) Weeks Worked in 1989 | (5) Hours Worked per Week in 1989 | (6) (N) |
|---|---|---|---|---|---|---|
| U.S.-born non-Hispanic whites | 45.4 | 10.7 | 38.2 | 27.3 | 22.6 | 41,172,352 |
| U.S.-born African-Americans | 43.8 | 10.1 | 34.5 | 30.6 | 26.3 | 3,201,282 |
| Hispanics | | | | | | |
| U.S.-born | 39.8 | 9.4 | 34.2 | 27.0 | 32.7 | 1,405,504 |
| Foreign-born | 38.8 | 7.9 | 28.2 | 22.7 | 21.1 | 1,898,873 |
| Chinese | | | | | | |
| U.S.-born | 43.3 | 12.0 | 44.6 | 32.3 | 26.3 | 44,645 |
| Foreign-born | 42.1 | 10.3 | 37.3 | 29.5 | 26.4 | 277,797 |
| Japanese | | | | | | |
| U.S.-born | 49.7 | 11.2 | 41.1 | 30.1 | 24.5 | 117,683 |
| Foreign-born | 38.8 | 11.9 | 42.5 | 15.3 | 12.8 | 51,844 |
| Filipinos | | | | | | |
| U.S.-born | 38.6 | 11.0 | 35.8 | 34.9 | 29.6 | 25,605 |
| Foreign-born | 43.3 | 12.0 | 37.8 | 38.2 | 32.7 | 186,311 |
| Foreign-born Asian Indians | 37.6 | 12.2 | 42.6 | 28.3 | 25.0 | 170,054 |
| Foreign-born Koreans | 40.0 | 11.3 | 34.0 | 26.9 | 26.3 | 125,729 |
| Foreign-born Vietnamese | 37.3 | 8.9 | 30.1 | 27.8 | 24.8 | 81,683 |

[a] Race/ethnicity of household is identified by the race/ethnicity of husband.
[b] The numbers are weighted back to the total population.

prestige (31.1) and also work fewer hours (33.2) and weeks (37.1) in 1989 than all other groups of husbands. African-American wives fall between foreign and U.S.-born Hispanic wives in terms of their occupational prestige and the number of hours worked, but African-American wives work more weeks in 1989 than either group of Hispanic wives.

The distribution of couples by the work status of the husbands and wives and their ethnicity is presented in Table 3. Minority couples generally have both spouses working in higher proportions than white couples. Only three of the twelve minority groups considered here—immigrant Japanese, immigrant Hispanic, and immigrant Korean couples—have lower proportions of dual workers than whites. U.S.-born and foreign-born Filipino couples are most likely to be dual-worker couples (77 percent). Among the other Asian couples, the proportions of dual-worker couples vary from 66.7 percent among U.S.-born Chinese to 60.1 percent among Vietnamese. On balance, the proportion of dual-worker couples is highest among Asian-Americans, followed by African-Americans, then U.S.-born Hispanics, and last by whites. It is also interesting to note that whites are more likely to have neither spouse working (13.5 percent) than most of the minority groups, which may partly be a reflection of the older age composition of white couples.

In short, Asian-American couples rank the highest in the labor force participation rates: they are most likely to be dual-worker couples; they not only work longer in 1989 but do so in higher prestige jobs. Hispanic husbands and wives work more (weeks and hours per week) than white couples but work in jobs that are of lower prestige than the jobs of whites. A similar pattern—of longer weeks and hours worked but in lower prestige jobs—holds for wives in African-American families. In contrast, African-American husbands have the lowest labor force participation levels on all three indicators.

## ASSESSMENT OF ECONOMIC WELL-BEING OF VARIOUS RACE/ETHNIC COUPLES

How do these human capital and labor force participation differences among the race/ethnic groups relate to the family's economic well-being and the economic contributions that the couples make? The results are shown in Table 4. Asian-American couples have the highest overall family income of all groups considered here (Panel 1). With the exception of Vietnamese couples, every other group of Asian-American couples has higher family incomes than the $48,642 reported for white couples. Similar differences exist between Asian-American and white couples even when only dual-worker couples are considered (Panel 2) and to a lesser extent when only the husband and or wife works (Panels 3 and 4).

*Table 3.* Work Status of Couples by Race/Ethnicity of Household:[a] 1990 U.S. Census 5% PUMS Data[b]

| | (1) Both Work (%) | (2) Only Husband Works (%) | (3) Only Wife Works (%) | (4) Neither Works (%) | (5) Total (%) | (6) (N) |
|---|---|---|---|---|---|---|
| U.S.-born non-Hispanic whites | 59.7 | 22.4 | 4.4 | 13.5 | 100.0 | 41,172,352 |
| U.S.-born African-Americans | 62.6 | 16.8 | 7.9 | 12.8 | 100.0 | 3,201,282 |
| Hispanics | | | | | | |
| U.S.-born | 60.9 | 25.7 | 4.4 | 8.9 | 100.0 | 1,405,504 |
| Foreign-born | 53.3 | 35.1 | 3.9 | 7.7 | 100.0 | 1,898,873 |
| Chinese | | | | | | |
| U.S.-born | 66.7 | 20.4 | 4.5 | 8.5 | 100.0 | 44,645 |
| Foreign-born | 62.7 | 23.7 | 4.8 | 8.8 | 100.0 | 277,797 |
| Japanese | | | | | | |
| U.S.-born | 60.7 | 18.0 | 6.7 | 14.5 | 100.0 | 117,683 |
| Foreign-born | 35.1 | 59.7 | 1.6 | 3.7 | 100.0 | 51,844 |
| Filipinos | | | | | | |
| U.S.-born | 77.0 | 15.3 | 3.6 | 4.1 | 100.0 | 25,605 |
| Foreign-born | 77.1 | 11.8 | 5.8 | 5.4 | 100.0 | 186,311 |
| Foreign-born Asian Indians | 65.2 | 31.5 | 1.7 | 1.6 | 100.0 | 170,054 |
| Foreign-born Koreans | 59.5 | 32.4 | 3.3 | 4.8 | 100.0 | 125,729 |
| Foreign-born Vietnamese | 60.1 | 25.2 | 3.0 | 11.7 | 100.0 | 81,683 |

[a] Race/Ethnicity of household is identified by the race/ethnicity of husband
[b] The numbers are weighted back to the total population.

*Table 4.* Mean Family Income ($) by Work Status of Married Couples by Race/Ethnicity of Households:[a] 1990 U.S. Census 5% PUMS Data[b]

| | (1) Total | (2) Both Work | (3) Only Husband Works | (4) Only Wife Works | (5) Neither Works | (6) (N) |
|---|---|---|---|---|---|---|
| U.S.-born non-Hispanic whites | 48,642 | 54,836 | 48,467 | 32,890 | 26,742 | 41,172,352 |
| U.S.-born African-Americans | 38,351 | 46,024 | 30,590 | 27,901 | 17,377 | 3,201,282 |
| Hispanics | | | | | | |
| U.S.-born | 38,302 | 44,732 | 31,835 | 25,224 | 19,124 | 1,405,504 |
| Foreign-born | 34,066 | 40,548 | 28,676 | 25,466 | 18,094 | 1,898,873 |
| Chinese | | | | | | |
| U.S.-born | 69,756 | 76,134 | 63,731 | 49,923 | 44,538 | 44,645 |
| Foreign-born | 51,423 | 59,434 | 43,929 | 32,749 | 24,794 | 277,797 |
| Japanese | | | | | | |
| U.S.-born | 62,162 | 70,389 | 59,920 | 49,123 | 36,600 | 117,683 |
| Foreign-born | 64,476 | 64,511 | 67,399 | 47,252 | 24,115 | 51,844 |
| Filipinos | | | | | | |
| U.S.-born | 51,063 | 54,055 | 42,838 | 46,593 | 29,475 | 25,605 |
| Foreign-born | 28,451 | 63,098 | 50,185 | 41,524 | 28,204 | 186,311 |
| Foreign-born Asian Indians | 64,799 | 70,611 | 56,261 | 39,702 | 22,729 | 170,054 |
| Foreign-born Koreans | 49,571 | 57,047 | 42,935 | 27,198 | 17,316 | 125,729 |
| Foreign-born Vietnamese | 41,165 | 50,780 | 30,498 | 26,735 | 18,525 | 81,683 |

[a] Race/Ethnicity of household is identified by the race/ethnicity of husband
[b] The numbers are weighted back to the total population.

On the other hand, Hispanic and African-American couples do not differ significantly in their overall family income as well as in the family income in each of the couple's work status categories. The family incomes of both groups are generally lower than that of Asian-American couples. Hispanic and African-American families also have lower incomes than white families even when both husband and wife work.

Table 5 presents the earnings and income contributions of husbands and wives to the family income. Husbands' earnings represent between 42 percent (African-Americans) and 79.6 percent (immigrant Japanese) of the fam-

*Table 5.* Contribution (%) of Husband and Wife to Family Income by Race/Ethnicity of Households:[a] 1990 U.S. Census 5% PUMS Data [b]

| | *1989 Earnings of:* | | | *1989 income of:* | |
|---|---|---|---|---|---|
| | *(1)* *Husband* | *(2)* *Wife* | *(3)* *Couple* | *(4)* *Couple* | *(5)* *Other Family Members* |
| U.S.-born non-Hispanic whites | 46.5 | 24.2 | 70.7 | 94.5 | 5.5 |
| U.S.-born African-Americans | 42.0 | 27.5 | 69.5 | 92.0 | 8.0 |
| Hispanics | | | | | |
| U.S.-born | 57.6 | 22.2 | 79.8 | 92.7 | 7.3 |
| Foreign-born | 57.9 | 19.4 | 77.3 | 87.2 | 12.8 |
| Chinese | | | | | |
| U.S.-born | 54.3 | 24.1 | 78.4 | 94.2 | 5.8 |
| Foreign-born | 52.7 | 23.8 | 76.5 | 90.0 | 10.0 |
| Japanese | | | | | |
| U.S.-born | 46.3 | 21.3 | 67.6 | 91.8 | 8.2 |
| Foreign-born | 79.6 | 11.4 | 91.0 | 98.1 | 1.9 |
| Filipinos | | | | | |
| U.S.-born | 57.3 | 26.4 | 83.7 | 92.2 | 7.8 |
| Foreign-born | 46.3 | 32.9 | 79.2 | 87.8 | 12.2 |
| Foreign-born Asian Indians | 67.4 | 21.4 | 88.8 | 94.0 | 6.0 |
| Foreign-born Koreans | 63.8 | 21.9 | 85.7 | 93.5 | 6.5 |
| Foreign-born Vietnamese | 51.8 | 21.8 | 73.6 | 88.0 | 12.0 |

[a] Race/Ethnicity of household is identified by the race/ethnicity of husband
[b] The numbers are weighted back to the total population.

ily income (Panel 1 in Table 5). Wives generally contribute less than half of what the husbands do.

There is, however, ethnic variability in husbands' and wives' earnings contributions. Asian-American husbands, who on average have the highest levels of human capital and labor force participation of all groups included in this analysis, contribute the most compared to all other groups (ranging from 79.6 percent among immigrant Japanese husbands to 46.3 percent among U.S.-born Japanese and immigrant Filipino couples). Despite their comparatively lower levels of human capital, Hispanic husbands, both U.S.-born and immigrant, contribute more than white husbands. Hispanic husbands may contribute more than white husbands by working more weeks and hours. African-American husbands contribute the least to the family income perhaps because of their lower levels of human capital and labor force participation. Ethnic differences in wives' contribution are the converse of the husbands' patterns (Panel 2 in Table 5).

The combined earnings of the husband and wife contribute between 70 and 90 percent of the family income in all groups (Panel 3 in Table 5). The balance in the family income is made up of income from two sources: (1) individual income from sources other than employment or self-employment (namely, interest, dividends, or net rental or royalty; Social Security; public assistance; retirement, and other sources); (2) income from children and other relatives who live with the family.

Again ethnic differences exist in the proportion contributed by the couple through their wage, salary, and self-employment earnings. Asian-American and Hispanic couples contribute more (more than 75 percent) to the family income than white or African-American couples. White and African-American couples' earnings contribution to the family income is about 70 percent. Wives in African-American families (whose contribution ranks highest among wives) make up for the difference in the contribution of their husbands relative to white husbands.

When the contribution that couples make through their income (from all sources) is examined (Panel 4 in Table 5), several interesting patterns emerge. When income rather than earnings is considered, the contributions of the couples increase to more than 90 percent for most groups (with the exception of foreign-born Hispanics, Filipinos, and Vietnamese). But the highest jump in contribution levels is seen among white, African-American, and U.S.-born Japanese couples. *Almost a quarter of the income contribution* that these three groups of couples make to the family comes from sources *other than wages, salary, and/or self-employment.* In contrast, under 10 percent of the contribution of Hispanic and Asian-American couples comes from non-employment-related sources. Further, other family members (children and other relatives) contribute more to the family income in almost all the minority families than in white families (Panel 5 of Table 5). Foreign-born families receive the most contribution from other family members (12.8 percent in the Hispanic, 10 percent in the Chinese, 12.2 percent in the Filipino, and 12 percent in the Vietnamese families).

## CONCLUSION AND DISCUSSION

This exploratory analysis has found interesting ethnic variations in economic well-being of families in the United States and the strategies used by couples to maintain their families' economic status. Ethnic differences in family income appear to follow the human capital differences observed. Asian-American couples have the highest levels of human capital and family income, followed by white couples. Hispanic couples, particularly the U.S.-born, and African-American couples appear similar in their location below Asian-American and whites on both criteria.

Differences also exist in the strategies used to maintain family economic well-being. Asian-Americans are the most likely to be dual-worker couples, work in higher prestige jobs, and work more hours and weeks than other groups. They also have the highest family incomes among dual-worker couples of all ethnic groups, perhaps due to their high human capital and labor force participation. On the other hand, African-American and Hispanic couples, despite their lower (than white) levels of human capital are more likely to be dual-worker couples than white couples. However, compared to white couples, Hispanic and African-American couples work longer hours but in lower prestige jobs. It is quite likely that the challenges African-American and Hispanics face in the labor market because of their position on the dominant-minority hierarchy require that both partners work and work longer hours to make the family economically viable, even if their incomes fall short of the incomes of white families.

In terms of the contributions to family income, Asian-American husbands contribute the most, followed by Hispanic, white, and African-American husbands. Among wives in the different race/ethnic groups, African-American wives contribute the most. Further, Hispanic and Asian-American couples rely more on their employment or self-employment income than on other sources to maintain their family's economic well-being. While white and African-American couples also do the same, almost a quarter of their contribution comes from other sources (such as investments, social security, and public assistance). Family members other than the couple are likely to contribute more in foreign-born families among Hispanic and Asian-Americans than in the U.S.-born families.

The variability in the strategies for maintaining the family's economic well-being found between whites and the minority groups as well as among Asian-Americans, African-Americans, and Hispanic Americans points to the need for broadening the focus of the sociological literature on ethnic relations in the United States from biracial to multiracial. Such an analysis can also be extended to variations in family form.

## NOTES

1. Because Native Americans are quite segregated from the urban opportunity structures in the United States, they will be excluded from this analysis.

2. The census identifies information of head and spouse in a household. Not all heads are male, and not all spouses are female. In order to control for possible gender differences, data for heads and spouses are converted into data for husbands and wives. A new variable was created in which if the head of household was male he was treated as the husband (score of 0), and if the head was female she was treated as the wife (score of 1). Similarly, if the spouse was a male, he was the husband (score of 0 on the same new variable), and if the spouse was a female she was the wife (score of 1).

3. The numbers are weighted back to the total population.

4. The U.S. Census Bureau distinguishes between income and earnings: An individual's total "income" is the algebraic sum of income reported separately from the following sources: wage or salary income; net nonfarm self-employment income; net farm self-employment income; interest, dividend, or net rental or royalty income; Social Security or railroad retirement income; public assistance or welfare income; retirement or disability income; and all other income. Individual "earnings" includes only wage or salary income and net income from farm and nonfarm self-employment (Bureau of the Census 1992b).

5. Families with incomes of 0 or below were not included because of computational difficulties (division of head and spouse's earnings by 0 family income) in the contribution variable.

6. Because couples are the unit of analysis in this chapter, the ethnicity and nativity of wives are defined by ethnicity and nativity of their husbands, irrespective of the wives' own ethnicity and nativity.

## REFERENCES

Barringer, H., R. W. Gardner, and M. J. Levin. 1993. *Asians and Pacific Islanders in the United States.* New York: Russell Sage Foundation.

Bonacich, E. and J. Modell. 1980. *The Economic Basis of Ethnic Solidarity: Small Business in the Japanese American Community.* Los Angeles: University of California Press.

Bureau of the Census. 1992a. *Census of Population and Housing, 1990: Public Use Microdata Sample, U.S.* [machine-readable data files]. Washington: Author.

———. 1992b. *Census of Population and Housing, 1990: Public Use Microdata Sample, U.S. Technical Documentation.* Washington: Author.

Farley, J. E. 1995. *Majority-Minority Relations,* 3rd ed. Englewood Cliffs, NJ: Prentice Hall.

Farley, R. and W. R. Allen. 1987. *The Color Line and the Quality of the Life in America.* New York: Russell Sage Foundation.

Feagin, J. R. and C. B. Feagin. 1996. *Racial and Ethnic Relations,* 5th ed. Upper Saddle River, NJ: Prentice Hall.

Fernandez, M. and K. C. Kim. 1995. "Self-Employment Rates of Asian Immigrant Groups: An Analysis of Intra-group and Inter-group Differences." Paper presented at the annual meetings of American Sociological Association, August, Washington, D.C.

Hurh, W. M. and K. C. Kim. 1989. "The 'Success' Image of Asian Americans: Its Validity and Its Practical and Theoretical Implications." *Ethnic and Racial Studies* 12:512–38.

Kim, K. C. and W. M. Hurh. 1991. "The Extended Conjugal Family: Family-Kinship System of Asian Immigrants." Pp. 115–33 in *The Korean-American Community: Present and Future,* edited by T. H. Kwak and S. H. Lee. Seoul: Kyungnam University Press.

Light, I. and E. Bonacich. 1988. *Immigrant entrepreneurs: Koreans in Los Angeles.* Los Angeles: University of California Press.

Marger, M. N. 1991. *Race and Ethnic Relations,* 2nd ed. Belmont, CA.: Wadsworth.

Massey, D. S. and N. A. Denton. 1993. *American Apartheid: Segregation and the Making of the Underclass.* Cambridge, MA: Harvard University Press.

Queen, S. R., W. Habenstein, and J. S. Quadagno. 1985. *The Family in Various Cultures.* New York: Harper & Row.

Schaefer, R. T. 1996. *Racial and Ethnic Groups,* 6th ed. New York: Harper Collins.

Stevens, G. and J. H. Cho. 1985. "Socioeconomic Indexes and the New 1980 Census Occupational Classification Scheme." *Social Science Research* 14:142–68.

Tang, J. 1993. "The Career Attainment of Caucasian and Asian Engineers." *Sociological Quarterly* 34(3):467–96.

U.S. Commission on Civil Rights. 1988. *The Economic Status of Americans of Asian Descent: An Exploratory Investigation,* Clearinghouse Publication 95. Washington, DC: U.S. Commission on Civil Rights.

———. 1992. *Civil Rights Issues Facing Asian Americans in the 1990s: A Report of the United States Commission on Civil Rights.* Washington, DC: U.S. Commission on Civil Rights.

Voydanoff, P. 1984. *Work and Family: Changing Roles of Men and Women.* Palo Alto, CA.: Mayfield.

Wilson, W. J. 1987. *The Truly Disadvantaged: The Inner-City, the Underclass, and Public Policy.* Chicago: University of Chicago Press.

Yinger, M. *Ethnicity.* Albany, NY: State University of New York Press.

# Being a Part-Time Manager: One Way to Combine Family and Career * 7

Phyllis Hutton Raabe

A major work-family problem in the United States is *having time* for family caring (Galinsky, Bond, and Friedman 1993). This is largely because, next to Japan, the average full-time worker in the United States works the most annual hours among industrial nations (Schor 1991). In striking contrast to Western Europeans, employed Americans have much less paid nonwork time in holidays, vacations, and other leaves—for example, eight weeks a year less than a full-time German (Schor 1991; Hewitt Associates 1995).

Since women and men increasingly are combining family activities with work and careers, the high demands of work in the United States have stimulated questions about the necessity of forty- to more than sixty-hour work weeks, rigid work schedules and locations, and continuous career tracks for successful work and careers (Bailyn 1993; Galinsky et al. 1993; Rodgers and Rodgers 1989; Rodgers 1992). As Hochschild noted in *The Second Shift*, while individual and family coping on the home front is important, people trying to integrate family and career achievement also "need careers basically redesigned to suit workers who also care for families" (Hochschild 1989:x).

Interests in alternative, reduced work time arrangements have led many—particularly women—to work part-time schedules (Barker 1993; Callaghan and Hartmann 1991). In the United States, part-time work often has involved work and career penalties: subordinated work, low pay, inadequate benefits, blocked career ladders, and employment insecurity. However, part-time work *can* be in "good" formulations, for example, on an interim basis, with proportionate wages and benefits, and with inclusion in viable career paths (Barker 1993; Schwartz 1989; Tilly 1992).

While part-time jobs frequently are available in lower-level white-collar occupations and can be one way of combining "work and family," a major question has been about their existence in professional and managerial

*This research project on part-time managers in the U.S federal government was conducted in collaboration with the U.S. Office of Personnel Management and supported by a grant from the Louisiana Center for Women and Government.

work—areas that are central to career achievement (in the sense of upward mobility) in the United States. That is, given the prevalent hierarchy of occupations and jobs, does part-time work mean forgoing higher-level occupations and jobs, plateauing, and career derailment? When part-time work options are available to professionals and managers, their *use* often has meant career subordination and "career suicide" (Schwartz 1992). This policy construction by work organizations has constrained the use of part-time schedules. As one man put it:

> "I am committed to my profession, and I want to be taken seriously, but I don't want to be working all hours. I want some time with my children. I wish it were possible to work part-time without losing my foot on the ladder." (cited in Cooper and Lewis 1994:16).

## THE PART-TIME MANAGER OR PROFESSIONAL ALTERNATIVE

To what extent are part-time professional and managerial positions first of all available and then compatible with career achievement—either on an interim basis with reentrance to regular career paths or as permanent, equitable part-time work with viable alternative career ladders? These constructions of jobs and career paths are expressions of what has been called "work and career pluralism" in which there is *equivalence* of a variety of work and career arrangements—where reduced work time (through leaves and part-time work over the life course) is not viewed as substandard but is included within an expanded frame of legitimate, standard work (Raabe 1996; Morgan 1986; Sirianni 1991).

In terms of their existence, part-time professional and managerial jobs exist, and there has been growth in the numbers and proportions of part-time professionals and managers (Association of Part-Time Professionals 1992). Part-time career innovations for professionals such as *part-time law partners* (Loveman 1990; New Ways to Work 1990), and *tenure for part-time faculty* (Lomperis 1990) have been developed. Despite these career innovations for professionals, management work has seemed especially resistant to reduced work time configurations due to traditional expectations about the necessity of long hours and pervasive supervision involved in management work (Bailyn 1993; Rodgers 1992; Schwartz 1989). Since management comprises such a high proportion of upper-level jobs, this is a pivotal area for the issues of career achievement and stratification. If management must involve long hours and unmitigated levels of commitment, women and men who want to work reduced hours will suffer career penalties. However, traditional definitions of management have been changing, and the increased emphasis on worker self-management and on decentralized, participatory management (Kanter

1989; Walton and Lawrence 1985) may be one foundation for management on a part-time basis.

Part-time managers exist at companies and in government (Olmsted and Smith 1994). For example, 120 managers at NationsBank had reduced their work time schedules through the bank's Select Time program by 1992 ("Bank Adds . . . ," 1991; Galinsky, Friedman, and Hernandez 1991). Wells Fargo also has managers on part-time schedules. A 1991 survey of large companies found that 53 percent had part-time managers (Parker and Hall 1993). Since 1984, thousands of professionals and managers in New York State's Voluntary Reduction in Work Schedule program have reduced their work schedules from 5 to 30 percent while remaining in their career-path positions (M. L. Ackley, State of New York, Governor's Office of Employee Relations, private communication, 1993; Dudak 1993; Olmsted and Smith 1994).

Among U.S. employers, the U.S. federal government was an early pioneer in endorsing systematic part-time options with The Federal Employees Part-Time Career Act of 1978 [U.S. Merit Systems Protection Board (USMSPB) 1991]. As with the NationsBank and New York State programs, part-time work in the federal government under this act is a more legitimate, equitable, and viable construction of part-time employment. It is available to professionals and managers as well as other workers, involves at least proportionate remuneration and benefit coverage, and maintains career opportunities. In these ways, part-time work in the federal government represents an instance of work and career pluralism and constitutes a site where questions about the characteristics and conditions associated with possible positive outcomes can be examined. In turn, greater knowledge about positive constructions of part-time management in which both practitioners and organizations benefit may contribute to the further development of part-time management positions—and to their availability as one mechanism for integrating family involvement with career achievement.

While the number of part-time managers is a small proportion of the federal work force, they constitute a much larger number at a point in time than generally found at other employers: for example, there were 500–600 part-time managers in 1990 and 1992 and 342 in December 1993 (U.S. Office of Personnel Management 1992a, 1992b, 1995).

What are the characteristics of these part-time managers, their careers, and managing on a part-time basis? To what extent and in what ways is managing on a reduced work time schedule successful and compatible with career achievement? In collaboration with the U.S. Office of Personnel Management, a survey was sent to all part-time managers in the federal government in 1994. Of 293 part-time managers employed at that time, 144 surveys (49 percent) were returned.

## U.S. FEDERAL GOVERNMENT PART-TIME MANAGERS AND FAMILY-CAREER COMMITMENTS

As with the overall part-time profile in the federal government [U.S. Office of Personnel Management (USOPM) 1992a, 1992b, 1995], the majority of part-time manager respondents were women: 63 percent, while 37 percent were men. Most of the managers were well-educated: 83 percent had a college degree or higher (30 percent had a masters degree, 14 percent had a doctorate), and fairly high-level in rank: 67 percent were in grades 12, 13 and 14, and 76 percent manage more than three people.

These part-time managers manifest high commitments to both family and career. On a scale of 1 (high) to 5 (low), respondents overall ranked family as very important (1.1.), as they did work accomplishment (1.2) and career achievement (1.8). Their main reasons for being a manager on a part-time basis were caring for children (76 percent) and "an interest in a more balanced life (work/nonwork)" (46 percent); "meeting family responsibilities" was the most important factor in relation to career plans for the next three to five years. At the same time, respondents strongly agreed that "part-time employees are as committed to this agency as full-time employees" (1.5 average score), and that they are willing "to put in a great deal of effort beyond that normally expected to help this organization be successful" (1.8 average score). Indeed, 63 percent work overtime: 51 percent average one to five hours, 11 percent more than five hours a week.

## WORK AND CAREER PLURALISM: "WIN-WIN" PERSONAL AND ORGANIZATIONAL OUTCOMES

The U.S. federal government's part-time work system has flexibility and provides diverse scheduling options. These part-time managers worked a variety of reduced work time arrangements: 44 percent worked less days a week, 25 percent worked reduced hours every weekday; 6 percent worked reduced hours over a two-week period; and 25 percent had other variations.

The career structure also is flexible, as employees move between full-time and part-time schedules. In becoming part-time managers, 48 percent of respondent managers were full-time and then reduced hours, 23 percent already were part-time and proposed another part-time job, and 10 percent applied for an established part-time position. Career fluidity also is indicated by these managers' career plans. While 61 percent said they were not seeking any change in position in the next three to five years, 13 percent expect to seek promotion to *another* part-time position, 14 percent expect to seek promotion to full-time, 14 percent might move laterally to another part-time position, while 8 percent were interested in a full-time position with a compressed work schedule.

In terms of career progression, rather than part-time management definitely being a career dead-end, promotions also occurred: 29 percent of respondents had been promoted as a part-time manager. In addition to career opportunities, these part-time managers cited other positive personal, family, and organizational outcomes associated with being a part-time—in comparison with being a full-time—manager (see Table 1).

Despite working reduced hours, 85 percent of these part-time managers asserted that they accomplish as much work as a full-time manager (57 percent strongly agreed, 28 percent agreed). In another question comparing managing on a part-time and a full-time basis, 59 percent said there was "no change" in the *quantity* of their work as part-time managers with 11 percent reporting an increase. In relation to the quality of their work, 81 percent reported "no change," while 14 percent said their work quality increased. Job performance evaluations also indicated work accomplishment: 58 percent stated that their most recent performance rating was "outstanding," 30 percent had achieved "exceeds fully successful," and 11 percent, "fully successful." [These ratings of sample respondents were higher than those reported by both full-time and part-time managers in the 1992 Survey of Federal Employees (USOPM 1992b).]

How can reduced work time be compatible with maintained or improved productivity? In addition to the increased mental health, motivation, and family-work balance reported in Table 1, these part-time managers emphasized the importance of increased personal work efficiency, use of innova-

*Table 1.* Some Positive Outcomes of Being a Part-Time Manager, U.S. Federal Government Sample, 1994

| | *Percentage of Part-Time Managers Reporting:* | |
|---|---|---|
| | *Increase* | *No change* |
| Quantity of time available for family/personal life | 86 | 9 |
| Overall quality of your employment arrangement | 81 | 14 |
| Overall quality of family/personal life | 79 | 16 |
| Mental health | 65 | 29 |
| Quantity of time available for social/recreational life | 53 | 35 |
| Ability to concentrate while working | 50 | 41 |
| Overall motivation | 49 | 46 |
| Level of creativity in work | 45 | 46 |
| Level of initiative in work | 44 | 49 |
| Physical health | 36 | 59 |
| Interest in work | 31 | 62 |

*Table 2.* Management Dimensions and Activities, U.S. Federal Government Sample, 1994

| | *Percentages Reporting:* | | |
|---|---|---|---|
| *Part-time in comparison to full-time manager* | *No change* | *Increase* | *Decrease* |
| My work efficiency | 44 | 51 | — |
| Use of innovative communication measures | 42 | 51 | — |
| Postponement of less important tasks | 43 | 54 | — |
| Prioritization of tasks | 60 | 36 | — |
| Accessibility in nonwork times | 59 | 30 | — |
| Coordination of work | 63 | 31 | — |
| Delegation of tasks | 62 | 26 | — |
| Accessibility in nonwork times | 59 | 30 | — |
| Supervision of subordinates | 63 | 4 | 27 |

tive communication measures, and postponement of less important tasks. Table 2 delineates some management components that were assessed as changed or maintained when managing as a part-time manager was compared with managing on a full-time basis.

This survey's findings about the work flexibilities, career mobility options, and work and career accomplishments of U.S. federal part-time managers indicate that the U.S. federal government constitutes an example of work and career pluralism. Further, being a part-time manager is one way to combine "family and career" over the life course, and one that can result in positive personal and organizational outcomes. As one part-time manager put it,

> I had a 3 year old coming out of diapers, and an 83 year old mother going in them. . . . My 4 years of part-time management employment have been superb. My director has been marvelous, and swears she had more work from me in 3 days than some others in 5.

Another noted,

> Being part-time in the same position that I had as a full-time position has made a total difference in my outlook on work and family life and also has definitely affected my health. I am much more productive while at work, and I am much happier at home. . . . I have always been a manager who delegates a great deal of responsibility to the people I manage and I have always said that the sign of a good manager is that the department should run the same with the manager there or not there. I am very fortunate in having extremely good people under me, but I feel that certainly part of that is due to the management style.

The statement of one part-time manager indicates the possible win-win outcomes of pluralistic work and career arrangements in general and part-time management in particular that work organizations have yet to fully appreciate:

> My overall impression is that part-time managers represent a considerable bargain for the Federal Government. Highly motivated individuals following a part-time schedule on their own initiative tend to accomplish a larger workload than is commensurate with the reduced hours. This is done because the individual has a personal motivation to make the work arrangement succeed and to be viewed as successful while working on a part-time basis. My experience is one of working more effectively and reducing to a minimum the "down" time that most employees take as a matter of course on the job. My experience on an organizational basis has been that although the "official" position is to support and make available part-time professional positions, the culture of the organization still views these positions as a negative. The standard of judgment remains the full-time position, and a part-time position is of a lesser caliber. . . . What is needed is more up-front, explicit support by the organization for part-time professional positions—both managerial and nonmanagerial.

However, there are some negatives. The reduced wages—even if proportionate and equitable—are a constraining factor for many people wanting to reduce work time (Galinsky et al. 1993). Among these part-time managers—who already had "voted with their feet" and were engaged in part-time work—majorities stated that they were "willing to forgo some income in order to have reduced work time" (63 percent strongly agreed and 23 percent agreed with the statement). One recent divorcee with a young child illustrated the view that time with family is worth a wage cut: "I want to see if we can financially survive on working 4 days a week—it's that important to me!"

In addition to wage loss, there also continue to be organizational barriers to part-time management being a pluralistic work and career arrangement that facilitates combining family and career.

## CULTURAL AND STRUCTURAL BARRIERS TO PART-TIME MANAGEMENT

While assessments of part-time management were largely positive, respondents indicated some work and organizational problems. Although 70 percent reported "no change" in communication difficulties when being a part-time manager in comparison with full-time, 24 percent cited increased communication difficulties. Similarly, while the majority (61 percent) stated that there was no change in workplace accessibility to subordinates and in co-worker sociability, 28 percent said there were decreases in accessibility to subordinates, and 31 percent said there were decreases in co-worker sociability. According to one part-time manager, strengths and weaknesses are experienced in part-time management:

> It is very difficult to get a full-time management job done in fewer hours, but it can be done. Working fewer hours makes you a better manager in the following ways: better delegator, focus only on important tasks, better time-management. Working fewer hours makes you a worse manager in the following ways: less time to talk with co-workers, less time to see things "first hand."

Since long hours, full-time work, and continuous careers remain the dominant organizational norms, many part-time managers cite cultural and structural organizational obstacles. For example, respondents indicate gaps between what is important for working as a part-time manager and what exists. While the most important factor cited was "support from my immediate supervisor/manager," and 92 percent said it is *very important,* a smaller percentage, 62 percent, said it occurs "to a great extent." In terms of "a supportive organizational culture," 62 percent said it is very important; however, only 26 percent said it exists "to a great extent," 57 percent said "to some extent," while 17 percent said "not at all."

Although most said that as part-time managers there was "no change" in their general worker status as perceived by others in their organizational unit or in chances for a fulfilling career, significant minorities saw a decrease in their worker status (28 percent) and in chances for a fulfilling career (30 percent). Further, many part-time managers continue to experience difficulties and frustrations in gaining acceptance and recognition for part-time management work. The following quote illustrates the perceived stigma and difficulties those part-time managerial positions encounter:

> My choice to go part-time was made easy because my supervisor at that time was also part-time. Since then, I have held three other positions, due to realignments and job growth. It is becoming more difficult to retain my part-time status due to pressure from my immediate supervisor. Although I am performing all aspects of my job at a successful level, there is a true "stigma" to being part-time. Other managers assume you have less dedication, don't care about your "mission," etc. My boss wants me here every hour he works—"just because." My true belief is that managers are the best people to allow part-time hours—*if* they have properly empowered, trained and delegated to their employees. I do not produce a product. I monitor, plan, assign and report. I do this quite well 4 days a week. I am missed on my days off only because of my absence, not because of any voids.
>
> My chief was against my being part-time when she first came; she had to be convinced I was getting the job done well. Many other chiefs are openly negative/skeptical. . . . Part-time workers are often considered second class, because family is "supposed" to be secondary to your job.
>
> As a part-time supervisor, some people feel that I am not as dedicated as a

> full-time manager. This is not true. I work extremely hard and get all my work done accurately and in a timely manner. I was told that I would not be promoted from a GS-9 to a GS-11 until I return to work full-time. This is not fair. I feel that promotions should be based on quality of work, not on whether you work part-time or full-time.

## CONCLUSION

The long hours and rigid schedules of past mechanized, industrial work are increasingly incongruent with the nature of postindustrial work and the interests of men and women in combining family time with career success. Part-time work is one way to construct more family time. However, in the United States, part-time work often has been unavailable in upper-level work or has meant "career suicide." Some workplace situations are more supportive of combining family time with career progression. The U.S. federal government with its work and career flexibilities and equitable salaries and benefits for part-time as well as full-time employees provides the opportunity for a more pluralistic work and career system.

The U.S. federal government—along with other U.S. employers—is experiencing a conflict between traditional, "standard" modes of work and career arrangements and new, flexible, pluralistic forms (Bailyn 1993; Raabe 1996). This survey of U.S. federal part-time managers provides evidence that, for many, being a part-time manager is a "win-win" situation that benefits individuals, families, and work organizations. It is clear that supervisors of part-time managers and aspects of organizational culture and structure can either facilitate or undermine part-time management as a positive, pluralistic work and career arrangement. As one part-time manager commented, "A supportive higher level manager is a must. I have worked as a part-time manager in both positive and negative situations. Everything can fall apart—communication, delegation, planning work goals, etc., if management doesn't back you."

Within the overall institutionalized federal government part-time system, some experience constraints and difficulties. Yet many part-time managers are in supportive, pluralistic environments. The evidence of positive experiences is especially important in showing that part-time management work can be constructed in ways that benefit both individuals and work organizations. Further it is one way that women and men can integrate more family time with career achievement.

Large majorities of part-time manager respondents advocate that "the Federal Service should develop more part-time managerial positions" and that "the Federal Service should do more management training about the possibilities and process of developing upper-level part-time positions." Currently, being a part-time manager remains a "contested terrain" with supportive, pluralistic experiences but also some negative, constraining ones. Indeed, it is an option, however, that appears to serve both its participants and employer well.

## REFERENCES

Association of Part-Time Professionals. 1992. "Number of Part-Time Workers Up Slightly." *Working Options* 12(4):1.

Bailyn, L. 1993. *Breaking the Mold.* New York: Free Press.

"Bank Adds Manager Training to 'Select-Time' Program." 1991. *National Report on Work & Family* 4(4):2–3.

Barker, K. 1993. "Changing Assumptions and Contingent Solutions: The Costs and Benefits of Women Working Full- and Part-Time." *Sex Roles* 28-1/2:47–71.

Callaghan, P. and H. Hartmann. 1991. *Contingent Work.* Washington, DC: Economic Policy Institute.

Catalyst. 1993. Flexible Work Arrangements II: Succeeding with Part-Time Options. New York: Author.

Cooper, C. L. and Lewis, S. 1994. Managing the New Work Force. San Diego: Pfeiffer.

Dudak, J. J. 1993. *Voluntary Reduction in Work Schedule Program.* Albany: State of New York, Governor's Office of Employee Relations.

Galinsky, E., J. T. Bond, and D. E. Friedman. 1993. *The Changing Workforce: Highlights of the National Study.* New York: Families and Work Institute.

Galinsky, E., D. E. Friedman, and C. A. Hernandez. 1991. *The Corporate Reference Guide to Work-Family Programs.* New York: Families and Work Institute.

Hewitt Associates. 1995. Salaried Employee Benefits Provided by Major U.S. Employers in 1994. Lincolnshire, IL: Author.

Hochschild, A. 1989. *The Second Shift.* New York: Avon.

Kanter, R. M. 1989. "The New Managerial Work." *Harvard Business Review* (Nov.–Dec.):85–92.

Lomperis, A. M. T. 1990. "Are Women Changing the Nature of the Academic Profession?" *Journal of Higher Education* 61(6):643–77.

Loveman, G. W. 1990. "The Case of the Part-Time Partner." *Harvard Business Review* (Sept.–Oct.):12–29.

Morgan, G. 1986. *Images of Organization.* Newbury Park, CA: Sage.

New Ways to Work. 1990. "Update: Alternative Work Schedules in Law Firms." *Work Times* 9(1):4–5.

Olmsted, B. and S. Smith. 1994. *Creating a Flexible Workplace,* 2nd ed. New York: ANACOM.

Parker, V. and D. Hall. 1993. "Workplace Flexibility: Faddish or Fundamental?" Pp. 122–55 in *Building the Competitive Workforce,* edited by P. Mirvis. New York: Wiley.

Raabe, P. H. 1996. "Constructing Pluralistic Work and Career Arrangements." Pp.

128–41 in *The Work-Family Challenge: Rethinking Employment,* edited by S. Lewis and J. Lewis. Newbury Park, CA: Sage.

Rodgers, C. S. 1992. "The Flexible Workplace: What Have We Learned?" *Human Resource Management* 31(3):183–299.

Rodgers, F. S. and C. Rodgers. 1989. "Business and the Facts of Family Life." *Harvard Business Review* 67:65–76.

Schor, J. B. 1991. *The Overworked American.* New York: Basic Books.

Schwartz, F. 1989. "Management Women and the New Facts of Life." *Harvard Business Review* 67:65–76.

———. 1992. Breaking with Tradition—Women and Work. New York: Warner.

Sirianni, C. 1991. "The Self-Management of Time in Postindustrial Society." Pp. 231–74 in *Working Time in Transition,* edited by K. Hinrichs. W. Roche, and C. Sirianni. Philadelphia: Temple University Press.

Tilly, C. 1992. "Dualism in Part-Time Employment." *Industrial Relations* (Spring):330–47.

U.S. Merit Systems Protection Board (USMSPB). 1991. *Balancing Work Responsibilities and Family Needs: The Federal Civil Service Response.* Washington, DC: Author.

U.S. Office of Personnel Management. 1992a. *A Study of the Work and Family Needs of the Federal Workforce.* Washington, DC: Author.

———. 1992b. *Survey of Federal Employees.* Washington, DC: Author.

———. 1995. *Balancing Work and Family Demands Through Part-time Employment and Job Sharing.* Washington, DC: Author.

Walton, R. and Lawrence, P. (eds.). 1985. *Human Resource Management.* Boston: Harvard Business School.

# Economic Transition in a Company Town: The Politics of Work and Possibility in Postindustrial Rochester 8

Andrew J. Perrin

Much recent work in academia as well as in the popular press has focused on "downsizing" and a cluster of related changes in the American workplace, ranging from the shift from manufacturing to service industries to the rise in temporary and other contingent employment. Academic research on the topic tends to deal with the business implications of these shifts (Illes 1996; "Economic Anxiety") or, at times, with economic and workplace impacts (Rifkin 1995; Aronowitz and DiFazio 1994), but does not address the ways these changes affect the communities in which they take place. Popular media accounts conflict with one another—ranging from the *New York Times*'s "Downsizing of America" series in the spring of 1996 to rebuttals to that series (Samuelson 1996; Rattner 1996) claiming that downsizing is a largely irrelevant phenomenon masking an essentially robust economy.

Another body of research examines community and worker impacts of plant closings and other traumatic economic events (Dudley 1994; Abedian 1995; Bensman and Lynch 1987; Dandaneau 1996); however, these singular, dramatic events, which often have unmistakable effects on the communities in which they are located, offer limited lessons for interpreting Rochester's recent path. These communities experience the short-term dramatic downfall of institutions that were central to the region, while Rochester (and, I argue, the United States in general) has undergone a more gradual process. This difference is important since it means Rochester and communities like it are not drawn into an apocalyptic, communitywide "social drama" (Turner 1980) that would produce a communitywide common perception of loss.

In industrial communities like Rochester, major corporate actors once formed the core around which common identities and notions of community cohesion were written. [1] The industrial mode of organizing work was integral to the formation of the area's physical and social communities. The dramatic shift in the relationship between these institutions and their employees and communities is an important driving force behind the widely observed decline in community involvement. Furthermore, ironically, the same shift decreases the community's available store of social and cultural capital—the resources individuals use to build social connections—thus constraining public notions of political possibility and the ability of community and labor organizations to organize effectively to counteract the negative effects of downsizing.

I argue that downsizing and related changes in the structure of work in Rochester reduce the employment relationship to little more than an exchange of labor for money. This is devastating to Rochester and to industrial communities like it not because their economies are devastated, but rather because the social and financial resources that help hold the community together are products of a fuller employment relationship. Thus downsizing has significant effects on the social composition of industrial communities, even though its immediate effect on employment may be ameliorated by growth in employment by small employers.

## THE INSTITUTIONAL CONTEXT

Rochester is a midsized industrial city in western New York State, located halfway between Syracuse and Buffalo on the southern shore of Lake Ontario. The Rochester Metropolitan Statistical Area has a population of just over one million, and a work force of around 623,000 (United States, Department of Commerce. Bureau of Economic Analysis 1994). Rochester is home to three major corporations—Kodak, Xerox, and Bausch & Lomb—as well as numerous other branch plants and smaller companies. I use the term "industrial anchors" to refer to these large corporations whose financial, cultural, and social involvement in civic life help constitute the community's very meaning.

The past fifteen years in Rochester have brought significant deindustrialization, manifested in two ways. The first expression of deindustrialization is the straight measure of manufacturing jobs as a proportion of nonfarm employment (Cohen and Zysman 1987; Hill and Negrey 1987), which has declined from 32.8 to 21.2 percent since 1981. The second expression is the decreasing significance of the industrial anchors (Kodak, Xerox, and Bausch & Lomb) as a proportion of manufacturing employment (Figure 1). These two factors combine to produce a nearly 50 percent drop in the "big three's" share of Rochester nonfarm employment (Figures 1 and 2).

Approximately thirty thousand people lost jobs during the wave of corporate downsizing beginning in Rochester in 1983 (Brockelman 1995; Center for Governmental Research 1993; Phil Ebersole, personal communication, June, 1996). Kodak alone cut employment by 39 percent from 1983 to 1995, and Xerox, Bausch & Lomb, and a host of smaller employers followed suit.

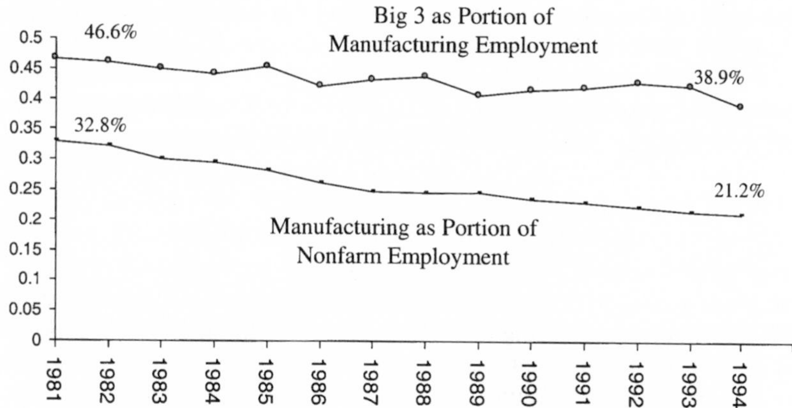


*Figure 1.* Employment structure, 1981–1984, Rochester, NY, MSA. Source: REIS 1969–1994, and Rochester Democrat and Chronicle.

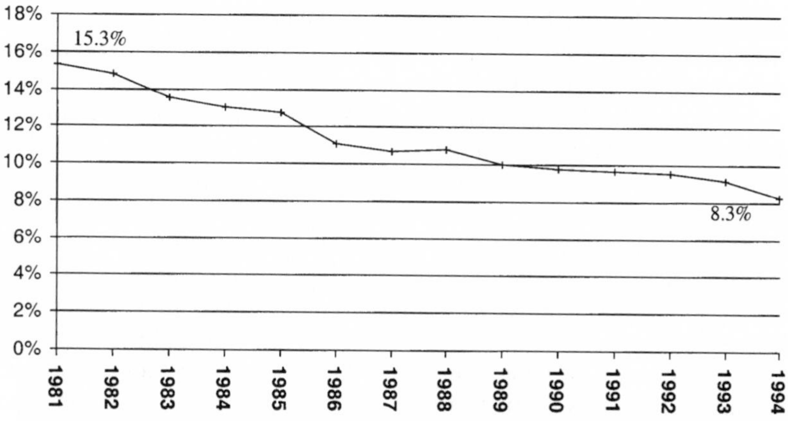


*Figure 2.* "Big 3" employment as portion of total nonfarm employment, 1981–1984, Rochester, NY, MSA. Source: REIS 1969–1994, and Rochester Democrat and Chronicle.

Rochester is not a devastated manufacturing town like those studied by Kathryn Dudley (1994), Bruce Nissen (1995), and others. Indeed, its fortunes have been better than those of its neighbor, Buffalo. Partially because of the nature of its businesses and partially because those businesses were based in the area, Rochester's deindustrialization experience has been more gradual and, perhaps, less apocalyptic, than many described in the plant-closing literature. Nor is Rochester experiencing Rifkin's "end of work"; indeed, unemployment is very low and has remained substantially lower than state and national levels for some time. Rather, my focus groups show that Rochester's employees are feeling a dramatic decline in the formal and informal *security* offered by work; their employers are increasingly a source only of income, and they no longer provide the social and cultural capital that came out of real work security and formed the basis for Rochester's community.

## THE EXPERIENCE OF DOWNSIZING

This study consisted of two sets of focus groups (see Focus Group Details at end of chapter). I use Erving Goffman's scheme of frame analysis to describe the analytic structures that shape participants' thinking about their experiences. [2] For Goffman, frames are essentially basic elements of analysis by which people organize their understanding of their experiences. Keys are analytic lenses individuals use to invest these frame elements with social meaning (Goffman [1974] 1986:10–11, 46). Frame analysis allows for an understanding of the ways respondents understand their social surroundings—the logic by which they interpret experiences.

The participants in the first set [3] of focus groups—made up of people who had been directly affected by downsizing—presented four major keys of analysis through which they viewed the central frame, which I term *violation-(re)action.* The four recurring keys are *individuation,* or discussion of the difference between the speaker and others in similar situations (often expressed through what I term *positivity,* or the claim that the speaker expects the situation to improve soon); *community,* discussion of participants' experiences as they relate to a group to which they belong, their neighborhood, or Rochester as a whole; *emotion,* the frank discussion of grief, loss, and anger in relation to layoffs; and *family,* often linked with emotion, the discussion of effects on family life. The central frame—*violation-(re)action*—encompasses the sense of victimhood and the process of coping with or trying to change the origin of that violation. The relation between the violation-(re)action frame and the analytical key through which it is articulated give insight into the individual and community impacts of the issues being discussed.

## THE FRAME: VIOLATION-(RE)ACTION)

All the participants felt that, at some point along the way, their employers or social forces in general had violated some norm of appropriate behavior. Most felt bitter toward their former employers; a few used an analytical scheme allowing them to picture the employer as simply an unwilling actor in a broader global economic game. All, however, agreed that downsizing was a problem that deserved at least a discussion, and generally some sort of response.

The theme of (re)action refers to the possibilities for responding to that violation. These include governmental assistance with education, job training, and an attractive business climate; legal action; personal development (education, image and presentation, etc.); and collective action. Violation as a theme is viewed through all the keys (individuation, community, emotion, and family); (re)action is most likely to be viewed in the individuation and community keys, although it comes up in the other keys in the form of coping with the changes associated with unemployment.

### *Key I: Individuation*

Each participant's first response to the opening question of the groups of downsized workers—"why you responded to the announcement in the paper" (1:79–80)—consisted at least in part of such a story, differentiating him or her from the generic story of downsizing. Participants attempted to make their stories special—anomalies in a context where downsizing has become routine. This key, which I call *individuation*, is by far the predominant mode of understanding used by members of these focus groups. [4]

The strategy of individuation is pursued by many participants throughout the groups. The notion that, in general, it is substandard workers who are laid off pervades participants' analytic frame. The names below have been changed to protect the identities of persons interviewed. Richard Farrell, a fifty-seven-year-old former Xerox worker, provides a paradigmatic example of individuation:

> I asked them when they tapped me on the shoulder, who's going to take over? You know, cause I knew nobody could take over, cause I'd been doing the same job for eight years, and I kind of knew then, I was a finisher. On the copier, on the 5100, I was Mr. Finisher, to tell you the truth. They came to me for answers. I didn't know if they could replace me, so the first thing I asked was, well, who's going to take over? (2:225–30)

Farrell's response displays two other important characteristics that correlate with individuation. First is the pride he shows in his work; his understanding of the machine he worked on and the belief in the job he did are unsurpassed.

Joe Nixon, a thirty-three-year-old former biotechnology worker, adjusted his self-conception when he was told where to go on the day of his layoff:

> I got into the room I was supposed to be in, and I realized that was not the room to be in. Because some others in the room were not the better workers. So immediately I knew I was in deep trouble. It was a situation I didn't want to be

> in. It was my son's first birthday. So I was real excited, we were going to have, you know, cake and I come home to my wife and say, hey, I don't have a job today. (2:171–75)

Nixon's own presence in the wrong room was not enough to convince him that merit was not the sole criterion for layoffs. Rather, his observation of the other members of his group told him what he was dreading. In the face of new information, he changes his assessment of his own competence rather than reevaluating his idea of whom downsizing effects.

Not surprisingly, the individuation key colors the theme of (re)action, so that strategies for coping with the layoff are individual as well. Workers convinced that job loss was a private, individual event seek private, individual ways to address it. The most common strategy is education—even though that is not always successful. Jim MacDee, a forty-three-year-old former factory worker, points out "what an irony it is; I've got over 250 college credits totaled up on my side of the board, but you hear that same thing" (3:73–34). Access to education is considered an appropriate governmental response to the crisis of downsizing—a strategy that reinforces the notion that individual characteristics are the primary predictor of employment success.

### *Key II: Community*

Participants in the focus groups did view downsizing as a collective violation as well as an individual one, although they revealed few ideas on how to address it collectively. Through the community key, though, they consider the collective and social impacts of downsizing. Jim MacDee, a former DuPont worker, discussed his view of community impacts:

> Part of the reason I decided not to take the opportunities that large corporations offer in these times of downsizings is my sense of community. Having lived here for nearly 30 years. . . . It just seemed to me with the skills I have and the kind of community, the opportunities here, the extended family, and the benefits to my kids, that it would be more valuable for all of us to maintain that sense of community. I thought about it, and I said, "Look." It's like looking in the mirror and in the mirror you see in the background the statue of Mercury and you see Frontier Field. These things are a part of you, all the things that you see as part of your background. If you go to another community elsewhere, and pull yourself away from all that, the picture isn't nearly as clear. The corporations downsizing just took that mirror and, pssh, smashed it; and now there's all these little pieces. You can make something happen and have a lot that is in that mirror piece, but things are very unclear for a long period of time. (3:498–513)

For varying reasons, all participants considered leaving the Rochester area a last resort. For example, Susan White, a manager for a national drugstore company, has moved several times for the company. When she was laid off, she was offered another move, this time to New Jersey, but she declined, feeling that her job would be tenuous in the new location as well. Several others, though, mentioned family and friends as ties to Rochester that they would be unwilling to cut.

The sense of violation is as strong in the community key as in the individuation key. MacDee's statement above expresses the common view that companies cause serious damage to community relations when they change the way they relate to their host cities. Frank Showers, a former white-collar Kodak employee, suggests that companies also hurt their own long-term interests when they abandon the notions of solidarity that connect them with their communities:

> I was taught in the military, take care of your people and they'll take care of you. And it works. George Eastman's ashes down the road a little bit must be churning around a lot faster than Brownian motion can account for, because George understood you take care of your people. He did the Eastman Dental Center, he did all the hospital things; and I don't think it was because he was a particularly altruistic person. But he understood that if he took care of his people and they didn't have to worry about those things, they were more productive workers. He got more out of them. (3:891–98)

In the third focus group, the prospect of reinvigorated unions arose spontaneously. This was the clearest expression of a *collective* sense of reaction to violation; participants said specifically that the notion of a union would protect individuals from the unpredictability of corporate decision-making:

> Frank Showers: *used to be you started off a radical and you got more conservative as you got older. But I find in my case, I'm getting more radical as I get older. We were brought up to see these things in one way, and now we realize that the system does not work in the way that we thought it was advertised to work. Maybe there are some other approaches that may make more sense. I was always fairly antiunion. My first job was with Ford Motor Company, I saw all the excesses there. And now I realize that although unions have problems, there is a need for unionlike organizations. And so I think we are finding ourselves more radicalized as we get older.*
>
> Jane Greck: *I, I, I have been thinking union. And you brought it up to begin with, and now you're saying . . .*
>
> Susan White: *I'd like to see more of a management union.*
>
> Jane Greck: *You know, we needed some sort of a union. Some sort of a support to protect us. If we were doing the job and doing it well, and that's very important, because as my husband says, there were people at Xerox that were laid off and I can see why they were.*

*He said there were people that were not performing. And, not that he was patting himself on the back, but his being laid off was the biggest shock in the world. He never expected he was going to be one of those people. But do the unions protect the non-performers?*

Mike Nichols: *Yes.*

Susan White: *They protect everybody.*

Frank Showers: *Oh yes, and that's one of the failings but . . .*

Jane Greck: *But they protect people who are performing and just happen to be in the wrong spot. (3:1096–1128)*

Even in this setting, where participants acknowledge a need for collective involvement to protect employees, the sense that poor individual performance is, or ought to be, a reason for a layoff remains strong. Indeed, even Mike Nichols, who believes that a union at Kodak might have prevented his layoff, is deeply skeptical about the union members he worked with while on contract at Xerox, and therefore he retains a strong antiunion stance.

Participants also agreed that being laid off has contradictory effects on neighborhood and community involvement. Richard Farrell noticed that a laid-off neighbor has "more time to take care of his yard" (2:515); but the primary understanding of community and neighborhood impacts is revealed in this interaction:

Sebby Wilson Jacobson: [5] *What does it do to your neighborhood; do you see a change in your neighbor because . . .*

Nina Bullock: *Terrible. Terrible.*

Richard Farrell: *He doesn't know what to do with himself. And he smokes, and his wife won't let him smoke in the house. So you see him outside [laughter], I mean in the dead of winter!*

Nina Bullock: *And he wants to move south and he doesn't have the money to move south now. And he's trying to start his own business being a middleman for other phone companies, doing it at home. But he misses the social contact.*

Richard Farrell: *He's missed the interaction.*

Sebby Jacobson: *This is why I asked . . .*

Nina Bullock: *You become one-dimensional. (2:485–501)*

"Missing the social contact" is a recurring theme: while people who have been subjected to a job loss have more time to do things, they also lose the connection with others that stems from a primary social role at work. As Mike Nichols says:

Mike Nichols: *Yes. Yes, I was hoping to get called back at Xerox in some kind of capacity, but they had an article in the paper just the other day with their offering another retirement package. They're going to get rid of a lot of temps anyway, so I don't know. I'm*

> *still trying to get back in there. I have gone to all kinds of job fairs and I've got resumes floating all over the place. You know it kind of affects you too because you used to interact with a lot of people and, you know, like belonging to like a bowling league. I was president of my bowling league, and of course no income, can't bowl. Then I was working nights at Xerox, so I couldn't bowl anyway, but I mean you lose contact with people and . . . (3:342–51)*

This sense of disconnection from neighbors and former associates is balanced by three processes of connection with others: the discussion of unions described above, the idea of class-action lawsuits against companies for age discrimination (which occurs in three separate occasions in the focus groups), and, perhaps most interestingly, the idea of mutual emotional support by neighbors, as described here by Joe Nixon:

> Joe Nixon: *My neighbor got laid off too. But he's 62 years old, so he considers it time to retire. So he takes it as a positive; this is the third time he's been laid off, that is, downsized. He's more of a financial accountant type person, so he's always been able to find something someplace. This time he said, I guess I will just work part time, and just find something to do for the social end of it. Money's tight, but he needs the social end of it, too. I don't think it did anything to the neighborhood. You know it'll happen, you get used to it. Then they get the guy you know. I live in a town house. And so way down one side he's screaming, you're working overtime, I'd like to be working; and this guy over here, he's just enjoying retirement. So it's kind of all three. (2:516–29)*

Nixon and his neighbors, though, do not come up with common critiques that illuminate all of their different satisfactions with their work lives. This social connection, therefore, operates more as emotional support than as social solidarity.

### *Key III: Emotion*

Many of the participants said they decided to participate in the focus groups in order to "vent," or to express their anger and feelings about their situations. Others wanted to share those experiences with others in similar situations, hoping to gain a sense of connection through the groups. For most participants, being laid off carries a strong feeling of loss: work, even when it was neither rewarding nor interesting, provided a sense of self-worth and identity, and the sudden absence of work produces a strong emotional reaction. Susan Fiske tells of going to a required meeting at her company, run by an executive from the company's headquarters:

> Probably one of the worst things that I had to go through was when I was told I was going to be losing my job in three months after I'd been with this company for 18 years. One of the higher ups came down from Blue Bell, and we all had to go into a meeting, and listen to how great the corporation was going to be doing that year, what great profits they were going to have. Sure they were going to have some cutbacks. But there was 20 of us sitting in that room that were going to lose our jobs. We had to sit there and listen to how great the corporation was going to do. And if you don't think that doesn't hurt and make you mad and angry. They have no feelings. (1:347–54)

Fiske tries hard to manage her emotions, using the positivity subframe to suggest that a bright outlook is important to eventually gaining a job:

> I know I'm going to have to pick myself up. Get out there and maybe, even, just take a job in a store waiting on customers, or something. But I still have that room for hope, that phone's going to ring. I'm going to get an interview, a good one, and be able to land that job, and maybe keep it for a year or two. That's all I can hope for. (1:656–59)

Don Drew and Steve Morrison discuss the emotional impacts of being laid off. Morrison suggests, previously, that the optimal situation would be "for everybody to be doing something that they like doing whether they're getting paid for it or not." But for Drew, the alienating effects of unemployment are stronger:

> Don Drew: *I find myself watching television more than I should. More than I want to be. I'm not watching, just . . .*
> Steve Morrison: *Oh, yeah, staring at it, more like it.*
> Don Drew: *. . . because I don't handle rejection real well, and I got one rejection today, or two today, and pretty soon I find that the rest of my day, I'm pretty busy feeling sorry for myself.*
> Steve Morrison: *Trying to get the shoe out of your gut. (1:722–31)*

This exchange points to the social importance of emotional responses—Drew's reaction is to watch television, an activity Putnam (1996:46) suggests breeds isolation and lack of community involvement.

The immediate reaction to an emotional violation is coping behavior, not targeted reaction or collective activity. Commitment to family, however, is strongly connected to emotions, and has important community impacts, as illustrated by Alice Smith's emotional story of her dismissal:

> My kids come first. I had my son drop out of one thing that he wanted to do because it was costing money, and I couldn't afford it. Now this summer he wants to play baseball and he says, mom, I know you're not working, the money's not coming in, I don't have to do it if we can't afford it. He says but I would like to do it. And its like I want to do things for him, and yet money's not

> there. And that hurts, and I know you can see it in his eyes; he hurts, and you just sit and watch, and you don't know what to do. (1:659–65)

Emotional reactions to being laid off take two general forms: reactive emotions such as anger and resentment and debilitating emotions such as resignation and isolation. Clearly, the first form holds potential for involvement not only in community activities per se but in organizing projects aimed at changing or ameliorating the effects of downsizing. The second, though, represents an important decline in social capital brought on not, as Putnam suggests, by television, but rather by a dramatic change in the emotional and social inputs available from involvement in work.

As Rothbell suggests, "The image of an individual successfully enacting numerous roles supports an impression of competency and of a well balanced personality" (1991:23). The loss of such a major role as a work-based identity leads to what Rothbell calls "the stigma of the single role." This role, often, is that of the family member, since involvement in a family is seen by focus group participants, male and female, as the central reason for sustaining both work and community commitments. This "retreat to the family" is understood as a withdrawal from boarder social commitments.

### *Key IV: Family*

The connection between family and community is summed up by an exchange in the third focus group. Several of the preceding comments talk about commitment to employment as a family-type involvement, such as John Matthews, who was laid off from Xerox: "It's like a death in the family, literally" (2:551).

For many of the participants, particularly women (for whom entering the work force was a significant social statement), the return to family is framed as a failure. Much as in Rothbell's role-theory example, they had hoped they could play a series of competent roles including family member and worker. Now, though, their loss of the worker role makes it difficult for them to hold either of these primary roles thoroughly, and the retreat to the family is insulation against the violation of social and work life and the betrayal they feel at the hands of former employers. Furthermore, as it has become more necessary for women to work to support a family (Gordon 1996), being unable to fulfill the role of employee also leads to insecurity about the role of mother.

## THE RIPPLE EFFECT: DOWNSIZING AFFECTS THOSE STILL EMPLOYED

On the initial survey of participants in the second set of focus groups, [6] over two-thirds of the respondents marked "Unemployment and Corporate

'Downsizing'" as "Important" or "Very Important" on a five-point scale ranking a series of seventeen social issues. Of those who considered the issue less important than most others, one-half still believed its overall impact on Rochester had been bad; all of the other respondents agreed. Three-quarters of respondents believed downsizing would continue in Rochester; the others expected it to end soon. From a list of possible causes of downsizing, "corporate greed" and the "need for efficiency" were the most commonly selected items; "globalization of the economy" and "technological changes" were selected next most often. Interestingly, neither "unions" nor government policies ("local and state government policy" and "federal government policy") was selected more than twice. [7]

## FRAME: COMMUNITY DECLINE

The primary frame used by participants in these groups was *urban decline*: Rochester's descent from a good city and a good place to live to a problem-ridden, divided location. Stories of Rochester's golden years are most often based upon ideas about employment in the area, particularly on stories of "the big yellow box," the local nickname for Kodak:

> Well I remember when I first came to Rochester, I went to school not too far from here, and the first reception I remember well. I didn't know anything about Kodak or Xerox, I knew the companies, but I didn't really know much about Rochester at all. The first impression I had of Rochester, like for instance, Kodak, was that . . . it was like this large country club type atmosphere. You know, once you started working there, you belong to the club. (6:251–61)

Participants use two keys to understand urban decline: *city vs. suburbs* and *the changing face of work*. While both keys are relevant to the argument here, for reasons of space I concentrate on the *changing face of work*.

Even among participants who were still working, downsizing and the attendant shift toward contingency and insecurity at work has taken its toll. This is particularly clear among technical workers at Xerox and Kodak, who report longer work hours and a significant decrease in security. Terry Luellen, an engineer at Xerox, suggests:

> It's not the downsizing, what is really bothering me more is the stress level generated because of the downsizing in the industry and in family life. Today when I was coming here, I was listening to the news and one of the educators said each parent has to spend thirty minutes at a time with children when they read. I mean that's well and good, but then you have a whole family out working, and a very high stress level at the work because of downsizing. How do we

> expect them to spend any time with the kids? There is so much impacted by all this downsizing. (5:230–42)

Jeffrey Lawson, also an engineer at Xerox, agrees, and claims that the competitive, insecure atmosphere produced by downsizing and increasing work hours operates to defeat Xerox's famous team-based work environment:

> We have this false culture around us that says we should work together as a team. But a lot of these qualities are not really very team oriented when you get right down to it. They're not really team based qualities that a lot of these companies are searching for. They're looking for clones. They're looking for, you know, clones that will basically follow in the paths of someone with a CEO like nature. You know, the type of people that will function, make decisions, sometimes without using a conscience. (5:521–31)

In addition to insecurity at existing work sites, employment at temporary and contract firms—work formally considered *contingent*—has also grown tremendously in Rochester. According to the National Association of Temporary Staffing Services (NATSS), temporary agencies alone have increased average daily employment [8] in the area by 53 percent from 1987 to 1995, and annual payroll has increased by 108 percent over the same time period. These figures do not include the growth in employment through long-term contract firms, nor do they include growth in independent contracting and "outsourcing"—work contracted out by large firms to be done by outside individuals and small businesses. Some participants in the focus groups report that their jobs are now being done by temporary and contract employees for lower pay and less benefits. [9] As Henson (1996), Rogers (1995), Spula (1994), and others have suggested, employment through a temporary or contract arrangement is very likely to provide less pay and benefits; in addition, it provides less social connection, since workers often change workplaces, tasks, and colleagues.

## COMMONALITIES: FRAMING INSECURITY AND COMMUNITY DECLINE

Rochester's employees were at one time concentrated largely in a few large corporations—institutions that gave their employees and community a sense of common identity. These companies' shift toward outsourcing, downsizing, and true globalization of production has not meant an aggregate decline in the *quantity of work* done in Rochester. It has, however, meant an increase in the insecurity of work and in the social resources that security once generated. Workers laid off during the waves of downsizing commonly find their new jobs with smaller firms or on temporary contracts, and usually at lower pay. Those who remain in large corporations find higher levels of stress and uncertainty over their future because of the new work environment.

Clearly, employment insecurity has a major impact, even on employees who are not the direct victims of downsizing. Rochester's large employers have produced a general social environment in which work is insecure and in which the social capital they once provided is increasingly scarce. People who have lost jobs feel that loss essentially as a "private fact" (Schlotzman and Verba 1979); the loss of capital—both cultural and real—makes it difficult, if not impossible, for them to frame their experience as a political event. They therefore are also unable to conceptualize an envelope of political possibility that would allow for collective action. For those who are still working, the environment of downsizing produces a profound insecurity that translates, again, into a decline in the personal and social resources available to them for community involvement. This is best illustrated by the fact that those respondents in the randomly recruited groups who were most pessimistic about urban revitalization were also those closest to the working class; those who were most optimistic were clearly somewhat insulated from the profound insecurity of contemporary work.

## INSECURITY, COMMUNITY, AND THE POLITICS OF POSSIBILITY

Large corporations provided, among other things, common senses of identity among workers and among residents of communities where they were located. Downsizing does two related things to employees and workers. First, it is profoundly personally demoralizing (Illes 1996); second, it simultaneously withdraws the resources needed both for "re-selfing" (Wexler 1996) and for engaging in collective responses such as community and labor organizing (Schlotzman and Verba 1979; Rogers 1995). Insecurity and a perception of powerlessness make what McAdam (1982:48) calls "cognitive liberation"—a substantive vision of political change—increasingly difficult. Increasing alienation (Rogers 1995) with increasingly contingent work thus forms a "vicious cycle"—it is personally debilitating and it inhibits people's ability, either individually or in groups, to address that debilitation.

Workers thus have a dramatically constrained sense of potential—a small envelope of political possibility. Since they have no sense that organizing or policy could make a difference, they choose instead to engage in isolated, individual strategic moves to preserve individual achievements—moves that are subject to the same workplace insecurity to which they are responding. In order to escape this vicious cycle, the perception of political possibility needs to be widened. Given the notion that alternative configurations of work and community are available, individuals might participate in community and workplace organizing to get there. What they need are the individual and social resources to redraw the envelope.

## PUSHING THE ENVELOPE

Labor unions provide one opportunity for individuals to gain a sense of political efficacy. Rochester has not traditionally been a heavily unionized city; Kodak's famous paternalistic policies managed to keep organizers at bay, and Bausch & Lomb is also unorganized. The city's conservative politics and relatively high-status manufacturing industries have kept unions far weaker than they are in Buffalo, just seventy miles to the west. Furthermore, many local unions have found themselves struggling to maintain working standards for their members; increasing the breadth of possibility is not really a feasible goal, even for the most politically minded unions (Bruce Popper, personal interview, August 1, 1996).

Although Rochester once had a militant community organizing project run by Saul Alinsky, that project is now defunct, and the organization that grew out of it is, much like the local unions, engaged as much in social service type work as it is in any kind of organizing activity. Numerous neighborhood organizations continue to exist, but in general they also address their members' and communities' immediate concerns, rather than concentrating on the broad economic and social issues facing the Rochester area.

What kind of event or institution might infuse Rochester's residents with the social capital necessary to reinvigorate political imagination? Valelly offers the notion of "public policy for reconnected citizenship" (1993:241), suggesting that government policies targeted at reconstructing social capital could rebuild political participation and community activism—precisely the phenomena downsizing has whittled away.

Skocpol (1996) and others have shown repeatedly that the relationship between public policy and democratic participation is not unidirectional. State actions do not simply flow from popular opinion; they also have a strong role in shaping popular opinion. Americans are operating in a political environment in which there is a shared assumption of political impossibility—government is incapable of solving problems, and corporations are and should be essentially independent of local and national control. A bold set of social policies designed specifically to change this ideology of defeatism could be the first step toward democratic renewal and, ultimately, to rebuilding communities undermined by the disappearance or metamorphosis of their industrial anchors.

## FOCUS GROUP DETAILS

All groups were held at the *Rochester Democrat and Chronicle,* Editors' Conference Room, Rochester, New York. Citations in the text are in the form (*x*:*yyy*), where *x* is the focus group number and *yyy* is the line number in the transcript.

Group 1: February 16, 1996, 11:00 A.M.
Group 2: March 15, 1996, 6:00 P.M.
Group 3: March 16, 1996, 10:00 A.M.
Group 4: June 13, 1996, 6:30 P.M.
Group 5: June 17, 1996, 6:30 P.M.
Group 6: June 19, 1996, 6:30 P.M.

## NOTES

1. See Anderson (1991) for more on the construction of culture around technological anchors.

2. For more on the interpretation of qualitative data using frames, see Morgan (1988), Gamson (1992), and Sasson (1995).

3. Two sets of focus groups were run for this study, with three groups each. The focus groups were cosponsored by Gannett Rochester Newspapers, Inc., and held at the Editors' Conference Room at the newspaper's office building in downtown Rochester. The first set was held in February and March 1996. Subjects were recruited using advertisements in the local paper for individuals who had been "affected by downsizing." A total of fifteen subjects participated in three focus groups. There was no financial incentive for their participation, although they were reimbursed for travel expenses and provided with refreshments before the discussion. The second set of focus groups was held in June 1996; subjects were recruited by random telephone interview, were paid $15 for their participation, and were also reimbursed for expenses and given refreshments. This research protocol was approved by the Committee for the Protection of Human Subjects at the University of California, Berkeley, and was issued Project number 96-2-58.

4. Goffman's *Asylums* (1961:151) provides a similar outlook on inmates in mental hospitals, each of whom gave an individual story as to why his or her internment was a mistake. Also see Wexler (1996) for a discussion of attempts at "re-selfing" in the face of discouraging events.

5. Jacobson is the special projects editor for the *Democrat and Chronicle.*

6. Participants were recruited for the second set of focus groups by means of telephone calls from a randomized list from an electronic telephone directory. They were paid $15 plus expenses for their participation. The survey was given to participants before the focus group began.

7. Since the number of respondents is so small (sixteen), no claim is made to statistical significance; this survey merely shows the preexisting attitudes of participants in the groups before the discussions began.

8. Average daily employment (ADE) is a measure often used to track the growth of temporary services, since many temporary employees are "employed" by numerous firms over the course of a single year. Hence measures concerning the overall annual payroll of a temporary firm are misleading.

9. See Henson (1996:22–23) and Uchitelle (1996) for more on the practice of rehiring ex-employees through temporary agencies.

## REFERENCES


Abedian, Julia. 1995. *Exposing Federal Sponsorship of Job Loss: The Whitehall Plant Closing Campaign and "Runaway Plant" Reform.* New York: Garland.

Anderson, Benedict. 1991. *Imagined Communities,* rev. ed. London: Verso.

Aronowitz, Stanley and William DiFazio. 1994. *The Jobless Future: Sci-Tech and the Dogma of Work.* Minneapolis: University of Minnesota Press.

Bensman, David, and Roberta Lynch. 1987. *Rusted Dreams: Hard Times in a Steel Community.* Berkeley: University of California Press.

Brockelman, Stephen R. 1995. "Corporate Downsizing in Rochester NY: Economic Development Responses and the Transition from Manufacturing to Services." Unpublished M.A. Thesis, John F. Kennedy School of Government, Harvard University, Cambridge, MA.

Center for Governmental Research. 1993. *The State of a Greater Rochester.* Rochester, NY: Center for Governmental Research.

Cohen, Steven S. and John Zysman. 1987. *Manufacturing Matters: The Myth of the Post-Industrial Economy.* New York: Basic Books.

Dandaneau, Steven P. 1996. *A Town Abandoned: Flint, Michigan, Confronts Deindustrialization.* Albany: State University of New York Press.

Dudley, Kathryn Marie. 1994. *The End of the Line: Lost Jobs, New Lives in Postindustrial America.* Chicago: University of Chicago Press.

"Economic Anxiety." 1996. *Business Week* (March 11):cover story.

Gamson, William A. 1992. *Talking Politics.* New York: Cambridge University Press.

Goffman, Erving. [1974] 1986. *Frame Analysis: An Essay on the Organization of Experience.* Boston: Northeastern University Press.

———. 1961. *Asylums: Essays on the Social Situation of Mental Patients and Other Inmates.* Garden City, New York: Anchor.

Gordon, David M. 1996. *Fat and Mean: The Corporate Squeeze of Working Americans and the Myth of Managerial "Downsizing."* New York: Free Press.

Henson, Kevin D. 1996. *Just a Temp.* Philadelphia: Temple University Press.

Hill, Richard Child and Cynthia Negrey. 1987. "Deindustrialization in the Great Lakes." *Urban Affairs Quarterly* 22:4(June):580–97.

Illes, Louise Moser. 1996. *Sizing Down: Chronicle of a Plant Closing.* Ithaca: Cornell University ILR Press.

McAdam, Doug. 1982. *Political Process and the Development of Black Insurgency, 1930–1970.* Chicago: University of Chicago Press.

Morgan, David L. 1988. *Focus Groups as Qualitative Research.* Sage University Paper Series on Qualitative Research Methods, Vol. 16. Beverly Hills: Sage.

Nissen, Bruce. 1995. "Fighting for Jobs: Case Studies of Labor-Community Coalitions Confronting Plant Closings." Albany: State University of New York Press.

Putnam, Robert. 1996. "The Strange Disappearance of Civic America." *American Prospect* 24(Winter):34–49.

Rattner, Steven. 1996. "Downsizing the Downsizing Crisis." *New York Times* (October 16):A21.

Rifkin, Jeremy. 1995. *The End of Work: The Decline of the Global Labor Force and the Dawn of the Post-Market Era.* New York: Putnam.

Rogers, Jackie Krasas. 1995. "Just a Temp: Experience and Structure of Alienation in Temporary Clerical Employment." *Work and Occupations* 22(2, May):137–66.

Rothbell, Gladys. 1991. "Just a Housewife: Role-Image and the Stigma of the Single Role." Pp. 21–36 in *Social Roles and Social Institutions: Essays in Honor of Rose Laub Coser,* edited by Judith R. Blau and Norman Goodman. Boulder: Westview.

Samuelson, Robert J. 1996. "Fear of Firing." Washington Post (February 7):A19.

Sasson, Theodore. 1995. *Crime Talk: How Americans Construct a Social Problem.* Hawthorne, New York: Aldine de Gruyter.

Schlotzman, Kay Lehman and Sidney Verba. 1979. *Injury to Insult: Unemployment, Class, and Political Response.* Cambridge, MA: Harvard University Press.

Skocpol, Theda. 1996. "Unravelling from Above." *American Prospect* 25(March–April):20–25.

Spula, Jack Bradigan. 1994. "Work in the '90s: A Temporary Permanence." *City Paper* (Rochester, New York) (April 28):5.

Turner, Victor. 1980. "Social Dramas and Stories about Them." *Critical Inquiry* 7(1):141–68,

Uchitelle, Louis. 1996. "More Downsized Workers Are Returning as Rentals." *New York Times* (December 8):1.

United States, Department of Commerce. Bureau of Economic Analysis. 1994. Regional Economic Information System (REIS) 1969–1991 [computer file available at http://govinfo.kerr.orst.reis-stateis.html].

Valelly, Richard M. 1993. "Public Policy for Reconnected Citizenship." In *Public Policy for Democracy,* edited by Helen Ingram and Steven Rathgeb Smith. Washington, DC: Brookings Institution.

Wexler, Philip. 1996. *Holy Sparks: Social Theory, Religion, and Education.* New York: St. Martin's.

# Negotiating Parental Involvement: Finding Time for Children 9

Kerry J. Daly and Anna Dienhart

Scholars have approached the study of parental involvement in many ways. Early efforts unwittingly focused on mother involvement, as if it were parental involvement. This was followed by efforts to address this bias by trying to understand father involvement by looking at the father-child relationship (see, for example, Lamb 1976, 1981). Throughout, considerably less effort has been devoted to understanding the relationship between father and mother involvement. In this chapter, we emphasize the social and contingent nature of parental involvement, while focusing specifically on the nature of father involvement. We seek to go beyond models of father involvement that focus only on the father-child relationship; rather, we emphasize father involvement as an experience that is co-constructed with, and contingent on, the experience of mother involvement. A considerable body of evidence has accumulated that indicates that there is a strong relationship between marital quality and parental involvement (Cummings and O'Reilly 1997). In order to further our understanding of this relationship, we argue that men and women are engaged in a complex set of negotiations regarding parenting that involves both internal dynamics and external constraints. In this regard, we adopt a framework that is both systemic and social constructionist in nature: it views father involvement as a complex process of negotiation involving mothers, fathers, and children within a cultural and institutional context (Doherty 1997). This is consistent with more recent trends in fathering research that look at the relationship between fathers and children "as parts of complex social systems (notably, the family) in which each person affects every other reciprocally, directly and indirectly" (Lamb 1997:3).

Time is of central importance for understanding parental involvement. In an earlier work of father involvement (Daly 1996b), time emerged as a dominant metaphor for the way that men described their relationships to their children: They lamented about not having enough time with their children, they strategized about how to make time to be with their children, and most importantly, they repeatedly emphasized the value of spending time with their children. Diligence to time is centrally important for understanding the systemic and socially constructed properties of parental involvement.

In this chapter, we examine the relationship between father involvement, mother involvement, and time on two levels. First, we explore how parents live and carry out their responsibilities within an external culture of time. Although parents exercise some autonomy in how they carry out their parenting repertoires, they must do so within a broader context of temporal values, norms, and expectations that contains some traditional imperatives about how time should be allocated. We are particularly interested in the dynamics of control over time that exist between parents and the work culture of which they are a part. Institutional practices in the workplace have been identified as an important barrier to paternal involvement (Lamb 1997). Second, we examine how fathers who are committed to sharing parenting have had to work with their partners to create new ways of dealing with time in their relationship. These new ways of working with time are typically within a time culture oriented to parenting practices that are carried out in a more traditional fashion. Here, we examine not simply how much time each parent contributes, but how they construct and reconstruct the form of that time, the activity that fills that time, and importantly, the meanings and values associated with that time.

## METHODS

Qualitative research methodologies are particularly pertinent for the study of family experiences (Gilgun, Daly, and Handel 1992). Consistent with the assumptions of these methodologies, the goal of this research was to look into the deep texture and meanings as they emerge out of the everyday experiences of men and women working together to raise their children. In this study, men and women were interviewed, both individually and as a couple, in order to explore the ways that both men and women co-construct "fatherhood"—their beliefs, expectations, behaviors, and reflective experiences.

A sample of eighteen intact families was obtained through several "convenience" referrals initially and "snowball" referrals later. This sample was unique insofar as both the man and the woman agreed that he was an active and fully participating father in everyday family life. In addition, two other criteria had to be met: first, the couple had to have at least one child between the ages of two and six years, and, at the time of the first interview, none of their children were in their teen years; and second, they had to be an intact family (in order to avoid confounding issues of stepparenting, or divorce and remarriage). This convenience sample is by no means random, and therefore it is limited in its generalizability. The goal of grounded theory and associated qualitative research, however, is not to generalize about how many or what kind of people share a particular characteristic, but to capture the "complex assumptions, meanings, and contradictions that enter into the process of experiencing and constructing" (Daly 1993:515–16) everyday lives.

The average age of the couples in this study was, thirty-eight years and thirty-six years for men and women, respectively. The men and women were generally from the dominant Caucasian culture and were generally well educated. There was a range of educational and occupational experiences among both the men and the women. The eighteen families represented several different configurations of family structure: three families were dual-earners, three families job-shared, in four families the woman worked part-time, in two families the man worked part-time, there were three stay-at-home dads, and there were three stay-at-home moms. The annual income for the eighteen couples was reported to range from $10,000 (one family) to just over $140,000 (one family), with an average income of approximately $45,000. Two families had only one child, eleven families had two children, and five families had three children.

The research design followed the open and emergent tenets of grounded theory (Glaser and Strauss 1967; Strauss 1987; Strauss and Corbin 1988) and the long qualitative interview (Marshall and Rossman 1989; McCracken 1988). Thematic and constant comparative analysis of the thirty-six accounts revealed a diversity of possibilities for men and women to re-create fatherhood in the interactive environment of sharing parenting. While time was not the specific focus of these research interviews, talk about sharing parenting frequently turned to talk about time and men's and women's phenomenological experiences of family time.

## DISCUSSION: NEGOTIATING PARENTAL INVOLVEMENT WITHIN THE CULTURE OF TIME

The culture of time is characterized by the values of speed and efficiency leaving families feeling somewhat tyrannized by the escalating demands of a tightly scheduled clock culture (Daly 1996a). Although "family time" and "spending time with children" are cherished values in our culture, they are routinely sabotaged by an intensifying work ethos that leaves families with less time for each other than ever before. Families live in a world of accelerated time demands. In response to forces such as industrialization, information technology, and the globalization of the world economy, families are caught in an ever-tightening spiral of efficiency and speed. Couples who are committed to shared parental involvement must be very deliberate in their efforts to surmount the countervailing forces of the larger culture that place increasing temporal demands on family members.

In our North American culture, the masters of time are perceived as the school, the employer, and all other events that arise to impose various temporal demands on the family. However, none of these is as important as the expanding work ethic, which has resulted in parents dedicating more of their time to the activities of paid work. The economic imperative to support one's family is closely linked to issues of controlling time. For dual-earner couples, both incomes are often considered necessary to keep the family going. If this is the case, then the master of time is more likely to be the employer's schedule, whereby husbands and wives work on an ongoing basis to meet their responsibilities of full-time work while at the same time trying to patch together a set of caregiving relationships that will provide continuous coverage for the children.

For many shared-parenting families, however, the parents have made intentional life-style decisions that partially extricate them from that external master's control. At the center of their life-style choices lies a firm commitment for both parents to be significantly present in the daily lives of their children. This often means these people make intentional trade-offs between access to family time and higher family income. The men and women in these shared-parenting families endeavor to actively manage their time and the external demands on it.

Centrally important for managing their time was the requirement that they reconcile how their family would engage in life-style patterns they thought to be in contrast with the valued norms in our society. Similar to Schor's reference to the "insidious cycle of work and spend" (1991:107), the men in shared-parenting families spoke with some disdain about the insidious presence of the "culture of materialism" and the potential of its temptations to keep both men and women trapped in an overly demanding work schedule. They outlined their efforts to escape its potentially destructive grip on their family. By no means were these families threatened by poverty-line existence, nor were they completely escaping the tug of materialism. They did, however, make family decisions that they hoped would minimize the external drain on family time. For example, as in the excerpt below, some parents chose to locate their family home in an more affordable area so that they could live comfortably on less income and have more time for the children:

> We'd been living in Port Credit and we moved to Sunnyside where it was cheaper because we made this decision that we had to reduce our expenses [so that one of us could cut back to part-time work]. I now work some evenings and on weekends when he can be home with the children. (Rick and Karen)

This excerpt also demonstrates another dimension of shared-parenting arrangements. In shared-parenting families there is a substantial presence of on-off shifting, where one parent is on duty while the other is at work. This tag-team type of arrangement is seen as essential for balancing the external draws on their time with their intentions to be involved parents (Dienhart

1998). These men and women negotiate flexible work hours with their employers so that they can take turns being with the children and thus minimize the need for external day care. For the shared-parenting fathers, this typically meant they made transitions in their career paths so they could get more involved in the lives of their children.

Corresponding with this, their wives did not have to make all the compromises and sacrifices in their jobs and careers because they now had children. Not all the career transitions made by these involved fathers were as marked as Rob's, noted here, but they were significant in the impact they had on the family's ability to manage their time and remain consistent with their family values. Rob and Donna provide just one example of how couples made intentional choices. As with several couples, their negotiations resulted in notable transitions in his career, allowing him to get very involved in the daily childrearing. Rob is in his early forties; they have two children under the age of six. He said:

> [W]hen we had a second child it put a lot of demands on us all and we came to the conclusion jointly, although I think Donna was much more perceptive than I, that something had to give, and I was quite willing and ready to leave the brokerage business. I then went to work at the bookstore, and consequently we were able to come to a plan where we would share the store and the kids because we both felt strongly that we wanted to raise our children and not have 12 nannies looking after them.

It seems men's willingness to shift their careers, thus maximizing their potential to be involved fathers, rests on challenging the dominant claim that work makes on their time. As Rob's narrative hints, these families highly value family time and place great importance on the parental influence in the lives of children. This value of parental availability and engagement is bedrock for these men and their partners. Further, to be involved fathers, these men recognize they will be called to lay aside a culturally sanctioned power to privilege their call on time outside the family—be it for work or leisure—over their partner's. As Dan said:

> I think in our move, I stood to lose a lot and Liz stood to gain a lot and it became quite clear to me that I had quite a powerful hand to enable or disable Liz's chances in her career. Enabling Liz meant my life changed. That was the point where I realized that I could lay aside power and control for my self-protection, and instead use it creatively. When our first child came along, it was again a decision that I knew I could probably have Liz work a quarter-time if I'd pushed—it wouldn't have been difficult—but again it was quite clear to me that wasn't what Liz had been called to do and by then I was beginning to understand that.

For those men who did not make significant moves to shift their career work, other accommodations were made to maximize their time for family involvement. This often meant the man carefully scrutinized his work commitment and the external demands accompanying his paid employment. These men found a combination of strategies that enabled them to resist an employer's implicit demand to make work the central focus in their lives. A basic strategy involved using whatever flex-time arrangements were generally available and/or negotiating special flex-time deals with their boss. A second strategy involved efforts to make clear distinctions between priorities at work and priorities at home. For example, some of the men talked about being careful to evaluate how they were being called to respond to a crisis at work or the demands of extra work loads rather than simply doing what was asked of them in a knee-jerk way. They spoke about taking pause to determine whether they must sacrifice family time to handle the situation. Several men mentioned they found this strategy revealed a false urgency in many situations they previously thought of as imperative. Jason gave an example of what he discovered about the importance of this strategy in his life. He is a father in his early forties; he and his wife have two children. Jason works full-time and his wife is training in a new profession nearly full-time. He said:

> There's two kinds of deadlines in business. The one is really there and there's nothing, not anything you can do about it. There's the other kind of deadline that's either self-imposed or corporate, culturally imposed. . . . [I]t's realizing wait a minute, maybe this [deadline at work] isn't that important. [I've observed when] you have more balance in your life [between work and family] then you have less anxiety and less fear. You drop that anxiety and fear and it becomes easier, then you do what you can do [at work] and you do the best job you can [when you're there].

The culture of time is dominated by the cultural values of work. Being involved in the lives of their children meant that these parents had to be diligent in standing guard against the invasive forces of work. In addition, it meant changing some traditional time practices within the family that had been deeply internalized.

## PARENTS RECONSTRUCTING THE GENDERED EXPERIENCE OF TIME

The struggle for these couples to create and maintain shared parenthood required that they not only reconcile a set of external demands, but also align a set of internal dynamics associated with how women and men experience time as they play out the parenting role. To fully comprehend the different experience of time for men and women means going beyond the "accounting" approach that is typical of time-diary studies. In time-diary research, it is consistently shown that men devote more hours to paid employment than women (Firestone and Shelton 1994), women commit more hours to housework and child care than men (Demo and Acock 1993; Pleck 1997), and overall women have less leisure time than men (Coverman and Sheley 1986; Hochschild 1989; Shaw 1992). Although these studies are essential for understanding disparities in time use between men and women, many questions remain concerning the values, meanings, and commitments of time as they are experienced on a daily basis.

There are many conflicts that men and women experience over time. Power and control over time are rooted in the values that are assigned to time through family responsibilities, money, position, and status. As Coser (1974) pointed out some time ago, it is not a simple matter of incompatible time allocations that arise from the demands of family and work. However, it is a fundamental contradiction in the values that underlie the allocation of time that women are now expected to be committed to their work just like men but at the same time maintaining a priority to family. By today's standards, fathers face a similar contradiction: men live in a culture where there are new expectations that they be committed to family just like women (see for example, LaRossa 1988; Daly 1993) while at the same time maintaining their role as the primary provider (Cohen 1993).

There are some indications that these different cultural expectations are at the root of a phenomenologically different experience of time for men and women. Hall (1983), for example, has suggested that men are monochronic in their experience of time (a pattern of sequential behavior that is shaped by schedules, is task-oriented, and is open to evaluation of success or failure) whereas women are polychronic in their experience of time (patterned by a set of simultaneous interactions, focused on the present, and shaped by the involvement of people in transactions). Monochronic time dominates the traditional institutional domains of business, government, the professions, entertainment, and sports, while polychronic time is most prevalent in the domestic domain, especially in traditional homes, where women are more likely to be engaged concurrently in multiple tasks and responsibilities. There is, however, some limited empirical support for the idea that women's experience of time as polychronic. Hochschild (1989), for example, in her research on dual-earner families, reports that women, more than men, often do two or more things at once while in the home. Similarly, Davies (1994), based on her work in Sweden, argues that women have a simultaneous capacity that allows them to carry out several activities at once.

Although these examples of previous research may hold for many men and women locked in traditional gendered patterns of family life, we would argue that women and men who are committed to shared parenting must both be capable of managing the multitasked, polychronic demands of family life. Involved fathers noted clear awareness of how their full participation in the responsibilities and activities of family life required them to have wider repertories than was typically required in their work outside the home. Women in these couples also noted the differences they experienced in their paid employment and their family life. In this, the men and women were more similar than different; both recognized the need to have flexible and expansive repertories to effectively collaborate as a parenting team. Rob, a midforties father of two children under the age of six, spoke quite eloquently about recognizing the contextual differences and how narrow specialization is prized in his previous business experience:

> [At home I] had to take much more responsibility for everything I did when I got out of business. [In business] you are a very specialized individual and you have a lot of support so that you can perform your specialized duties, which made up a very unreal situation. . . . [At first, when I was home with the children on my "parent days"] I was very surprised and loved doing all the little things—seeing all tasks through from A to Z. It gave me a much better feeling in myself. Whereas before, I just told someone else to do it! On the home-front . . . the time is unstructured essentially, or being structured around the baby which is intense.

Heather, a woman in her midforties who returned to work full-time after each of her children was born noted how the predictability and control in the workplace was comforting and in notable contrast to the unpredictability of being with children. Similar in some respects to Hochschild's (1997) notion of reversed worlds wherein women can feel more in control of their lives at work, Heather said this:

> I was glad to go back to work. . . . I can go to work and finish drinking a cup of coffee. . . . I am good at my job and I like it. . . . I can really feel confident about what I am doing at work. I could say before I had kids, I just had my world together and I just knew I was going to do this and this and this. That I knew how to raise children and I knew how to do just about everything until I had kids and then I realized I don't know anything. . . . It's much easier to be in control in the work force.

These two excerpts suggest that indeed the work context typically involves more structure, control, and discrete expectations. In contrast, both Rob and Heather mention how parenting requires them to be less structured and requires that they give up some of the control that they feel at work. As parents, both men and women found the terrain was always changing, requiring them to be both unstructured and intensely structured, depending on the parenting situation at hand. Ross talks about the shift in control when he became a parent:

> For me, when I work in the store, I work very much in high gear. . . . [When] you're walking with [the kids] or taking them to the park, you really have time to slow down and my job was old hand and, as I say, I was really just coming from a different place with it so it's wonderful for me to be able to let go of control. . . . When I'm in the store, I'm like the business person, you know, controlling it hard and then around the children, I would be soft. . . . I would say letting go of that control was a big part of it for me.

Previous research similarly points to differences in how men and women relate to the work that is done in the family. Women are more likely to report family time with children as an experience of mixed leisure and work (Shaw 1992). For the men in this study, there seemed to be similar experiences of the blurred boundaries between time in the family being work and leisure. Women in these couples also noted the similarities in their experiences of time and work in the family and what they believed their partners, as involved fathers, experienced. For example, Janice, an at-home parent for most of the week, talked about noticing her partner takes on a routine task and involves the children to increase his enjoyment of the work. She said:

> I usually do the Monday to Friday cooking and it's like I say to the kids "You go and watch TV or something, mommy's just preparing dinner." Whereas, Chris [husband/father] likes to cook. . . . [H]e'll spend Saturdays and Sundays cooking up big batches of things to freeze and he'll let them help. They have fun with him doing things that are to me tasks, whereas they all have fun doing it. I guess he makes everything more fun—but I wouldn't necessarily say he gets to have all the fun and I do all the work because I have a lot of fun with them during the day—doing crafts, going to the park, reading books.

Here we see the father taking a more polychronic approach to a family task, introducing enjoyable elements and relationship opportunities into a routine task. In combining the routine task with a time to be with his children and have fun, he is also doing the work of teaching his children useful life skills. Janice, on the other hand, takes a more segmented approach: she seems to have special times during the day that she "plays" with the children and other times when she does routine tasks while monitoring them at some distance. When Janice "plays" with the children she is also interacting in ways that help them learn life skills; she may be thinking about other things she intends to do (e.g., creating a shopping list, or the craft may become a present for the birthday of someone she is thinking about). Both are demonstrating polychronic orientations to time, in different ways and perhaps to different degrees.

Another important dimension in the phenomenology of time for men and women is how they define their time spent in family and in doing family tasks. In contrast to time-diary studies, which de facto define time spent doing family tasks as "family work," most men and women in these shared-parenting couples seldom talked about their time in family as work. These men and women did not portray themselves as slaves of the "second shift" (Hochschild 1989). They talked about their time in family as a very different kind of experience. It was seen as time spent doing the work of raising their children, but it was also time invested with high rewards of personal enjoyment and satisfaction. For those men and women who worked either full-time or part-time outside the home, time with the children was experienced as a kind of leisure relative to the demands of their paid employment; they enjoyed the time with their children. This was especially evident when they talked about the long-term perspective and the spiritual dimensions of participating in the growing-up of another human being.

## CONCLUSION

In order to fully understand parental involvement, we argue that research needs to focus more on the systemic properties that either enhance or constrain that involvement. We examine these properties at two levels in this chapter: (1) a system of cultural values and expectations that reinforce work as a dominant claim on both women's and men's time; and (2) the dynamics of the parenting partnership that involves the reconstruction of traditional experiences, routines, and expectations of time for both fathers and mothers.

For couples who were committed to shared parenting, there was a deliberate effort to do things differently. In spite of the hurried pace of their lives, they sought to align themselves with the schedules of their children. In fact, by arriving at unique patterns of sharing the parenting between the mother and the father, these parents were able to escape, at least partially, the scarcity of family time. Having both mothers and fathers engaged in sharing the routines of daily family life meant that they were able to juggle their work and family life, while minimizing their reliance on outside caregivers. These men and women either worked with their employers, they made intentional choices to be in careers that allowed flexibility, or they blended part-time work and full-time work across the couple. They intentionally created these work patterns so they could manage to have one parent with the children for a majority of the time during the work week. They did this by agreeing to be flexible in the way they managed their work schedules and to maximize the potential to complement each other's designated at-home parent time. Whichever parent was the designated at-home parent took primary responsibility for the children, thus minimizing the need to have children fit into adult schedules dictated by work. The children's experiences of being rushed out to day care on their parents' way to work was minimized. For this to work for these families, the men had to make a commitment to be fully involved fathers, and, importantly, both the men and women had to negotiate flexible work schedules and actively work to reconstruct traditional patterns of time use.

The sample from which these ideas have emerged is unique and exceptional. Critics might rise to the temptation to dismiss such a sample as privileged, unrepresentative, and not at all indicative of the typical experience of father involvement. However, it is precisely the unique character of these families that offers some insight into the micropolitics associated with achieving some success in the challenge of shared parental involvement. The men in this study *are* exceptional insofar as they have been able to do what many men are unable to do: break the traditional chains of work to become committed, actively engaged, and involved fathers.

What is not exceptional in this study, however, are the challenges that both women and men faced in working toward the goal of being involved parents. These challenges exist for all families. Work and the centrality of earning persists in a tyrannizing way for women and men as they strive to make time for their parenting role. Freeing themselves from the expectation that they give priority to their work required an ongoing diligence to the needs of their children and families. For men and women who wish to move into and sustain fully involved parenting, there is a need to change the way that they think about and structure time, especially as dictated by external institutions, so that they can be responsive to the multiple demands of their children and the home.

## REFERENCES

Cohen, T. 1993. "What Do Fathers Provide? Reconsidering the Economic and Nurturant Dimensions of Men as Parents." Pp. 1–22 in *Men, Work and Family,* edited by J. C. Hood. Newbury Park: Sage.

Coser, L. 1974. *Greedy Institutions: Patterns of Undivided Commitment.* New York: Free Press.

Coverman, S. and J. F. Sheley. 1986. "Change in Men's Housework and Childcare Time." 1965–1975, *Journal of Marriage and the Family* 48:413–22.

Cummings, E. M. and A. W. O'Reilly. 1997. "Fathers in Family Contexts: Effects of Marital Quality on Child Adjustment." Pp. 49–65 in *The Role of the Father in Child Development,* 3rd ed., edited by M. E. Lamb. New York: Wiley.

Daly, K. J. 1993. "Reshaping Fatherhood: Finding the Models." *Journal of Family Issues* 14:510–30.

———. 1996a. *Families and Time: Keeping Pace in a Hurried Culture.* Newbury Park, CA: Sage.

———. 1996b. "Spending Time with the Kids: Meanings of Family Time for Fathers." *Family Relations* 45:466–76.

Davies, K. 1994. "The Tensions between Process Time and Clock Time in Care-work: The Example of Day Nurseries." *Time & Society* 3:276–303.

Demo, D. and A. Acock. 1993. "Family Diversity and the Division of Domestic Labor." *Family Relations* 42:323–31.

Dienhart, A. 1998. *Reshaping Fatherhood: The Social Construction of Shared Parenting.* Newbury Park: Sage.

Doherty, W. 1997. "A Conceptual Model of Influences on Father Involvement and the Transition to Fatherhood." Paper presented at the Theory Construction and Research Methodology Workshop, NCFR, Crystal City, VA, November 6.

Firestone, J. and B. A. Shelton. 1994. "A Comparison of Women's and Men's Leisure Time: Subtle Effects of the Double Day." *Leisure Sciences* 16:45–60.

Gilgun, J. F., K. Daly, and G. Handel (Eds.). 1992. *Qualitative Methods in Family Research.* Newbury Park, CA: Sage.

Glaser, B. G. and A. L. Strauss. 1967. *The Discovery of Grounded Theory.* Chicago: Aldine.

Hall, E. T. 1983. *The Dance of Life: The Other Dimension of Time.* Garden City, NY: Anchor Press/Doubleday.

Hochschild, A. 1989. *The Second Shift.* New York: Avon.

———. 1997. *The Time Bind: When Work Becomes Home and Home Becomes Work.* New York: Metropolitan Books, Henry Holt.

Lamb, M. E. 1976. *The Role of the Father in Child Development.* New York: Wiley.

———. 1981. *The Role of the Father in Child Development,* 2nd ed. New York: Wiley.

———. 1997. "Fathers and Child Development: An Introductory Overview." Pp. 1–18 in *The Role of the Father in Child Development,* 3rd ed., edited by M. E. Lamb. New York: Wiley.

LaRossa, R. 1988. "Fatherhood and Social Change." *Family Relations* 37:451–58.

Marshall, C. and G. B. Rossman. 1989. *Designing Qualitative Research.* Newbury Park, CA: Sage.

McCracken, G. 1988. *The Long Interview.* Newbury Park, CA: Sage.

Pleck, J. 1997. "Paternal Involvement: Levels, Sources and Consequences." Pp. 66–103 in *The Role of the Father in Child Development,* 3rd ed., edited by M. E. Lamb. New York: Wiley.

Schor, J. B. 1991. *The Overworked American.* New York: Basic Books.

Shaw, S. 1992. "Dereifying Family Leisure: An Examination of Women's and Men's Everyday Experiences and Perceptions of Family Time." *Leisure Sciences* 4:271–86.

Strauss, A. L. 1987. "Qualitative Analysis for Social Scientists." Cambridge: Cambridge University Press.

Strauss, A. L. and J. Corbin. 1990. *Basics of Qualitative Research: Grounded Theory Procedures and Techniques.* Newbury Park, CA: Sage.

# New Considerations for the Twenty-First Century IV

# Working Mothers, Welfare Mothers: Implications for Children in the Twenty-First Century 10

Toby L. Parcel

## INTRODUCTION

As our society continues to struggle with how to lower welfare expenditures and define what levels of support are appropriate to families in need, some researchers are inquiring about how the parental transition from welfare to work might affect children. In this chapter, I address this concern by pursuing three issues. First, I argue that it is inappropriate to assume that there is a strict dichotomy between mothers who work and those who rely on some form of welfare support. Rather, I show that a sizable group of individuals both work and rely on welfare support. In addition, I argue that all mothers work. To allow appropriate comparisons among families, I identify four groups of mothers as relevant to thinking about the effects of welfare and work on children: those who neither work for pay nor receive welfare; those who work for pay and do not receive welfare; those who both work for pay and receive welfare; and those who do not work for pay but do receive welfare. Second, I show that personal and family resources vary significantly across these four groups. Based on theory and prior research, I argue that these resource differences have implications for the well-being of the children in these respective households. Third, I show how the characteristics of those who voluntarily leave welfare and those who remain on welfare after two years differ from those who are more persistently employed over the same time period. I conclude by suggesting how the transition from welfare to work for mothers may have implications for their children.

## "WORKING MOTHERS" VERSUS "WELFARE MOTHERS"

Several streams of literature combine to sensitize us to the likelihood that attempting to dichotomize mothers into those who "work" and those who accept "welfare" is not a useful exercise. First, literature on the "working poor" suggests that some families remain poor even when an adult in the household is employed (Corcoran and Hill 1980; Harris 1993). Recent analysis of data from the National Longitudinal Survey of Youth's Child-Mother data set demonstrates that out of a sample of 1040 women who had at least one child aged three to six in 1986, over 10 percent both worked and received welfare (Parcel and Menaghan 1997).

Definitions of welfare also influence the extent to which such overlap is possible. If one uses a singular definition of welfare to suggest that someone must be receiving AFDC in order to be defined as on welfare, the percentage of those both working and on welfare will be smaller than if a broader definition is used. The most common definition of being on welfare is more general, and in addition to accepting AFDC, also includes those receiving food stamps or a housing subsidy. Since some families may qualify for one form of support but not the others, the group being supported in some form is necessarily larger than a group receiving only one form of support.

Two strands of literature help us to understand how parental work status affects child well-being. Early studies concerned themselves with whether children of mothers who worked would be at a disadvantage relative to children of mothers who did not engage in paid employment (Bradley and Caldwell 1980, 1984; Farel 1980; Schachter 1981; Easterbrook and Goldberg 1985). Many of these studies, however, produced inconclusive results or had serious methodological problems. No consensus existed as to how to measure maternal employment, with some studies creating two or three categories of employment (Schachter 1981; Easterbrook and Goldberg 1985) and others failing to measure this construct (Haskins 1985). In addition, many studies on the topic were of relatively short duration and were conducted on small samples (Farel 1980; Schachter 1981; Easterbrook and Goldberg 1985). A more recent literature explores how variation among working mothers may influence child well-being (Parcel and Menaghan 1990, 1994a, 1994b; Menaghan and Parcel 1991, 1995; Geschwender and Parcel 1995).

Other relevant arguments include those suggesting that all mothers work, while only some of them are paid. Feminist perspectives have done a good job of sensitizing us to this reality. Arlie Hochschild's classic book *The Second Shift* (1989) suggests that women who work outside the home face a second shift of work in terms of running the household and rearing children. By focusing on the work that women do to maintain households and rear children and by naming this work "the second shift," Hochschild encourages us to view work more broadly than activities that are monetarily compensated. Although women likely delegate some of the work involved in these activities while they are pursuing paid employment, the responsibility for completing these tasks remains theirs. For Hochschild, the problem is why this second shift of work is delegated largely to mothers, and what strategies women use to encourage/require their spouses to share in the work and in the responsibility. Ferree (1991) and Wharton (1994) develop compatible arguments.

As influential as this work has been, its implications for the problem we are considering here are important. The original idea behind AFDC was to support widows in completing child rearing and household maintenance while their children remained dependent on them. Thus what is second-shift work for working mothers was the only shift of work for mothers being supported on AFDC; at the time the program was conceptualized in the 1930s, the proportions of mothers with spouses, where the mothers were also employed outside the home, was low. Thus, the intent was to support children of widows so that they could have some semblance of the economic resources that intact two-parent families could provide. More recently AFDC has become associated with supporting families where fathers are absent for reasons other than death, and at the same time, by the mid-1980s substantial proportions of mothers were employed outside the home (Hoffman 1989; Parcel and Menaghan 1994b). If these working mothers can manage a second shift, why should other mothers be exempt from these responsibilities? Obviously, rearing children and maintaining a household for them involves a lot of work. This is true even for those households where one spouse works for pay and another provides household maintenance; although this type of household is a minority among household forms (U.S. Bureau of Labor Statistics 1997), it forms a logical comparison group when considering the implications of changes in work status for mothers with dependent children.

For these reasons, I view all mothers as working, but acknowledge that the mothers who work for pay both receive additional income as well as face a second shift of work and responsibility centered around their homes and children. And single mothers, whether they receive welfare support or not, have no one to assist with a second shift. A central question for this chapter, then, is what differences we might find among children reared in households that vary along these dimensions, and among their parents. This question takes on additional importance in times of social change precipitated by federal legislation allowing for the termination of welfare benefits "as we know them." We conceptualize the likelihood that some children who have been reared in households without a working adult but where welfare is accepted, will now live in households where some benefits are provided but where the primary caretaker either works, receives job training, or performs some community service outside the home.

In view of these arguments, I propose that it is appropriate to divide families into four categories defined by (1) whether the mother works for pay or not and (2) whether the family receives any form of welfare assistance or not. We conceptualize the likelihood that these groups of families will vary in terms of the personal resources they bring both to the labor market and to the task of rearing families. We expect that the most advantaged group of mothers will be those who neither engage in paid work nor accept welfare. The second most advantaged group will consist of those who work for pay but are not on welfare, followed by those who both work for pay and accept welfare. The least advantaged group should be those who do not work for pay but do accept welfare.

## PARENTAL RESOURCES AND CHILD WELL-BEING

We now consider what types of parental resources influence child well-being. Studies within the status attainment tradition (Blau, Duncan, and Tyree 1967; Featherman and Hauser 1976; Horan 1978; Kerckhoff, Campbell, and Trott 1982; Ishida, Muller, and Ridge 1995) clearly demonstrate that offspring socioeconomic status is importantly a function of educational attainment and that, in turn, educational outcomes are importantly influenced by parental socioeconomic status. Thus, the effect of parental socioeconomic standing on the socioeconomic well-being of their children is both important and indirect, operating through educational attainment.

Turning to younger children, Parcel and Menaghan (1994a, 1994b) suggest several categories of parental characteristics important to child well-being. They argue and demonstrate that parental working conditions have both direct and indirect effects on child well-being, the indirect effects operating through children's home environments. The parental working conditions they single out for attention include parental wage levels, parental work hours, and occupational complexity. Parental wages provide the material foundation for the household, and thus are fundamental to establishing the level of material resources on which parents draw during the child-rearing process. Persistent overtime work hours set the limits within which parents can interact with their children. Longer parental work hours, for both mothers and fathers, are associated with lower levels of child verbal facility (Parcel and Menaghan 1994a, 1994b), and higher levels of child behavior problems. Coleman (1988, 1990) worries that maternal paid employment will weaken and diminish the quantity of social capital available for child socialization, and these findings are not inconsistent with that hypothesis. At the same time, lower paternal work hours are associated with increased behavior problems (Parcel and Menaghan 1994b) while low maternal work hours are associated with lower levels of child verbal facility than are full-time maternal hours. Thus, lower work hours, by themselves, do not appear to be an asset to children. Parcel and Menaghan (1994b) also show that high parental work hours in combination with other major family and life changes such as birth of an additional child are associated with decrements in child well-being within a two-year time frame. Finally, following arguments by Mel Kohn and colleagues concerning the effects of adult work on adult personality and child-rearing values, Menaghan and Parcel (1991) show that higher levels of maternal occupational complexity are associated with stronger children's home environments, which in turn favorably affect child cognition and social adjustment (Parcel and Menaghan 1994b).

Other parental resources and family characteristics also influence children. Lower levels of parental schooling, in addition to being associated with lower levels of offspring adult socioeconomic achievement, signal reduced human capital available during the child socialization process. Parental ability levels may also influence child well-being, as may parental levels of self-esteem and locus of control. Parents who believe that they have substantial control over life events and a more positive self-image are more likely to take effective action in the socialization process with their children, and are likely to convey the potential for such control to their children; this may have particularly salutary effects on child social adjustment. Several researchers have demonstrated that increased family size is associated with lower levels of educational attainment (Downey 1995), lower levels of verbal facility (Parcel and Menaghan 1990, 1994a, 1994b), and increased levels of behavior problems (Parcel and Menaghan 1993, 1994a, 1994b). Having a mother who is married is also likely to be an advantage for children. Two-parent families will have greater access to adult supervision and personal resources useful in directing child activities. They are also likely to have greater material resources with which to rear children. We also consider whether children themselves vary across these four family types so as to rule out whether processes of social selection have somehow resulted in the differential distribution of children across families. For example, shyness may interfere both with developing cognitive skill as well as child social adjustment, and thus needs to be considered in predicting key outcomes.

Finally, children's home environments influence child well-being. As noted above, among working mothers, variations in children's home environments predict both child cognition and child social adjustment. Parcel and Menaghan (1997) have demonstrated that children's home environments are strongest in households where mothers work for pay, weakest in households where mothers rely solely on welfare, and intermediate in households where mothers both work for pay and receive some form of welfare support; they did not evaluate the home environments in households where the mothers neither worked for pay nor accepted welfare. Taken together, these arguments identify parental working conditions, parental characteristics, elements of household structure, and child characteristics as resources relevant to variation in child well-being. We now describe the empirical strategy and data sources we use to address the issues we have posed.

## DATA SOURCES AND EMPIRICAL STRATEGY

Addressing these issues requires a data source that contains variation in family type by employment status and welfare receipt, and contains a wealth of family, child and parental information useful in both describing and analyzing how types of families differ. It is also important to have good measures of child well-being. The NLSY Child Mother data set meets these criteria. In 1979 the NLSY began following approximately twelve thousand youths between the ages of fourteen and twenty-one, with annual interviews concerning their education, occupational, marital, and fertility experiences. By 1986 more than one-half of the NLSY women had become mothers; age-appropriate developmental assessments of both cognitive and social outcomes were completed on these children in 1986 and repeated on two-year intervals. We use data from 1986 since all children age three years and older were administered a measure of cognition that year, the Peabody Picture Vocabulary Test (revised; PPVT-R). This measure has high reliability and validity (Dunn and Dunn 1981; Baker and Mott 1989).

Our sample includes mothers of children who were three to six years old in 1986, and whose children lived with them. Truncating the sample at six years excludes older children who were born prior to the initial NLSY interviewing year. Thus, our sample represents children who are early or on-time births, and therefore necessarily leaves out children of the same age born to older mothers, who may have delayed childbearing to pursue higher education and/or paid employment. As such, these data likely understate the degree of inequality among the four groups we study since the groups with mothers who pursue paid employment are likely to postpone childbearing and thus appear in our sample with less frequency than they appear in the population. Truncating the sample to avoid the very oldest children in 1986 may result in disproportionate elimination from the sample of children in households receiving welfare. Thus our data exclude some children from both the higher SES and lower SES ends of the continuum.[1]

Table 1 summarizes the operationalizations of variables used in the analysis. I highlight additional details here. The PPVT-R measures a child's receptive or hearing vocabulary of standard American English.[2] Limitations of the test include the likelihood that the test underestimates verbal facility among minority children and among disadvantaged children (Lee, Brooks-Gunn, and Schnur 1988). Regarding parental working conditions, we dummied work hours to permit detection of nonlinear relationships between work hours and the dependent variables. Mothers who do not work for pay receive missing values on all work hour dummies, as do unemployed or absent fathers. All missing values are recoded to the mean. Thus, the work hours variables capture variations in work hours among employed parents. Maternal AFQT and self-concept are measured in 1979 and 1980, and thus are

*Table 1.* List of Variables

| *Variable* | *Description* |
|---|---|
| PIAT Math | Measured in 1988. This test taps math achievement from recognizing numerals to trigonometry concepts. |
| PIAT Reading | Measured in 1988. This portion of the test examines reading using measures of reading recognition and pronunciation ability from preschool to high school levels. |
| PPVT-R | Measured in 1986. This test taps receptive vocabulary of Standard American English. |
| Home Environment | Measured in 1986 and 1988. This scale examines the home environment mothers provide for their children. It includes items about physical environment, affect, and cognitive stimulation. |
| Behavior Problems | Measured in 1986 and 1988. This scale taps behavior problems with other children and at home, including problems with temper, dependence, and feelings of inferiority. |
| Occupation Complexity | Measured in 1986 and 1988 for mothers and 1985 and 1987 for spouses. This 19-item scale ( = .94) was developed by Parcel by first matching data from the Dictionary of Occupational Titles, 4th ed. (1977), to 1970 U.S. Census occupational codes and then performing factor analysis on the data. The scale measures three aspects of jobs including the education/training levels required for the work, the direction, control, and planning of activities, and the complexity of working with people and data. Nonemployed mothers received a missing value for this variable. |
| Usual Work Hours per Week | Measured in 1986 and 1988 for mothers and 1985 and 1987 for spouses. For mothers, dummy variables capture no work hours, low part-time hours (1–20), high part-time hours (21–34), full-time hours (35–40), and overtime hours (41+). For spouses, a dummy variable represents part-time (1–34), full–time (35-40), and overtime (40+) hours. For both parents, full-time hours are the reference group. |
| Maternal Nonemployment | Measured in 1986 and 1988. Mothers who reported no work hours were coded as nonemployed. |
| Hourly Wages | Measured in 1986 and 1988 for mothers and 1985 and 1987 for spouses. For both parents, this is captured by average hourly wage. For fathers, this measure was constructed by dividing average annual earnings by average hours worked |
| Marital Status | A dummy variable measuring mothers who were married or not married in 1986. Not married is the reference group. |

*Table 1.* List of Variables (*continued*)

| *Variable* | *Description* |
|---|---|
| Parental Education | Measured in 1986 for mother and spouse. Education is measured by number of years. |
| Parental Age | Measured in 1986 and 1988 for mother and mother's spouse. |
| Maternal Cognitive Skills | Measured by the mother's percentile score on the Armed Forces Qualifying Test (AFQT) given in 1980. This test measures paragraph comprehension, word knowledge, arithmetic ability, and numeric operational skills. |
| Maternal Self-Esteem | Measured in 1980 using a 10-item Rosenberg self-esteem scale. |
| Maternal Ethnicity/Race | Measured as a set of dummy variables capturing black, white, Mexican Hispanic, and other Hispanic groups. |
| Family Size | Measured in 1986 as the number of children the mother had in addition to the focus child. |
| Additional Children | Measured in 1988 as a dummy variable tapping whether the mother has had an additional child/children since 1986. |
| Child Gender | A dummy variable with female as the reference group. |
| Child Health Problems | Measured in 1986 and 1988. A dummy variable with no health problems that limit the child's participation in activities and school as the reference group. |
| Shyness and Anxiety | Assessed by the interviewer at the start of the 1986 interview. The scale ranges from 1 (not at all shy/anxious) to 5 (extremely shy/anxious). |
| Low Birthweight | A dummy variable distinguishing between children whose birth weight was below 5.5 pounds, weighing 5.5 pounds or more as the reference group. |
| Maternal Family of Origin | This variable examines whether the mother lived in a one-parent or a two-parent family when she was 14. One-parent families are the reference group. |
| Grandmother's Education | The child's maternal grandmother's level of education. |

causally prior to the child outcomes that we study. Home environment is measured as a *z*-score and taps physical environment, maternal warmth, and cognitive stimulation.

## RESULTS

Table 2 presents the results of ANOVA analyses that portray the differences in key outcomes and resources among the four groups identified above. We predicted that the most advantaged children would be those of mothers who neither worked nor accepted welfare (*N* = 381), followed by those who worked but did not receive welfare (*N* = 651); the least two advantaged groups would be those whose mothers both worked and received welfare (*N* = 130), followed by those whose mothers did not work but received welfare (*N* = 259).

We see that the four groups are ordered as predicted with statistically significant differences on verbal facility (PPVT-R), children's home environments, maternal age, presence of two parents in the home when the mother was fourteen years of age, and spouse's age. Several other variables show the strongest group to be mothers who work but do not receive welfare followed by those who neither worked nor received welfare, followed by the remaining two groups as predicted. These variables include several that are relevant to paid employment including maternal education, maternal AFQT, and maternal self-concept. Each of these factors can influence job placement and success. Also following this pattern is grandmother's education, our indicator of maternal class background.

The pattern of spouse variables tells a slightly different, although not incompatible story. Regarding spouse occupational complexity and wage levels, the most advantaged group is mothers who neither work nor accept welfare followed by mothers who work and do not accept welfare; the third most advantaged group is mothers who did not work but who received welfare. We need to remember however, that only 35 percent of these mothers have spouses, so these averages are computed on a relatively small number of cases. The least advantaged group of mothers in terms of spouse wages and occupational complexity are mothers who both work and receive welfare; 40 percent of them are married. Clearly, these families are the "working poor" that we identified above.

Spouse education follows the basic pattern outlined above, with the exception that spouses of mothers who do not work for pay but receive welfare are slightly more educated than mothers who both work for pay and receive welfare. This pattern mirrors the findings for spouse occupational complexity and wages. Households that receive welfare have spouses (when they are present) who are less likely to be working full-time or more as compared with households that do not receive welfare. Finally, there are significant differences in numbers of children across our household types; those with mothers who neither worked for pay nor received welfare, and those who did not work for pay but received welfare, have more children than the other two types. In addition, mothers who work for pay are less likely to have low birthweight babies than mothers who are not working for pay. Clearly the four household types we have identified differ significantly both in terms of parental resources and child outcomes.

We now turn to consideration of how this picture develops as we move forward two years to 1988. One of the advantages of the NLSY data set is that

*Table 2.* Means and ANOVAs for Mothers of 3- to 6-Year-Old Children in 1986, NLSY

| *Variable* | *Mothers Who Worked and Did Not Receive Welfare in 1986* | *Mothers Who Worked and Received Welfare in 1986* | *Mothers Who Did Not Work but Received Welfare in 1986* | *Mothers Who Neither Worked nor Received Welfare in 1986* |
|---|---|---|---|---|
| PPVT 1986 | 95.49*** | 89.83 | 85.47 | 96.22 |
| Home 1986 | .27*** | –.07 | –.60 | .28 |
| Child Characteristics | | | | |
| Male | .50 | .49 | .57 | .52 |
| Shy in Interview | –.01 | –.07 | .09 | –.16 |
| Low Birthweight | .06*** | .06 | .07 | .07 |
| Health Problems 1986 | .06 | .03 | .06 | .06 |
| Parental Characteristics | | | | |
| Mother's Age 1986 | 25.70*** | 24.92 | 24.85 | 25.81 |
| Mother's Education 1986 | 12.19*** | 11.69 | 10.95 | 11.92 |
| Black | .16*** | .31 | .37 | .10 |
| Mexican Hispanic | .04*** | .05 | .09 | .06 |
| White | .77*** | .59 | .50 | .80 |
| Other Hispanic | .03** | .05 | .04 | .04 |
| AFQT 1980 | 69.15*** | 59.95 | 50.41 | 66.16 |
| Self-Concept | –.02*** | –.23 | –.42 | –.12 |
| Two Parents at Age 14 | .80*** | .71 | .62 | .80 |
| Grandmother's education | 10.89*** | 10.69 | 9.67 | 10.85 |
| Spouse's Age 1986 | 28.79* | 28.69 | 28.03 | 29.18 |
| Spouse's Education 1986 | 12.28*** | 11.47 | 11.59 | 12.47 |

| | | | | |
|---|---|---|---|---|
| Maternal Work Characteristics | | | | |
| Occupational Complexity | –5.02*** | –8.96 | — | — |
| Wage | 5.84*** | 4.78 | — | — |
| Work 1–20 Hours | .14 | .17 | — | — |
| Work 21–34 Hours | .17** | .27 | — | — |
| Work 35–40 Hours | .57 | .48 | — | — |
| Work over 40 Hours | .12 | .08 | — | — |
| Spouse Work Characteristics | | | | |
| Occupational Complexity | –5.04*** | –9.17 | –6.69 | –4.19 |
| Wage | 9.57*** | 6.66 | 7.37 | 10.97 |
| Work under 35 Hours | .03*** | .16 | .19 | .02 |
| Work 35–40 Hours | .58*** | .50 | .63 | .50 |
| Work over 40 Hours | .39*** | .34 | .18 | .48 |
| Family Characteristics | | | | |
| Married | .75 | .40 | .35 | .88 |
| Number of Children | 1.84*** | 1.86 | 2.32 | 2.11 |
| *N* | 651 | 130 | 259 | 381 |

* $p < .05$ **$p < 01$. *** $p < .001$.

it allows us to trace in a very detailed way the work statuses of families over time. By 1988, a number of the mothers accepting welfare (in 1986) have voluntarily declined welfare assistance. Some mothers working in 1986 are no longer working, with a subset of these now accepting welfare. A number of those mothers not employed for pay in 1986 are employed for pay in 1988; indeed, a more detailed tracing of statuses would undoubtedly reveal even more complexities for some families who may have changed statuses more than once over the two-year period. In view of the recent Welfare Reform Act, it is very relevant to consider changes in family circumstances over a two-year period because some families may find their welfare benefits terminate after two years.

In this analysis I focus on the characteristics of three groups whom I label as work persisters, welfare persisters, and voluntary welfare escapees. Comparisons among these groups are interesting for several reasons. Comparing welfare escapees and welfare persisters is important because under the new legislation, those who would otherwise have persisted in accepting some forms of welfare may find themselves ineligible, and in many cases competing for the same types of jobs that welfare escapees are already occupying. If there are major differences in the profiles of these two groups favoring the welfare escapees, it suggests that the exit from welfare may be especially challenging for those who would not have left voluntarily. In addition, in a more global sense, both groups are competing with the persistent workers. We expect families of persistent workers to be advantaged relative to the other groups. It will be particularly interesting to compare child outcomes among the three groups; can we detect differences among the children that are comparable to differences in parental characteristics?

Table 3 presents the results of ANOVA analyses for parental and child characteristics across the three groups: work persisters (*N* = 487), welfare escapees (*N* = 91), and welfare persisters (*N* = 138). The top of Table 3 provides data regarding child well-being, and also allows us a picture of how different these three groups were in 1986. The groups are ordered as predicted in 1986 with children of persistent workers showing stronger verbal facility, fewer behavior problems, and stronger home environments than children in the other two groups; the differences between the children of persistent workers and those of welfare persisters are particularly large. These differences persist into 1988, with significant differences across the three groups in reading and especially math achievement, and even greater differences in behavior problems than were evident in 1986. Although home environments have improved for all groups during the two-year interval, significant differences remain.

Maternal resources also vary significantly across the three groups as predicted. Mothers who are persistent workers are older, more educated, less likely to be of minority racial status, higher in measured mental ability,

*Table 3.* Means and ANOVAs for Mothers of 5- to 8-Year-Old Children in 1988, NLSY

| *Variable* | *Persistent Workers* | *Voluntary Welfare Escapes* | *Welfare Persisters* |
|---|---|---|---|
| PPVT 1986 | 95.63*** | 92.54 | 80.72 |
| Math 1988 | 102.84*** | 100.71 | 93.77 |
| Reading 1988 | 105.72*** | 102.04 | 98.49 |
| Behavior Problems 1986 | −1.17** | 2.50 | 2.58 |
| Behavior Problems 1988 | −1.97*** | 3.26 | 3.59 |
| Home 1986 | .29*** | −.03 | −.88 |
| Home 1988 | .58*** | .30 | −.32 |
| Child Characteristics | | | |
| Male | .50* | .47 | .54 |
| Shy in Interview | −.05* | −.14 | .07 |
| Low Birthweight | .04 | .03 | .11 |
| Health Problems 1988 | .02*** | .07 | .05 |
| Parental Characteristics | | | |
| Mother's Age 1988 | 27.85*** | 27.24 | 26.64 |
| Mother's Education 1988 | 12.37*** | 11.58 | 10.95 |
| Black | .15*** | .18 | .48 |
| Mexican Hispanic | .04*** | .07 | .09 |
| White | .78*** | .71 | .38 |
| Other Hispanic | .03*** | .05 | .05 |
| AFQT 1980 | 70.62*** | 63.83 | 44.11 |
| Self-Concept | .07*** | −.24 | −.49 |
| Two Parents at Age 14 | .83*** | .76 | .56 |
| Grandmother's Education | 10.92*** | 10.70 | 9.35 |
| Spouse's Age 1988 | 31.40 | 30.54 | 29.79 |
| Spouse's Education 1988 | 12.40*** | 11.37 | 11.22 |
| Maternal Work Characteristics 1988 | | | |
| Occupational Complexity | −3.40 | −5.93 | — |
| Wage | 7.40*** | 5.42 | — |
| Work 1–20 Hours | .12*** | .09 | — |
| Work 21–34 Hours | .14*** | .18 | — |
| Work 35–40 Hours | .61*** | .56 | — |
| Work over 40 Hours | .13*** | .17 | — |
| Spouse Work Characteristics 1988 | | | |
| Occupational Complexity | −3.18*** | −7.31 | −8.79 |
| Wage | 9.62*** | 6.67 | 6.78 |
| Work under 35 Hours | .06*** | .00 | .23 |
| Work 35–40 Hours | .59*** | .76 | .45 |
| Work over 40 Hours | .35*** | .24 | .32 |
| *N* | 487 | 91 | 138 |

* $p < .05$.  ** $p < .01$.  *** $p < .001$.

stronger in self-concept, and come from more advantaged family backgrounds. They also have higher wages than those women who have voluntarily escaped welfare. Spouse characteristics also favor the families where mothers are persistent workers. These spouses are more educated, have more complex jobs, and earn higher wages.

## DISCUSSION AND CONCLUSIONS

Taken together, these findings suggest strong evidence in support of the idea that families in which mothers are persistent workers and where spouses are employed have strong economic and social advantages relative to families where the mother has recently escaped from welfare and especially relative to families where the mother is accepting welfare in both 1986 and 1988. These differences are significant for maternal and spouse characteristics and, as such, may not be very surprising. The magnitude of the differences, however, should not be underestimated. Consider AFQT as an example. These data suggest that there is a one-and-one-half standard deviation difference in the measured mental ability between persistent workers and welfare persisters. The differences in AFQT between the voluntary welfare escapees and the welfare persisters is close to one standard deviation. Differences in maternal years of schooling are also important, as are differences in self-concept. These characteristics are pertinent to success in paid employment, and suggest that those women who in 1988 were welfare persisters are likely to face very stiff competition as they attempt to enter the labor market as what we might call "involuntary welfare escapees." Additional analyses (not presented here) suggest that mothers who worked for pay in 1988 who had been working in the home in 1986 are similar on these characteristics to the persistently employed.

These data also speak to the issue of how early inequality begins. In short, the findings suggest that inequality begins very early. Not only do the children of these three groups appear very different in 1988 but comparable differences are also observed as early as 1986 when these children were three to six years old. These findings have implications for children as we consider work and family changes in the twenty-first century. Clearly, more of these children will be in families where their parents will be obtaining less support from various welfare sources than they would have obtained prior to the Welfare Reform Act. These children are competing with their more advantaged peers: they are already behind before welfare reform. Their parents will be struggling to manage "a second shift" of responsibility, while at the same time performing that juggling act with fewer resources than parents already engaged with these multiple roles.

What can be done to help these parents? Because individual states are in charge of this transition from welfare to work, there will be locational variation in the rules under which welfare recipients will make the transition, and the support that states will provide to families. There is likely to be locational variation in the success of this transition for both parents and children. Given these data, it seems wise for states to consider providing parenting training for this population as a form of investment in the next generation. Some welfare support programs already require participation in parenting classes. Such efforts, possibly as a part of a larger package of educational support, might help to promote child well-being during this period of important social experimentation and profound social change. Such investments might also have the salutary effect of lowering welfare receipt in the next generation.

## NOTES

1. We also excluded a few additional children with extremely low birth weights (less than 1,500 grams) who might therefore be at high risk for delayed development. When more than one child per mother was in the three- to six-year-old age group, we selected the younger to avoid overrepresenting mothers with high fertility.

2. The interviewer says a word, and the child points to one of four pictures that best matches the meaning of the word. The test becomes progressively more difficult as the child proceeds through it. The test has high split half and test-retest reliability (Dunn and Dunn 1981), high concurrent validity with broader measures such as the Stanford-Binet and the Wechsler Intelligence Scale for Children (WISC), and significant associations with standardized measures of reading comprehension, mathematics and later school achievement (Baker and Mott 1989).

## REFERENCES

Baker, Paula C. and Frank L. Mott. 1989. *NLSY Child Handbook 1989: A Guide and Resource Document for the 1986 National Longitudinal Survey of Youth Child Data*. Columbus, OH: Center for Human Resource Research, Ohio State University.

Blau, Peter M., Otis Dudley Duncan, and Andrea Tyree. 1967. *The American Occupational Structure*. New York: Wiley.

Bradley, Robert H. and Bettye M. Caldwell. 1980. "Home Environment, Cognitive Competence, and IQ among Males and Females." *Child Development* 51: 1140–48.

———. 1984. "The Relation of Infants' Home Environments to Achievement Test Performance in First Grade." *Child Development* 55:803–9.

Coleman, James S. 1988. "Social Capital in the Creation of Human Capital." *American Journal of Sociology* 94:S95–S120.

———. 1990. *Foundations of Social Theory*, Cambridge, MA: Belknap Press of Harvard University Press.

Corcoran, Mary and Martha S. Hill. 1980. "Unemployment and Poverty." *Social Service Review* 54(3):407–13.

Downey, Douglas B. 1995. "When Bigger Is Not Better: Family Size, Parental Resources, and Children's Educational Performance." *American Sociological Review* 60(5):746–61.

Dunn, Lloyd and Leona Dunn. 1981. *PPVT-R Manual*. Circle Pines, MN: American Guidance Service.

Easterbrook, M. Ann and Wendy A. Goldberg. 1983. "Effects of Early Maternal Employment on Toddlers, Mothers, and Fathers." *Developmental Psychology* 21:774–83.

Farel, A. M. 1980. "Effects of Preferred Maternal Roles, Maternal Employment, and Socioeconomic Status on School Adjustment and Competence." *Child Development* 51:1179–86.

Featherman, David L. and Robert M. Hauser. 1976. "Changes in the Socioeconomic Stratification of the Races, 1962–1973." *American Journal of Sociology* 82: 621–51.

Ferree, Myra Marx. 1991. "The Gender Division of Labor in Two-Earner Marriages: Dimensions of Variability and Change." *Journal of Family Issues* 12(2):158–80.

Geschwender, Laura and Toby L. Parcel. 1995. "Objective and Subjective Parental Working Conditions' Effects on Child Outcomes: A Comparative Test." *Research in the Sociology of Work* 5:259–84.

Harris, Kathleen Mullan. 1993. "Work and Welfare among Single Mothers in Poverty." *American Journal of Sociology* 99(2):317–52.

Haskins, R. 1983. "Public School Aggression among Children with Varying Day-Care Experience." *Child Development* 56:689–703.

Hochschild, Arlie. 1989. *The Second Shift*. New York: Viking.

Hoffman, Lois W. 1989. "Effects of Maternal Employment in the Two-Parent Family." *American Psychologist* 44:283–92.

Horan, Patrick M. 1978. "Is Status Attainment Atheoretical?" *American Sociological Review* 43:534–41.

Ishida, Hiroshi, Walter Muller, and John M. Ridge. 1995. "Class Origin, Class Destination, and Education: A Cross-National Study of Ten Industrial Nations." *American Journal of Sociology* 101:145–93.

Kerckhoff, Alan C., Richard T. Campbell, and Jerry M. Trott. 1982. "Dimensions of Educational and Occupational Attainment in Great Britain." *American Sociological Review* 47:347–64.

Lee, Valerie E., Jeanne Brooks-Gunn, and Elizabeth Schnur. 1988. "Does Head-Start Work? A 1-Year Follow-Up of Disadvantaged Children Attending Head Start, No Preschool, and Other Preschool Programs." *Developmental Psychology* 24:210–22.

Menaghan, Elizabeth G. and Toby L. Parcel. 1991. "Determining Children's Home Environments: The Impact of Maternal Characteristics and Current Occupational and Family Conditions." *Journal of Marriage and the Family* 53:417–31.

———. 1995. "Social Sources of Change in Children's Home Environments: The Effects of Parental Occupational Experiences and Family Conditions." *Journal of Marriage and the Family* 57:1–16.

Parcel, Toby L. and Elizabeth G. Menaghan. 1990. "Maternal Working Conditions and Child Verbal Ability: Studying the Transition of Intergenerational Inequality from Mothers to Young Children." *Social Psychology Quarterly* 53:132–47.

———. 1993. "Family Social Capital and Children's Behavior Problems." *Social Psychology Quarterly* 56:120–35.

———. 1994a. "Early Parental Work, Family Social Capital, and Early Childhood Outcomes." *American Journal of Sociology* 99(4):972–1009.

———. 1994b. *Parents' Jobs and Children's Lives.* Hawthorne, NY: Aldine de Gruyter.

———. 1997. "Effects of Low-Wage Employment on Family Well Being." Pp. 116–21 in *The Future of Children: From Welfare to Work,* vol. 7, no.1, edited by Richard E. Behrman. Los Altos, CA: Center for the Future of Children (David and Lucille Packard Foundation).

Schachter, F. F. 1981. "Toddlers with Employed Mothers." *Child Development* 52:958–64.

U.S. Bureau of Labor Statistics. 1996. *Employment Characteristics of Families Summary.* Washington, DC: Author.

Wharton, Carol S. 1994. "Finding Time for The 'Second Shift': The Impact of Flexible work Schedules on Women's Double Days." *Gender and Society* 8(2):189–205.

# Can All Children Learn to Read at Grade-Level by the End of Third Grade? 11

George Farkas, Jim Fischer,
Ralph Dosher, and Keven Vicknair

## INTRODUCTION: THE IMPORTANCE OF EARLY READING

In this chapter we seek to determine the feasibility of attaining the following goal: bringing *all* public school students up to reading at grade level by the end of third grade. We are concerned with the nation in general, and the Dallas Public Schools (DPS) in particular. Our focus is primarily on those groups of students whose disadvantaged status has led to schooling difficulties, which has put their own and the nation's future at greatest risk: central-city children from low-income households, largely black and Hispanic. It has long been recognized that for these children the cycle of disadvantage and failure begins quite early (Natriello, McDill, and Pallas 1990; Zigler and Styfco 1993). Relatedly, preschool and kindergarten are important settings for intervention if these children are to have an opportunity at school success. When many of these children begin first grade less than reading-ready, as is currently the case, they are unlikely to be able to meet the required curricular demand of reading by the end of the first semester. As a result, they are seriously behind in their schoolwork, and are beginning the cycle of failure in which their skills are below the level demanded by the curriculum, and their self-esteem, willingness to try, and time-on-task are inadequate to succeed at the assigned tasks. Thus, as noted by Madden et al.:

> Learning deficits must be prevented in a comprehensive approach emphasizing early education, improvement in instruction and curriculum, and intensive intervention at the earliest possible stage when deficiencies first begin to appear. . . . Once students have fallen seriously behind, they are unlikely to ever catch up to their age-mates because the experience of failure introduces problems of poor motivation, self-esteem, and behavior that undermine the effectiveness of even the best remedial or special-education approaches. (1993:125)

By second grade, the situation of these children worsens dramatically. The second-grade curriculum assumes that students can read acceptably, and the reading level expected increases substantially during this year. The teacher has little choice in moving the class on to higher reading levels; many other and related skills must be worked on—spelling, capitalization, punctuation, composing and writing essays and stories, and (sometimes) cursive writing. In addition, the students must be moving forward in their mathematics, social studies, science, music, art, and other subject matter instruction. All of these skills require substantial time on task, and many are themselves dependent upon the student's ability to read and write.

The third-grade curriculum is the last to include large amounts of basic skills instruction. By now, the assigned reading is quite demanding in terms of sophisticated vocabulary and reading comprehension. Reading is not to be done simply line by line. Instead, students are expected to keep the main theme of the piece in mind while observing the development of individual subthemes. Reading must be fluent, as must the student's ability to compose and write essays and stories. Cursive writing must also be mastered. As noted by Madden et al., "Disadvantaged third graders who have failed a grade or who are reading significantly below grade level are very unlikely to graduate from high school . . . and will experience difficulties throughout their school careers" (1993:125).

By fourth grade, the curriculum and teacher focus is no longer on basic skills, such as learning to read. Instead, students are now expected to be "reading to learn." The focus is on detailed subject matter in science, social studies, and so on. Language arts and mathematics assume the more basic skills and advance rapidly through more sophisticated material. Yet, by fourth grade the majority of central-city school children from low-income households have basic skills significantly below the grade level expected by the curriculum. At this point, where basic skills instruction is being reduced, they become essentially "lost to the system."

The mismatch between student reading level and that expected by the grade-level curriculum worsens over time. Most central-city children from low-income households spend the majority of their schooling years reading so far below grade level that they cannot read the assigned textbook. But teachers have no choice: they must attempt to "teach" this textbook anyway.

Research has shown that the most important predictor of dropping out of school is that of the student reading far below grade level. Further, the most important predictor of reading level at the end of each grade is the reading level at which the student began the grade. Thus, reading achievement, the foundation of schooling success, is a cumulative process, in which success in the early grades is crucial. The overwhelming importance of cognitive readiness at the kindergarten or first-grade level for later cognitive performance suggests that interventions occurring on or before school entry, with follow-ups in the early elementary years, are the most effective means of improving children's school achievement and preventing later academic problems (Slavin 1989; Madden et al. 1993; Slavin et al., 1994; Wasik and Slavin 1993; Reynolds 1992).

## THE CURRENT SITUATION

To assess the magnitude of the task of bringing all children up to grade level by the end of third grade, it is useful to understand the reading levels at which students currently end each of grades one, two, and three. We attempted to estimate these levels for the Dallas Public Schools (DPS) by using reading comprehension scores for district-administered Iowa Test of Basic Skills (ITBS) tests given during the spring of 1995, combined with Woodcock-Johnson test scores administered during this time period to students tutored by the Reading One-One program, but not administered the ITBS by the district.

Table 1 begins this analysis by showing the distribution of ITBS reading comprehension test scores for *tested students.* The categories represent ten-percentile groupings of the national distribution of ITBS scores. (Thus, for example, among first-graders, the lowest tenth of scores within the national percentile are those below a grade-equivalent of 1.2, interpreted as "mastering the material taught in the second month of first grade.") We see that among the 8,122 tested first-graders, 52 percent ended the year below the national average grade level score of 1.8 grade-equivalents. Among the 7,759 tested second-graders, 54 percent ended the year below the average grade-level score of 2.8. Among the 7,812 tested third-graders, 66 percent ended the year below the national average grade-level score of 3.8.

However, because of state regulations, these tested students are many fewer than those actually enrolled in these grades. That is, there are untested students in the school system and they are typically the ones most likely to read below grade level. Not surprisingly, the majority of untested students are Hispanic.[1] Accordingly, it is important that they be included in any attempt to bring all children up to grade level. As such, we estimated scores for these untested students and are attempted to determine the extent to which there was reading readiness for the first three grades.

When all DPS students are counted, we get the following estimated results. Among 13,391 first-graders, 64 percent end the year reading below grade level. Among 12,081 second-graders, 70 percent end the year reading below grade level. Among 12,172 third-graders, 78 percent end the year reading below grade level.

The third-graders are of particular interest. The number below grade level, and the amount each must improve to attain grade level, "sizes the problem" of bringing all children up to grade level by the close of third grade. Figure 1 shows the cumulative percentage below grade level, for the United States as a whole and for the DPS. We see that a relatively higher proportion of DPS students are below grade level.

*Table 1.* Dallas Public School's ITBS Reading Comprehension Scores, April 1995, Tested Students

| *National Percentile Ranges:* | | | *1–10* | *10–20* | *20–30* | *30–40* | *40–50* | *50–60* | *60–70* | *70–80* | *80–90* | *90–99* |
|---|---|---|---|---|---|---|---|---|---|---|---|---|
| *Grade-Equivalent Ranges:* | | | *K.1–1.19* | *1.2–1.39* | *1.4–1.59* | *1.6–1.69* | *1.7–1.79* | *1.8–1.99* | *2.0–2.19* | *2.2–2.59* | *2.6–2.89* | *2.9–4.7* |
| First Grade | Black | 5085 | 384 | 355 | 881 | 378 | 705 | 590 | 524 | 502 | 256 | 509 |
| | % | | 7.6 | 7.0 | 17.3 | 7.4 | 13.9 | 11.6 | 10.3 | 9.9 | 5.0 | 10.0 |
| | Hispanic | 1590 | 157 | 126 | 281 | 150 | 238 | 156 | 161 | 144 | 66 | 111 |
| | % | | 9.9 | 7.9 | 17.7 | 9.4 | 15.0 | 9.8 | 10.1 | 9.0 | 4.2 | 7.0 |
| | White | 1447 | 77 | 59 | 165 | 98 | 139 | 151 | 134 | 161 | 104 | 358 |
| | % | | 5.3 | 4.1 | 11.4 | 6.8 | 9.6 | 10.5 | 9.3 | 11.1 | 7.2 | 24.8 |
| | Total | 8122 | 618 | 540 | 1328 | 626 | 1082 | 898 | 819 | 806 | 426 | 978 |
| | % | | 7.6 | 6.6 | 16.3 | 7.7 | 13.3 | 11.1 | 10.1 | 9.9 | 5.2 | 12.0 |
| Cumulative % below Grade Level | | | 7.6 | 14.3 | 30.6 | 38.3 | 51.6 | | | | | |
| Grade-Equivalent Ranges: | | | K.4–1.69 | 1.7–1.99 | 2.0–2.19 | 2.2–2.59 | 2.6–2.79 | 2.8–3.09 | 3.1–3.39 | 3.4–3.79 | 3.8–4.59 | 4.6–7.0 |
| Second Grade | Black | 4798 | 598 | 723 | 440 | 689 | 444 | 712 | 451 | 189 | 343 | 211 |
| | % | | 12.5 | 15.1 | 9.2 | 14.4 | 9.3 | 14.8 | 9.4 | 3.9 | 7.1 | 4.4 |
| | Hispanic | 1579 | 168 | 220 | 145 | 204 | 155 | 255 | 158 | 69 | 116 | 88 |
| | % | | 10.7 | 14.0 | 9.2 | 12.9 | 9.8 | 16.2 | 10.0 | 4.4 | 7.3 | 5.6 |
| | White | 1382 | 60 | 87 | 85 | 107 | 85 | 166 | 145 | 81 | 222 | 343 |
| | % | | 4.4 | 6.3 | 6.2 | 7.8 | 6.1 | 12.0 | 10.5 | 5.9 | 16.1 | 24.8 |
| | Total | 7759 | 827 | 1030 | 670 | 1000 | 684 | 1133 | 753 | 339 | 681 | 642 |
| | % | | | 10.7 | 13.3 | 8.6 | 12.9 | 8.8 | 14.6 | 9.7 | 4.4 | 8.8 |
| Cumulative % below Grade Level | | | | 10.7 | 23.9 | 32.6 | 45.5 | 54.3 | | | | |
| Grade-Equivalent Ranges: | | | | 1.3–2.09 | 2.1–2.79 | 2.8–3.09 | 3.1–3.39 | 3.5–3.79 | 3.8–4.19 | 4.2–4.69 | 4.7–5.39 | 5.4– |
| 6.49 | | | 6.5–9.7 | | | | | | | | | |
| Third Grade | Black | 4605 | 643 | 856 | 798 | 477 | 523 | 259 | 266 | 238 | 227 | 318 |
| | % | | 14.0 | 18.6 | 17.3 | 10.4 | 11.4 | 5.6 | 5.8 | 5.2 | 4.9 | 6.9 |
| | Hispanic | 1943 | 212 | 327 | 326 | 230 | 270 | 129 | 128 | 116 | 110 | 95 |
| | % | | 10.9 | 16.8 | 16.8 | 11.8 | 13.9 | 6.6 | 6.6 | 6.0 | 5.7 | 4.9 |
| | White | 1264 | 69 | 106 | 126 | 99 | 134 | 80 | 96 | 128 | 148 | 278 |
| | % | | 5.4 | 8.4 | 10.0 | 7.8 | 10.6 | 6.3 | 7.6 | 10.1 | 11.7 | 22.0 |
| | Total | 7812 | 924 | 1290 | 1251 | 806 | 927 | 467 | 490 | 482 | 485 | 690 |
| | % | | | 11.8 | 16.5 | 16.0 | 10.3 | 11.9 | 6.0 | 6.3 | 6.2 | 6.3 |
| Cumulative % below Grade Level | | | | 11.8 | 28.3 | 44.3 | 54.7 | 66.5 | | | | |

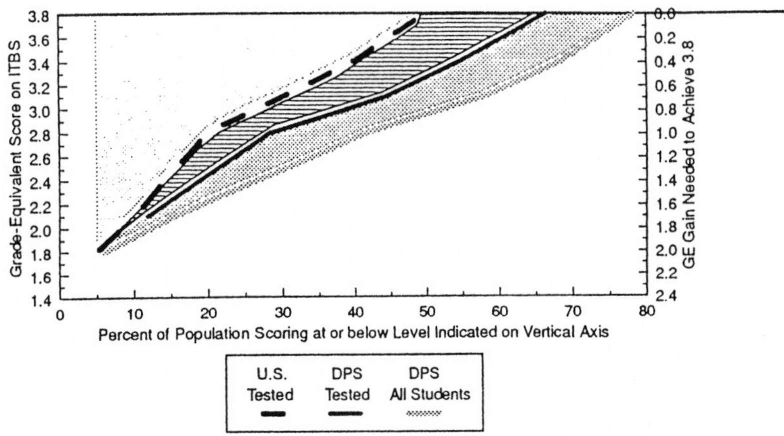


*Figure 1.* U.S. ITBS score distribution vs. DPS distribution, third grade reading comprehension.

Table 2 shows the third-grade students below grade level in detail. We see that these 78 percent of third-graders come to a total of 9,532 students, of whom 3,918 are black, 4,762 are Hispanic, and 852 are white. If most of these were only slightly below grade level, the problem would not be too great. Unfortunately, this is not the case. Instead, approximately, 5,000 of these students scored below 2.8 grade-equivalents, or more than one full school-year below grade level.

When data were examined in more detail, showing how much average improvement each group must achieve to reach grade level (grade-equivalent = 3.8), we found that approximately 10 percent of all third-grade students needed more than 1.7 additional grade-equivalents to reach grade level. Put another way, about 90 percent of DPS students can attain or exceed grade-level reading capability by the end of third grade if their cumulative achievement rises by an additional 1.7 grade-equivalents. As discussed in the following sections, we believe that this level of performance improvement is quite attainable by these students over the three- or four-year period between either first grade or kindergarten and the close of third grade.

But what about the bottom 10 percent? Can we realistically expect to bring all of these children up to grade level by the close of third grade? This raises the issue of Special Education, and the students who have been assigned there.

*Table 2.* Distribution of DPS Third-Grade Students below Grade Level (GE ≤ 3.70)

| | *Total* | | | *Black* | | | *Hispanic* | | | *White* | | |
|---|---|---|---|---|---|---|---|---|---|---|---|---|
| | *Number of Students* | *Percentage of Total Population* | *Cumulative Percentage* | *Number of Students* | *Percentage of Total Population* | *Cumulative Percentage* | *Number of Students* | *Percentage of Total Population* | *Cumulative Percentage* | *Number of Students* | *Percentage of Total Population* | *Cumulative Percentage* |
| GE 1.3–1.59 | 49 | 0.4 | 0.4 | 20 | 0.4 | 0.4 | 26 | 0.5 | 0.5 | 3 | 0.2 | 0.2 |
| GE 1.6–1.79 | 532 | 4.4 | 4.8 | 215 | 4.1 | 4.5 | 286 | 5.3 | 5.8 | 31 | 2.0 | 2.1 |
| GE 1.8–1.99 | 630 | 5.2 | 9.9 | 254 | 4.9 | 9.4 | 339 | 6.3 | 12.1 | 37 | 2.3 | 4.5 |
| GE 2.0–2.19 | 1438 | 11.8 | 21.8 | 518 | 9.9 | 19.3 | 841 | 15.7 | 27.8 | 79 | 5.0 | 9.5 |
| GE 2.2–2.39 | 1002 | 8.2 | 30.0 | 321 | 6.1 | 25.4 | 628 | 11.7 | 39.5 | 53 | 3.4 | 12.8 |
| GE 2.4–2.59 | 1045 | 8.6 | 38.6 | 335 | 6.4 | 31.8 | 654 | 12.2 | 51.7 | 56 | 3.5 | 16.4 |
| GE 2.6–2.79 | 369 | 3.0 | 41.6 | 118 | 2.3 | 34.1 | 231 | 4.3 | 56.0 | 20 | 1.3 | 17.6 |
| GE 2.8–2.99 | 1694 | 13.9 | 55.5 | 812 | 15.5 | 49.6 | 710 | 13.2 | 69.2 | 172 | 10.9 | 28.5 |
| GE 3.0–3.19 | 897 | 7.4 | 62.9 | 407 | 7.8 | 57.4 | 385 | 7.2 | 76.4 | 105 | 6.6 | 35.1 |
| GE 3.2–3.39 | 669 | 5.5 | 68.4 | 296 | 5.7 | 63.1 | 291 | 5.4 | 81.8 | 82 | 5.2 | 40.3 |
| GE 3.4–3.59 | 966 | 7.9 | 76.3 | 498 | 9.5 | 72.6 | 297 | 5.5 | 87.4 | 171 | 10.8 | 51.1 |
| GE 3.6–3.79 | 241 | 2.0 | 78.3 | 124 | 2.4 | 75.0 | 74 | 1.4 | 88.8 | 43 | 2.7 | 53.9 |
| Total | 9532 | 78.3 | | 3918 | 75.0 | | 4762 | 88.8 | | 852 | 53.9 | |

## SPECIAL EDUCATION

Children are selected for special education via a referral procedure, typically initiated by a parent or a teacher. The referral leads to a discussion and action by the school's Admission Review Discussion (ARD) team. Parental approval is required for Special Education placement. If the student *is* placed, an Individual Education Plan (IEP) is prepared for him or her.

Nationally, Special Education placements have trended upward over the past twenty years. Such placements constituted 8.5 percent of U.S. public school enrollments in 1977, but this percentage increased to 11.7 percent by 1992; by comparison, the 1992 DPS enrollment in Special Education was 9.8 percent of total enrollment. Also, of the 11.7 percent in Special Education nationally, the categories of *serious learning disorders* account for 7.5 percent of U.S. K–12 public school students; for DPS students the estimated level is 6.3 percent. For purposes of this report we have assumed that 3 to 5 percent of public school students in grades 1–3 have *serious learning disorders* (learning disabilities, mental retardation, and serious emotional disturbances), requiring very special treatments, including medical procedures. Another group of approximately 5 percent of the third-grade students have a cumulative deficit of more than 1.7 grade-equivalents and may be relatively slow learners, but do not have truly serious learning disorders. These students can be expected to achieve third-grade-level reading capabilities if they are provided the necessary support activities.

## A READING IMPROVEMENT STRATEGY

As noted by Robert Slavin, Edward Zigler, and others, it is much more cost-effective to seek to *prevent* school failure before or as it occurs, than to attempt to *remediate* it after the fact. As Slavin says:

> We cannot afford to allow children to start out on a path that begins with poor achievement and leads to truancy, behavior problems, delinquency, early pregnancy, and dropout. The economic costs, not to mention the social costs, of allowing this progression to unfold for so many students are intolerable. The negative spiral that begins with poor achievement in the early grades can be reversed. We know we can guarantee virtually all children adequate basic skills in the elementary school, and if we choose to do so , there is every likelihood that we could dramatically increase the school success of large numbers of students and consequently the quality of life of our society. (1989:4)

Despite such optimism, the task before us is large and requires the effective deployment of significant resources. The overall strategy is summarized by Figure 2. Here, the continuous line represents the distribution of student reading abilities before intervention. The dotted curve represents the students after an intervention has been applied to those performing below grade level. The intention is to take the below-grade-level students and provide customized, intensive intervention to each, so that all can be brought up to grade level. The result may be thought of as requiring the attainment of two milestones. The first is to move the distribution of student scores upward (to the right) so that it is centered on the grade-level score of 3.8. The second is to move all of the students who are still below grade level (on the left side of the curve) up to grade level. When both milestones have been achieved, the reading skills distribution will resemble the dotted curve of Figure 2, with the students formerly below grade level "piled-up" above the grade level cutoff.

The intensity of services necessary to achieve this goal will vary dramatically across students. For some, a small amount of remediation may be sufficient for them to get up to speed in their classwork. For others, much more intensive assistance will be required. Naturally, as the "easier cases" are successfully remediated, only those students facing the greatest challenges will remain. Some of these challenges will prove to be medical in origin; others will be associated with severely unfortunate home situations. We believe that, in principle, these children can be brought to their full potential and most can be brought to grade level in reading by the end of third grade. However, it is important to acknowledge that within this population, incremental gains will be achieved only at an increasing cost of resource allocation. That is, beyond some level, the cost of bringing each additional child up to grade level increases dramatically.

Finally, there is the issue of the timing of intervention within each student's school career. In view of the previously presented arguments for the importance of early intervention, combined with the fact that beginning earlier permits a longer span within which interventions can do their work prior to

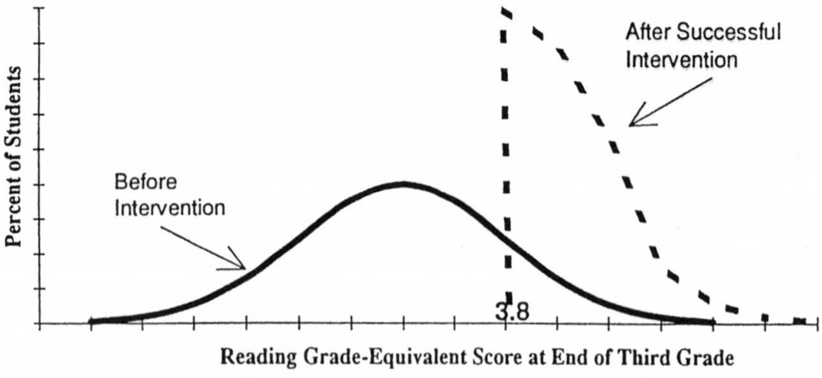


*Figure 2.* Strategy summary illustrated by reading capability distributions.

the end of third grade, we believe it best to begin intervening as early as preschool if possible, but certainly no later than the beginning of first grade. This and related issues will be discussed below, where we examine specific intervention strategies in more detail.

## MANAGEMENT IMPROVEMENT AND PROGRAM INTERVENTION POSSIBILITIES

Four elements are central to effective instruction for at-risk students: *quality of instruction, appropriate level of instruction, incentive, and time* (Slavin 1989:45). We discuss a variety of management improvements and program interventions which work directly on these critical elements.

### *Improved Teacher Effectiveness*

There are many outstanding public schools in the United States and many, many excellent teachers—even within low-performing schools. Unfortunately, there are also many ineffective teachers. Improving the effectiveness of low-performing teachers will be one of the highest leveraged activities in an overall program for helping *all* children read at grade level by the end of third grade. In the elementary grades, students spend five to six hours per day under the guidance of their classroom teacher. In terms of time available to influence the learning process, the teacher's opportunities are second only to the influence of the child's home life.

Individual student reading gains per school year, as measured by the spring standardized test scores, vary widely within large school districts. For the school year 1992–1993, individual second-grade classroom grade-equivalent gains—at the median—for over 500 DPS classrooms ranged from zero to over two full grade-equivalents. Some of this variation in reading gains resulted from differences in student ability and home life. However, within the same school with students from similar backgrounds, there are wide differences in the reading gains achieved in the various classrooms. For example, the students enrolled in the Julia C. Frazier School (K–3) in southeast Dallas are almost all black children from very low-income families. In the spring of 1994, the delta grade-equivalent (GE) gains in reading—at the medians—across the thirteen first-, second-, and third-grade classrooms varied from GEs of 0.1 to 1.5, a range of 1.4 grade-equivalents. In the spring of 1995, under the strong leadership of the Frazier principal, the average reading gain for the school increased by 0.4 GEs to 1.3 GEs, 30 percent above the average GE gains across the United States! Importantly, almost all of the classrooms improved their delta reading gains when compared with the previous school year. Not all, but the majority of the classes had their largest improvements with students who ranked in the lower half of the class in reading scores the previous year. Still, for the 1994–1995 school year GE gains across all thirteen classrooms varied from 0.8 to 2.2 GEs—a range of 1.4 grade-equivalents, the same as the previous year. Further, since these results occurred with a homogeneous student body, they show the large opportunity for gains in student reading capabilities through improvements in teacher effectiveness.

## QUALITY REMEDIAL READING INTERVENTION PROGRAMS

In recent years, a number of high-quality intervention programs have been developed to prevent and/or immediately remediate reading failure among early-elementary children. The most extensively researched of these are Reading Recovery (Ohio State University) and Success for All (Johns Hopkins). Both use highly structured one-to-one instruction (tutoring) provided on a daily basis by trained tutors. In a review of these and related programs, Wasik and Slavin suggest that one-to-one preventive (that is, early-elementary) tutoring "deserves an important place in discussions of reform in compensatory, remedial, and special education" (1993:198). This is because one-to-one tutoring combines all three of the remaining factors implicated in successful instruction: appropriate level of instruction, the student's incentive to work, and time on task. Only when a tutor provides one-to-one instruction can the level of instruction be customized to the student's current performance. Only within this format does the student receive the customized eye contact, warmth, and positive encouragement and feedback capable of providing the work incentive and concentrated time-on-task necessary to overcome the fear of failure and low self-esteem that is typical of students who are performing below grade level, even as early as first grade.

The issue is, What magnitude of effect can be delivered to first-, second-, and third-graders by such high-quality intervention programs? Fortunately, both Reading Recovery and Success for All have been extensively studied in a recent time-frame by reputable researchers. We shall rely on these studies (Madden et al. 1993; Slavin et al. 1994; Pinnell et al. 1994) to estimate the size of the gains that are achievable. In addition, we will report the effects achieved by a third program, Reading One-One, developed at the University of Texas at Dallas and currently operating within the DPS as well as school districts in Brownsville and San Antonio (Farkas and Vicknair 1995). Modeled on both Success for All and Reading Recovery, this program uses trained and managed paraprofessionals to directly address the chief drawback of the other programs—their cost. For as noted by Wasik and Slavin, "The major drawback to tutoring is its cost" (1993:179). As we shall see, Reading One-

*Table 3.* School-Year Gains Achievable via Quality One-One Tutoring (Grade-Equivalents[a])

| | *Average Gain* | *Average Gain From 60 sessions* | *100 sessions* |
|---|---|---|---|
| First Grade | | | |
| Success-for-All (Madden et al. 1993) | 0.2 | | |
| Success-for-All (Slavin et al. 1994) | 0.3 | | |
| Reading Recovery (Pinnell et al. 1994) | 0.3[b] | | |
| Reading One-One (Farkas and Vicknair 1995) | | 0.4 | 0.7 |
| Second Grade | | | |
| Success-for-All (Madden et al. 1993) | 0.5 | | |
| Success-for-All (Slavin et al. 1994) | 0.3 | | |
| Reading One-One (Farkas and Vicknair, 1995) | | 0.5 | 0.8 |
| Third Grade | | | |
| Success-for-All (Madden et al. 1993) | 0.5 | | |
| Success-for-All (Slavin et al. 1994) | 0.7 | | |
| Reading One-One (Farkas and Vicknair, 1995) | | 0.4 | 0.7 |

[a] Estimated from the Woodcock-Johnson Reading Inventory.
[b] Translated from the reported standardized effect estimates into grade-equivalents by relying on the correspondence between these reported in Slavin et al. (1994).

One delivers effects of a similar magnitude to those of Reading Recovery and Success for All, but at greatly reduced unit cost.

Table 3 summarizes the effects achieved by each of the three programs for each of grades 1, 2, and 3. These are reported as grade-equivalent gains in reading, measured by the Woodcock-Johnson Reading Inventory (although all studies use more than one measure, this is the only one they have in common).

For first grade, Success for All reports reading gains of 0.2 grade-equivalents in one study and 0.3 grade-equivalents in another. Success for All researchers (Slavin et al. 1994) discuss the tendency they observe for program effects, measured in grade-equivalents, to be larger at higher grade levels. They attribute this to the increased variance of this measure at higher grade levels. It is a tenet of Reading Recovery that the program only operates in first grade. The effect reported is 0.3 grade-equivalents (Pinnell et al. 1994).[2]

The Reading One-One researchers (Farkas and Vicknair 1995) used variation in the number of tutoring sessions received by different students to estimate the gains for each additional session. Among students participating in the program full-time, the average student received approximately sixty tutoring sessions. With this number of sessions, the average first-grader gained 0.4 grade-equivalents. Extrapolating to students who received the largest number of sessions—approximately 100—we get a potential gain of 0.7 grade-equivalents for them.

When these analyses are repeated for second-graders, we find gains of 0.5 and 0.3 grade-equivalents from Success for All; 0.5 and 0.8 grade-equivalents for, respectively, 60 and 100 Reading One-One sessions. For third-graders the estimates are 0.5 and 0.7 grade-equivalents for Success for All; 0.4 and 0.7 grade-equivalents for, respectively, 60 and 100 Reading One-One sessions.

Since versions of all three of these programs are currently up and running within the DPS, the means are at hand to use any or all of them within the sort of demonstration discussed later in this chapter.

Importantly, we now have sufficient operational experience with programs such as Reading Recovery, Success for All, and Reading One-One that we can be reasonably confident that they can be successfully implemented, and that high quality one-to-one tutoring can deliver the magnitudes of positive gains in reading reported in Table 3.

It is widely appreciated that in addition to improved teacher quality and quality direct instruction, student performance can be helped by both preschool preparation and programs that work with the student's family to increase their participation with her or his classwork. As one indication of the magnitude of gains achievable from these sources, Table 4 (Reynolds 1992:157) reports grade three reading achievement differences (in grade-equivalents) among students who (a) received no preschool, (b) received preschool alone, and (c) received preschool and some combination of positive factors, such as parent participation in schooling, cognitive readiness, and the teacher's rating of the student.

*Table 4.* End of Third-Grade Reading Scores (Grade-Equivalents) Achievable via Preschool, Family, and Related Interventions (Reynolds 1992)

| *Child Characteristic* | *Reading Achievement* |
|---|---|
| A. No preschool | 3.45 |
| B. Preschool | 3.70 |
| Mediating conditions | |
| C. Preschool and cognitively ready for school | 4.03 |
| D. Preschool, cognitively ready for school, and rated high by teacher | 4.24 |
| E. Preschool and rated high by teacher | 4.04 |
| F. Preschool, parent involved in school, and child does not change | 4.04 |
| G. Preschool, rated high by teacher, and continuously promoted | 4.08 |
| H. All five mediating conditions present | 4.38 |
| Difference between (A) and (H) | 0.93 |
| Change per year achieved over 4 years | 0.23 |

This study was conducted with 266 low-income, mostly black children and 125 comparison group children who were matched on neighborhood characteristics and were traced from kindergarten through the third year of school (1986–1989). Comparing the base group (no preschool) to the group that received all five positive "treatments" (preschool plus the other four conditions), we see that the "fully treated" group performed 0.93 grade-equivalents higher than the base group. If we think of this gain as being delivered bit-by-bit over four years, then it can be quantified as 0.23 grade-equivalents per year.

## THE TEXAS INSTRUMENTS FOUNDATION AND HEAD START OF GREATER DALLAS MARGARET H. CONE PRESCHOOL INITIATIVE

In March, 1990, the Texas Instruments Foundation with the cooperative efforts of Head Start of Greater Dallas, Inc., initiated a "model" preschool program with the opening of the Margaret H. Cone Head Start Center, located near the central business district in one of the poorest areas of Dallas. A majority of the neighborhood residents live in apartments that are owned and operated by the Dallas Housing Authority. Important parameters include:

- 90% of the families are black,
- 9% are Hispanic,
- 85% of the families earn less than $5,000 per year,
- 93% of the households are headed by a single parent,
- 94% of the families are on food stamps.

The Cone preschool program includes the following components:

- education,
- health/nutrition,
- social services/parental involvement,
- evaluation.

The center operates a full-day program year-round. During the first two years, a number of program goals were achieved in the health and social services areas, but little progress was made in the cognitive development domain, and children continued to leave the Cone Center to enter kindergarten functioning, on average, at a developmental level six months behind their chronological age. During the 1992–1993 school year, a special phonics program was developed by Southern Methodist University (SMU) and included in the Cone curriculum in April 1993 for Cohort 3. This SMU intervention program was

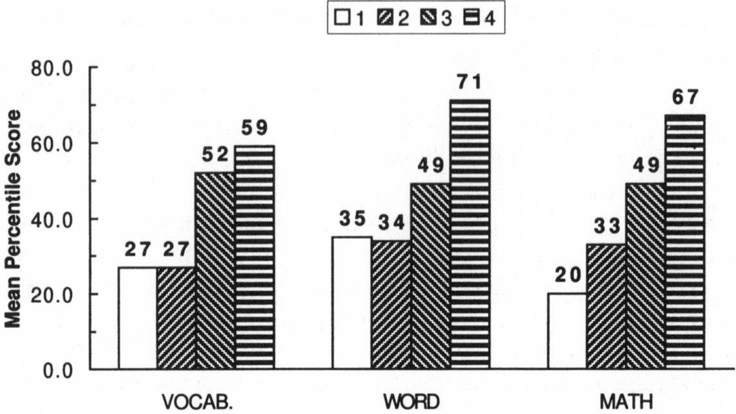


*Figure 3.* Kindergarten ITBS percentile scores.

continued and expanded during the following year for Cohort 4. The kindergarten ITBS scores for the first four Cone Center Cohorts (by year of Cone participation) are shown in Figure 3. Step-function improvements in scores were achieved by Cohorts 3 and 4 when compared to Cohorts 1 and 2. In this same time period, kindergarten score improvements were also being made by non-Cone students, but Figure 4 shows that Cone Cohort 4, in the spring of 1995, scored higher than non-Cone students in all three of the kindergarten ITBS subtests (kindergarten students do not take a "reading" test). In fact, on the word analysis test, the difference between the 71st percentile score for Cone

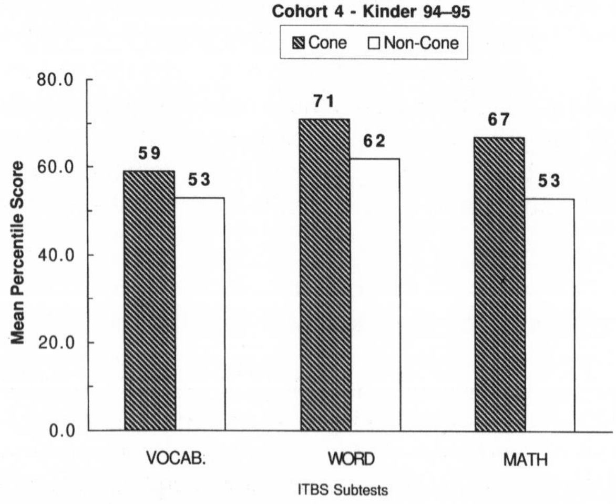


*Figure 4.* Kindergarten ITBS percentile scores.

Cohort 4 and the 62nd percentile score for the non-Cone students equates to grade-equivalents of approximately 1.27 and 1.06, suggesting that Cone students, on average, had higher scores by slightly over 0.2 grade-equivalents. This result is reasonably close to the 0.23 grade-equivalent per year potential gain indicated in the Reynolds 1992 study (Table 4) as available from *quality* preschool, family, and related interventions.

## PUTTING IT ALL TOGETHER

Table 5 shows the number of DPS third-graders currently at each reading level, with the gains each must achieve to attain grade level. We have added the average gain per year necessary to achieve grade level when this effort is spread over, respectively, two-, three-, or four-year periods. As we can see, if at least a three-year period is available, than an average of no more than 0.6 grade-equivalent gain per year will be sufficient to raise the great majority of children to grade level. An average of 0.7 grade-equivalent gain per year, for three years, would bring approximately 95 percent of the third-grade students to grade level. These average incremental gains per year are well within the reach of a strategy combining the sorts of management improvements and program interventions described above. For example, if the educational

*Table 5.* Third Grade: Gains in Reading Grade-Equivalent Scores Required to Achieve Grade Level of 3.8, Plus Gains per Year Required

| *Grade-Equivalent Range* | *Group Size* | *Average Grade-Equivalent* | *Average below GE of 3.8* | *Gain per Year Required to Achieve Grade Level*[a] | | |
|---|---|---|---|---|---|---|
| | | | | *2 yr* | *3 yr* | *4 yr* |
| GE 1.3–1.59 | 49 | 1.5 | 2.3 | 1.15 | 0.77 | **0.58** |
| GE 1.6–1.79 | 532 | 1.7 | 2.1 | 1.05 | 0.70 | **0.53** |
| GE 1.8–1.99 | 630 | 1.9 | 1.9 | 0.95 | 0.63 | **0.48** |
| GE 2.0–2.19 | 1,440 | 2.1 | 1.7 | 0.85 | **0.57** | **0.43** |
| GE 2.2–2.39 | 1,003 | 2.3 | 1.5 | 0.75 | **0.50** | **0.38** |
| GE 2.4–2.59 | 1,044 | 2.5 | 1.3 | 0.65 | **0.43** | **0.33** |
| GE 2.6–2.79 | 368 | 2.7 | 1.1 | **0.55** | **0.37** | **0.28** |
| GE 2.8–2.99 | 1,695 | 2.9 | 0.9 | **0.45** | **0.30** | **0.22** |
| GE 3.0–3.19 | 896 | 3.1 | 0.7 | **0.35** | **0.23** | **0.18** |
| GE 3.2–3.39 | 669 | 3.3 | 0.5 | **0.25** | **0.17** | **0.13** |
| GE 3.4–3.59 | 966 | 3.5 | 0.3 | **0.15** | **0.10** | **0.07** |
| GE 3.6–3.79 | 241 | 3.7 | 0.1 | **0.05** | **0.03** | **0.02** |
| GE 3.8 or greater | 2,640 | | | | | |
| Total students | 12,172 | | | | | |

[a] Boldface indicates cases for which the average annual gain needed is less than 0.6.

*Table 6.* Estimated Incremental Gains in Reading Grade-Equivalent Scores for Various Strategies

| *Activity/Program* | *Estimated K–3 Potential Δ GE Gain per Year* |
|---|---|
| Quality Preschool, Family and Related Interventions | 0.2–0.3 |
| Improved Teacher Effectiveness | 0.3–0.4 |
| Quality Reading Remediation Intervention Program (60 sessions) | 0.3–0.5 |
| Total | 0.8–1.2 |

experience of a low-performing third-grade student had included some or all of these activities, the incremental gains shown in Table 6 might have been attained per year.

Of course, the total gain for all three activities/programs taken together might be less than the sum of the gains when each is considered in isolation. Nevertheless, these impact levels suggest that a combination of these and/or other improvement activities could produce incremental gains of at least the required 0.6 to 0.7 GEs per year for most students.

## AN EXPERIMENT

In this section we briefly outline an experiment that could be conducted in any school district to determine the feasibility of the approach presented above. In so doing, we are guided by Slavin, who suggests the following:

> Adequate provisions for training, follow-up, and monitoring of project implementations are imperative. . . . Program implementations should start on a small scale, beginning with volunteers and only gradually expanding from a solid base of success. Second, districts should conduct their own evaluations of new programs, using random assignment or careful matching to compare program users and nonusers. (1989:47)

The experiment should be presented to principals and teachers as an opportunity. A group of three or more elementary schools should be chosen, so that the demographic and socioeconomic makeup of their total kindergarten–third-grade enrollment resembles that of the district as a whole.

The experiment must involve a multiyear commitment, so that current preschool and kindergartners can be observed through the end of third grade. However, interventions should also be introduced for current first-, second-, and third-graders, so that preliminary results and "learning by doing" are available within a shorter time frame.

Management improvements and program interventions must be decided in a timely fashion so that teacher buy-in can be achieved prior to the beginning of the first experimental year. An adequate research design, with supporting data collection, is essential if useful lessons are to be learned. The standard design requires before/after measurements on an experimental and control group. All studied students must be given appropriate test instruments (e.g., the Woodcock-Johnson reading inventory) both at the beginning and end of each school year. Study sample sizes must be large enough so that any program effects whose magnitudes are substantively significant can be measured with adequate precision.

Most important, an appropriate comparison group must be selected. Here, the most statistically powerful and widely accepted methodology involves random assignment to experimental and control groups. Second best is the selection of a matched comparison group, perhaps from "comparison schools." However, if the latter methodology is used, it is essential that sufficient and appropriate control variables be available to adequately adjust for possible differences between the experimental and comparison groups.

As for the specific management improvements and program interventions to be deployed, they should be chosen from the already existing inventory of successful practices and programs. However, whatever these may be, it is important that individualized attention be given each child. That is, after an initial measurement of their reading level at the beginning of the school year, they should be assigned to treatment and then tested at regular intervals (six-week periods may be appropriate) so that their progress can be measured. All cases should then be reviewed each period, and those whose progress is inadequate should be reassigned to more intensive treatment. This personalized approach will use resources most effectively while endeavoring to bring all children up to grade level in reading by the close of third grade.

## ESTIMATED PROGRAM COSTS AND POTENTIAL FUNDING SOURCES

While a proposed strategy has been defined, no doubt there are other approaches to achieve the desired goals. Any school district undertaking this type of reading improvement program should design the program elements to fit its particular situation and the principals and teachers involved should play key roles in the program planning. Obviously, the cost of any individual program will depend upon size and specific activities. However, for purposes of illustration, Table 7 shows estimated *incremental* cost ranges for an assumed "Three-School Experimental Program," with five grades per school (PK–3), and one hundred students per grade. Also, we have assumed that in addition to starting "official" cohorts at the preschool or kindergarten level, the experimental program would start the improvement process in all grades

*Table 7.* Experimental Reading Improvement Program Possibilities, Estimated *Incremental* Costs ($000s)

| | *Annual Operating Costs* | |
|---|---|---|
| *Program Element* | *Unit Costs* | *"Three-School Experimental Program" Costs*[a] |
| "Model" preschool similar to the TI Foundation–Head Start Cone Center (100 students per school) | $250–$300 per school | $750–$900 |
| Computer-based program similar to IBM's Writing-to-Read for Kindergarten and First Grade | $30–$50 per school ($20 per school one time capital cost) | $90–$150 ($60 one time capital cost) |
| Quality one to one remedial reading intervention in grades 1–3 (60 sessions per student) | | |
| UTD Reading One-One ($500 per student) | $75 per school[b] | $225 |
| Reading Recovery, Success-for-All ($2,000 per student) | $300 per school[b] | $900 |
| Teacher effectiveness improvements | Costs covered in District budgets | Costs covered in District budgets |
| Family K–3 support | | $100–$200 |
| Special treatments for students with serious learning disorders (approximately 5% of total population) | | $100–$250 |
| Program evaluation and administration | | $300–$500[c] |
| Total Annual Program Cost $1,565–$2,900[c] ($60 one-time capital cost) | | |

[a]Assumes three schools, five grades per school (PK–3), and 100 students per grade.
[b]Assumes an average of 50% of all students in grades one, two, and three (tutoring approximately 150 students per school.)
[c]Assumes no incremental costs for office space and equipment.

at the same time. In this way each grade would have the opportunity to experience the improvement process before the "official" cohort arrived. Under such a parallel process, approximately 1,500 students, in total, would be involved in some way in the program each year. Other schools and students might become part of the comparison group.

Table 7 is a very rough estimate of program cost ranges. These costs could be reduced with a smaller program size and/or fewer elements. Also, costs could be reduced further in some of the program elements already in place. For example, a DPS experimental program might include the Cone Center "model" preschool and Frazier's Writing-to-Read computer lab, reducing *incremental* annual operating costs by approximately $300,000 per year. Thus, a DPS "Three-School Experimental Program" might have incremental operating costs in the range of approximately $1,300,000 to $2,600,000 per year. As implementations expand after successful demonstrations in the experimental program, actual incremental costs should be reduced due to larger populations and cost improvements. As part of this experiment, the longer range goal of expanding the program should be considered.

Institutionalizing the program into all elementary schools might not be undertaken in the same fashion as the experimental program implementation. For example, the cognitive portion of the preschool program is very effective and yet requires only a small portion of the preschool costs. Also, gains might be achieved by offering additional tutoring sessions to at least some students. There is likely a cost trade-off between additional tutoring in first, second, and third grades and the preschool and kindergarten programs. A cost-benefit analysis would reveal where resources would be most effectively deployed.

However large these costs may appear, many studies (in particular, Slavin and others) have shown that achievement of the program goals will provide not only improved quality of life for the individual children and society at large but also long-run monetary gains (reduced prison costs, reduced welfare costs, increased taxes from higher-earning citizens, etc.) far in excess of the investments required.

## SUMMARY AND DISCUSSION

We have seen that when children whom Texas state regulations exempt from standardized testing are included back in the figures, approximately 78 percent of DPS third-graders finish the year below grade level in reading capability. We have also seen that a variety of already-existing management improvements and program interventions appear to be capable of delivering the average gains per year that, if instituted at the beginning of kindergarten or first grade, would bring the great majority of these students up to grade level by the end of third grade.

Four groups of students have been identified. The first of these, estimated to constitute 22 percent of DPS third-grade students, are already achieving grade level in reading. These require no further assistance. The second group, constituting approximately 68 percent of the total, require management and program interventions above those currently in place if they are to achieve grade level. However, they can be expected to respond quite well to these programs and policies, and to achieve grade level without the need for heroic efforts. The students in the third group, perhaps 5 percent of the total, are able to learn to read at grade level, but will do so only with some difficulty. These children will require special attention if they are to achieve grade-level reading. Such attention should be individualized, and might be expected to include psychological and medical attention, close monitoring of progress, and one-to-one tutoring with specially trained tutors over an extended period, perhaps including the summers. The children in the final group, approximately 5 percent of the total, are those most seriously at risk of school failure. They typically have very serious learning and emotional disabilities, or some form of mental retardation. Many of these students can learn, but raising them to grade level in reading by the end of third grade will require, in many cases, truly heroic efforts, including medical treatment for some, and even with such efforts this goal may still not be completely attainable. However, these students should be included in intervention planning, with the goal being to assist them to achieve their full reading-level potential.

As with any difficult, long-range goal, that of bringing *all* public school children up to grade level in reading by the end of third grade is best addressed as a series of shorter milestones to be achieved. For example, program milestones could include:

| *Milestone* | *Comments* |
|---|---|
| Bring all *tested* third-graders to the point where their end-of-year *median* reading score equals, or exceeds, a grade-equivalent of 3.8 | This milestone will probably be reached by the Dallas Public Schools within the next two or three years. |
| Bring the distribution of *all* third-grade students, including those currently *untested* by Texas law, to an estimated *median* reading grade-equivalent level of 3.8 | At this point, a minimum of 50 percent of all third-grade students would read at grade-level. |
| Bring *all* students in Group B (those who respond well to appropriate interventions) up to a reading level of 3.8 by the end of third grade. | When this goal is achieved, approximately 90 percent of third graders will end the year at grade-level. |
| Bring *all* students in Group C (those who can learn, but do so with difficulty) up to grade-level and bring *all* Group D students (those with serious learning disorders) up to their full potential by the end of third grade. | With this achievement, we would expect that, in any school district, over 95 percent of all third grade students in the program would read at grade-level by the end of the year. |

The last milestone represents the ultimate program goal and would require a number of years to achieve. We do believe, based on our research, that we can give an affirmative answer to the question, Can all children learn to read at grade level by the end of third grade?

Yes, *all* children who have the capability to learn can learn to read at grade level by the end of third grade. We also believe that children with serious learning disorders (perhaps 3 to 5 percent of the student population) can be helped to their full potential, greatly enriching the quality of their lives.

## APPENDIX: METHODOLOGY FOR CONSTRUCTING TABLE 2

The original data we obtained from the DPS were divided into ten broad grade-equivalent ranges as shown in Table 1 and column 1 of Table A1. In order to break down the distribution into finer categories it was necessary to estimate the internal distribution within each broad grade-equivalent range.

*Table A1.* Estimated Distribution of DPS Third-Grade Students Who Tested below Grade Level

| *Grade-Equivalent Range (from Table 1)* | *Detail Grade-Equivalent Ranges* | *Breakdown of Each Range (%)* | *Black* | *Hispanic* | *White* | *Total* |
|---|---|---|---|---|---|---|
| 1.3–2.09 | | | 764 | 1017 | 110 | 1891 |
| | 1.3–1.79 | 2.6 | 20 | 26 | 3 | 49 |
| | 1.6–1.79 | 28.1 | 215 | 286 | 31 | 531 |
| | 1.8–1.99 | 33.3 | 254 | 339 | 37 | 630 |
| | 2.0–2.09 | 36.0 | 275 | 366 | 40 | 681 |
| 2.1–2.79 | | | 1017 | 1966 | 169 | 3174 |
| | 2.1–2.19 | 23.9 | 243 | 475 | 40 | 759 |
| | 2.2–2.39 | 31.6 | 321 | 628 | 53 | 1003 |
| | 2.4–2.59 | 32.9 | 335 | 654 | 56 | 1044 |
| | 2.6–2.79 | 11.6 | 118 | 231 | 20 | 368 |
| 2.8–3.09 | | | 948 | 829 | 201 | 1978 |
| | 2.8–2.99 | 85.7 | 812 | 710 | 172 | 1695 |
| | 3.0–3.09 | 14.3 | 136 | 119 | 29 | 283 |
| 3.1–3.39 | | | 567 | 557 | 158 | 1282 |
| | 3.1–3.19 | 47.8 | 271 | 266 | 76 | 613 |
| | 3.2–3.39 | 52.2 | 296 | 291 | 82 | 669 |
| 3.4–3.79 | | | 622 | 371 | 214 | 1207 |
| | 3.4–3.59 | 80.0 | 498 | 297 | 171 | 966 |
| | 3.6–3.79 | 20.2 | 124 | 74 | 43 | 241 |
| Total range | 1.3–3.79 | 100.0 | 3918 | 4762 | 852 | 9532 |

The only individual-level data available to us were the data collected for Reading One-One tutored students. The first step was to collapse the individual ITBS scores into the subcategories in column 2 of Table A1. Once this was done we calculated each subcategory as a percentage of the original main grade-equivalent category. These percentages are shown in column 3 of Table A1. Once these percentages were calculated, we applied them to the total number of students in each of the original grade-equivalent categories to produce the figures in columns 4–7 of Table A1.

## NOTES

1. As used in this report, the terms *tested* and *untested* apply to the standard English-based ITBS and TAAS tests. The number of *untested* Hispanic students is large and the DPS has taken steps to measure the skills of these students. In the spring of 1995 about 70 percent of the ITBS *untested* students were, in fact, tested using the SABE and Woodcock-Munoz tests. These Spanish-language test scores will be used as the base line for 1995–1996 performance measuring. These scores will be factored into the DPS school ranking system. It is expected that 90 percent of the ITBS *untested* students will take the Spanish-language tests in 1996.

2. The authors only report the effect in "standardized coefficients," measured in units of the standard deviation of experimental and control groups. We have translated to grade-equivalents by utilizing the correspondence between these standardized coefficients displayed by Slavin et al. (1994), who report their effects in both formats.

## REFERENCES

Bender, William N. 1995. *Learning Disabilities: Characteristics, Identification, and Teaching Strategies.* Boston: Allyn and Bacon.

Farkas, George and Keven Vicknair. 1995. "Reading One-One Program Effects, 1994–95." Paper read at the session on "Raising Children's Test Scores" of the Conference on Social Programs That Really Work, sponsored by the Institute of Government and Public Affairs, University of Illinois, October 20, Chicago.

Madden, Nancy A., R. E. Slavin, N. L. Karweit, L. J. Dolan, and B. A. Wasik. 1993. "Success for All: Longitudinal Effects of a Restructuring Program for Inner-City Elementary Schools." *American Educational Research Journal* 30:123–48.

Natriello, Gary, Edward McDill, and Aaron Pallas. 1990. *Schooling Disadvantaged Children: Racing Against Catastrophe.* New York: Teachers College Press.

Pinnell, Gay Su, C. Lyons, D. DeFord, A. Bryk, and M. Seltzer. 1994. "Comparing Instructional Models for the Literacy Education of High-Risk First Graders." *Reading Research Quarterly* 29:9–39.

Reynolds, Arthur. 1992. "Mediated Effects of Preschool Intervention." *Early Education and Development* 3:157–70.

Slavin, Robert. 1989. *Effective Programs for Students at Risk.* Needham Heights, MA: Allyn and Bacon.

Slavin, Robert, M. Madden, L. J. Dolan, and B. A. Wasik. 1994. "Success for All: Longitudinal Effects of Systemic School-By-School Reform in Seven Districts." Paper presented at the Annual Meeting of the American Educational Research Association, April, New Orleans.

Wasik, Barbara and Robert Slavin. 1993. "Preventing Early Reading Failure with One-to-One Tutoring: A Review of Five Programs." *Reading Research Quarterly* 28:179–200.

Zigler, Edward and Sally Styfco (Eds.). 1993. *From Head Start and Beyond: A National Plan for Extended Childhood Intervention.* New Haven, CT: Yale University Press.

# Occupational Constraints on Women's Entry into Management

# 12

David J. Maume, Jr.

## INTRODUCTION

It is a truism that in the workplace "men control, women obey." Women's underrepresentation in positions of supervisory authority is well documented (Goldin 1990; Halaby 1979; Hill 1980; Kanter 1977; Wolf and Fligstein 1979), and this form of exclusion contributes to the gender gap in earnings (Reskin and Ross 1995; Rytina 1982; Spaeth 1985). Women's increased presence in managerial positions is a necessary condition for achieving gender parity in work rewards.

Recent evidence suggests women have made inroads into management. In 1970, 18 percent of managers were women; by 1990 two in five were women (Reskin and Ross 1995). Recent research on managers suggests progress toward gender equality. Olson and Frieze (1987) surveyed the literature and found small to nonexistent gender differences in starting salaries of new M.B.A. recipients. Jacobs (1992) examined Current Population Survey data to report that between 1969 and 1987 the ratio of women's to men's earnings among all managers improved from 56.9 to 61.1 percent; moreover, the gender ratio in earnings of managers approached parity as educational attainment increased.

On the other hand, women continue to face barriers as they advance through the ranks of corporations. Business magazines have documented the almost total absence of women from top positions within large firms (Cordtz 1994; Fierman 1990; Garland 1991; Konrad 1990). The emergence of the popular term "glass ceiling" suggests a belief in subtle barriers preventing women from achieving powerful positions within corporations.

The skeptical and optimistic views of women's position in managerial ranks can be reconciled. Because of changes in gender role and expanded educational opportunities for women since 1970, current cross-sectional data will show that younger women approach younger men in the salaries they receive at the beginning of their careers (as Olson and Frieze report above). It is also possible that few women currently hold top managerial posts because it requires thirty to forty years of experience to amass the credentials needed for assuming top leadership positions in firms (Hill 1980). As women's educational and work experiences converge on men's, women may increasingly assume leadership positions within firms.

Progress toward gender parity in career development should be assessed with longitudinal data. Rosenfeld (1980) showed that women and minorities receive starting salaries similar to those of white men, but over time, white men's salaries grow while the earnings of women and minorities stagnate. This is true as well for those with educational credentials. Olson and Frieze's (1987) review of studies of M.B.A. recipients showed that research conducted over a longer period of time revealed a significant gender gap in earnings later in the career. Many studies suggest that firms create ladders of opportunity that further the careers of some (usually white men) while others (women) are allowed to languish (Baron, Davis-Blake, and Bielby 1986; Kanter 1977; Rosenbaum 1979). Examining gender differences in the timing of promotions into managerial positions is crucial to an understanding of gender inequality in the labor market.

That is the purpose of this chapter. Using the Panel Study of Income Dynamics (PSID), transitions from nonmanagerial to managerial occupations will be examined. Before discussing the data and methods for this analysis, the next section reviews three perspectives on the mobility process.

## THEORETICAL MODELS OF MOBILITY

### *Rewards and Resources*

This perspective argues that workers have varying levels of resources (e.g., education, skills) they bring to a job, which affects their potential level of rewards (e.g., earnings and supervisory status). This model resembles the human capital model in economics in arguing that career changes are a function of skills and talents that reside in the individual. Research in this perspective has found that the higher the level of resources the higher the rate of upward job mobility (Sandefur 1981; Srenson 1977; Srenson and Tuma 1981; Tuma 1976). These studies also show a negative association between job tenure and the rate of job mobility, most likely because over time rewards are more likely to converge on resources, and/or because accumulating benefits raises the costs of switching jobs for workers.

Because the resources-rewards model of mobility directs its attention to individual factors, this perspective is perhaps better suited to explain voluntary moves out of a job (Hachen 1990). The resources-rewards model of mobility is limited in its applicability to job changes initiated by employers, such as promotions. For this reason this model has been supplemented in recent years by perspectives that assume institutional constraints on individual career paths.

### *The Internal Labor Market Model*

Researchers examining the ways in which workers are matched to jobs generally agree that different allocation mechanisms are found in different sectors of the labor market (Beck, Haran, and Tolbert 1978; Doeringer and Piore 1971; Edwards 1979; Farkas and England 1988). The major axis on which job conditions vary is firm size. Large firms face the problems of controlling workers and training them in the operation of complex technologies (Edwards 1979; Doeringer and Piore 1971). Consequently, large firms operating in oligopolistic industries construct job ladders and promise promotions in hopes of securing the commitment of their employees and to reduce turnover (Baron et al. 1986).

In emphasizing the creation of promotion ladders to meet the twin goals of imparting complex skills to workers and of reducing worker opportunism, analysts of internal labor markets assume implicitly that they are created with technical and efficiency considerations in mind. But it is not clear that efficiency arguments can be used to explain why women are shunted off to jobs that lack promotion opportunities and that pay less than the jobs held by men.

### *The Glass Ceiling Model*

Many analysts claim that gender is implicitly used in the job-matching process (Acker 1990; Baron and Newman 1990; Reskin 1988). That is, women are more likely than men to be confined to dead-end and nonsupervisory jobs, resulting in lower career earnings. There are several explanations for this practice in the literature.

Early research by Kanter (1977) showed that male managers preferred to interact with those who shared their background and life experiences (what Kanter calls "homosocial reproduction"). By definition, this excluded women from the ranks of management. When a few women were promoted to the ranks of manger, these "tokens" experienced pressure to outperform their male counterparts, or were stereotyped by their male colleagues, which negatively affected their work. To minimize disruption then, women were typically placed in positions in which they worked with other women, and failed to gain the experience needed to become supervisors.

The "social closure" explanation contends that men resist attempts at job integration in order to preserve their privileged positions within the firm (Acker 1990). By segregating women into "women's jobs" within the firm, men are free to compete among themselves for higher-paying jobs, which offer better career opportunities (Cockburn 1991; Halaby 1979, Tomaskovic-Devey 1993a, 1993b; Walby 1986). If women do acquire the qualifications needed to compete for jobs against men, men use their supervisory positions to change the rules to ensure women's continued subordination (Reskin 1988).

Others point to a process of "status composition," which constitutes a third way in which women are disadvantaged relative to men. In this case, jobs with large numbers of female incumbents are *devalued* in the eyes of the organization. Steinberg (1990) provides a good example of these dynamics in her analysis of bias against women in job evaluation systems. Women's jobs that involve the supervision of difficult clients (e.g., nurses or social workers) are routinely ranked lower than men's clerical jobs that require the supervision of organizational subunits. The hidden assumptions in evaluation systems is that women's nurturing skills are part of their psychological natures, while men's skills must be learned on the job and often involve working with machines. Researchers who investigated the devaluation of women's work find that jobs dominated by women and blacks are viewed as having lower skill requirements, lower pay, and fewer promotion opportunities (Acker 1990; Acker and Van Houten 1974; Baron and Newman 1990; Bielby and Baron 1986; Cockburn 1991; Steinberg 1990; Tomaskovic-Devey 1993a, 1993b; Walby 1986).

These explanations point to the importance of understanding the role of occupational segregation of women in determining work status and pay. That is, by virtue of their assignment to jobs with other female incumbents, women are prevented from attaining jobs with supervisory authority and better pay. The crowding of women into "typically female" jobs has been implicated as a major factor in the gender gap in pay (Baron and Newman 1990; Bridges and Nelson 1989; England, Farkas, Kilbourne, and Dou 1988; Jacobs and Steinberg 1990; Kilbourne, England, Farkas, Beron, and Weir 1994; Sorenson 1989; Tomaskovic-Devey 1993a). Estimates on the proportion of the gender gap in pay attributable to gender segregation range from 17 percent in Kilbourne et al. (1994) to 56 percent in Tomaskovic-Devey (1993a).

Unfortunately there are only a handful of studies examining the influence of occupational segregation on promotions, all of which have weaknesses. For example, Rosenfeld (1983) classified the jobs held before and after an employer change according to their gender typicality, and found no evidence that movement across the boundary between male- and female-typed jobs (in any direction) had an effect on wage mobility. But Rosenfeld (1983) defined wage mobility as a real wage gain of 5 percent or more, resulting in an unusually high number of women reporting a promotion (between 47 and 64 percent, depending on the age of the respondent).

Waite and Berryman (1986) found that the sex composition of the job had no impact on women's job turnover, while men lowered their turnover rates when employed in female-dominated jobs. Unfortunately, the dependent variable in this study—changing employers in the course of a year—does not directly address the issue of career development. Employer changes may stem from workers seeking a better job, or because they were laid off or fired.

Several other studies are well designed but are limited in their generalizability. For example, Hartmann (1987) used personnel records from a large insurance firm and found that percentage female in a job negatively affected the rate of promotion to a higher pay grade for women (but not men). This finding supports the glass ceiling model, but Hartmann sampled from within a single firm. Two other studies (DiPrete and Soule 1988; Steinberg, Haignere, and Chertos 1990) found that female co-workers limited the chances of a woman receiving a promotion, but the findings were limited by sampling from workers in the public sector.

In sum, little attention has been given to the impact of occupational segregation on career dynamics, particularly regarding movement into management. But a review of the segregation literature suggests that male-dominated jobs are more likely to be the "better" jobs in the work setting. Moreover, female-typed jobs are devalued within organizations, resulting in their incumbents receiving fewer skills, training opportunities, and promotions. Thus the following research hypothesis will be tested in this chapter:

H1: *Compared with those working in gender-balanced or male-dominated occupations, women working in female-dominated occupations are less likely to receive a promotion to a managerial position.*

## DATA, DESIGN, AND MEASURES

### *Data*

This chapter uses the Panel Study of Income Dynamics (hereafter, PSID; Institute for Survey Research 1992), a nationally representative longitudinal survey. Every year the PSID surveys workers about their current situations (e.g., employment status, current occupation and industry, employer tenure) and job changes over the prior calendar year. The observation window for this study begins with the 1981 survey year, which provides information on a worker's employment situation at approximately the start of the 1981 calendar year (respondents are contacted in late winter and early spring of every survey year; see Hill 1992). The 1982 survey year provides information on a worker's employment situation at the start of 1982, and job-related changes during 1981. This chapter will use the survey years 1981–1988 to examine work histories for the calendar years 1981–1987.

*Methodology*

A life-table analysis will be used to estimate managerial transitions on data organized for an event history analysis (Allison 1984; Teachman 1983). The strategy in event history analysis is to estimate the probability of receiving a promotion given the length of time a person has worked in a nonmanagerial job. The criterion for remaining in the risk set from year to year is that workers are employed full-time in a nonmanagerial job. Workers drop out of the sample either when they receive a promotion or otherwise leave the risk set. Then each paid survey year is treated as if it were a sample, and the surveys are pooled for all individuals. Pooling the calendar years 1981–1987 resulted in a total of 12,343 person-years of observations.

In any given survey year, it is possible to classify the gender type of the respondent's occupation and examine how long workers had been in the job. In addition, by examining a worker's status one year later, the probability of receiving a managerial promotion can be assessed. Using life-table techniques (Teachman 1983), I examined the survival curves for movement from a nonmanagerial to a management position by duration in a job. The results presented to the reader will be the cumulative proportion of respondents who have been promoted by the tenth year in a job.

## OCCUPATIONAL TYPE

The argument presented above suggests that the proportion female in the occupation affects the rate of promotion to management. The 1981 Current Population Survey (CPS) provided information on the demographic composition of occupations as of 1980 (Institute for Survey Research 1982). The percentage female in each occupation was calculated and the scores merged onto the occupations held by individuals (in all years) in the PSID. PSID respondents were defined as being in a *female-dominated* occupation when 80 percent or more of the incumbents were women; similarly, respondents were in a *male-dominated* occupation when 80 percent or more of the incumbents were men. All other respondents were in mixed occupations.

## FINDINGS

Table 1 presents descriptive statistics on the distribution of men and women across occupation type. The sample sizes are in person-years of waiting for a promotion to management, in which the population "at risk" was the pooled number of years workers were employed full-time in a nonmanagerial job. Table 1 shows that men and women are segregated by occupation type. Two-

*Table 1.* Distribution (%) across Occupation Type, by Gender, Full-Time Workers Ages 25–54 in Nonmanagerial Positions, PSID, 1981–1988

| *Occupation Type* | *Men* | *Women* |
|---|---|---|
| Males ≥80% (malocc) | 66 | 7 |
| 21% < males < 79% (mixocc) | 30 | 39 |
| ≤20% males (femocc) | 4 | 54 |
| Number of person-years | 7927 | 4416 |

thirds of the person-years that men spent waiting for a promotion are in occupations in which 80 percent or more of the incumbents are other men; only 4 percent of men's person-years are in positions in which 80 percent or more of the incumbents are women. By contrast, over half of women's person-years are in occupations dominated by women, and only 7 percent of women's person-years are in male-dominated occupations.

Using life-table techniques (Teachman 1983) the probability of receiving a managerial promotion by each year of tenure was examined. The duration-specific promotion chances were used to estimate the cumulative probability of waiting for a managerial promotion. Figure 1 presents figures on the cumulative percentage of respondents who had been promoted by their tenth year of tenure in a job. The three bars on the left are promotion rates for men broken down by the type of origin occupation, while the three bars on the right show the same information for women.

Figure 1 shows that the promotion process differs significantly by gender. Women are more likely to be promoted when they are in positions in which they *work primarily with men.* After ten years, 11.73 percent of women

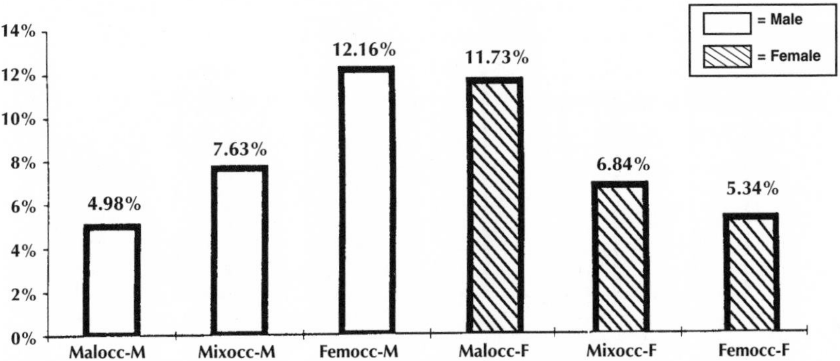


*Figure 1.* Percentage promoted after ten years by gender, and occupation type.

received a promotion if they were employed in male-dominated jobs. But, women employed in female-dominated jobs are less than half as likely to be promoted as women in male-dominated jobs (5.34 percent), and women in mixed occupations fare only slightly better (6.84 percent). On the other hand, men are *more likely* to receive a promotion when they work with other women (12.16 percent), compared with working in mixed occupations (7.63 percent) or with other men (4.96 percent). The high rate of promotion for women is understandable if one accepts the notion that male-dominated jobs are more highly rewarded in the labor market. But this does not explain why men's promotion chances are lowest in male-dominated occupations.

Before offering a substantive explanation for these results, the first issue that must be examined is that these figures may reflect differential job assignment by gender rather than differential valuation of occupations by employers. That is, if men work with other men in blue-collar or factory settings, they may enjoy high earnings but with the understanding that they will likely never receive a managerial promotion (Chinoy 1955; Kanter 1977). On the other hand if the women who work primarily with other men are in professional or sales positions, they may have higher promotion rates because these jobs are natural "stepping stones" into managerial occupations. Examining promotion chances among those in white-collar origin occupations takes this argument into account.

Figure 2 shows that most groups enjoy higher rates of promotion when employed in white-collar or stepping-stone occupations. However, some support is found for the differential job assignment of men, while the differential valuation argument is upheld for women. That is, men's low rate of promotion when working in male-dominated occupations (shown in Figure 1) may be due to their greater likelihood of working in blue-collar occupations; when the sample is restricted to those who work in white-collar or

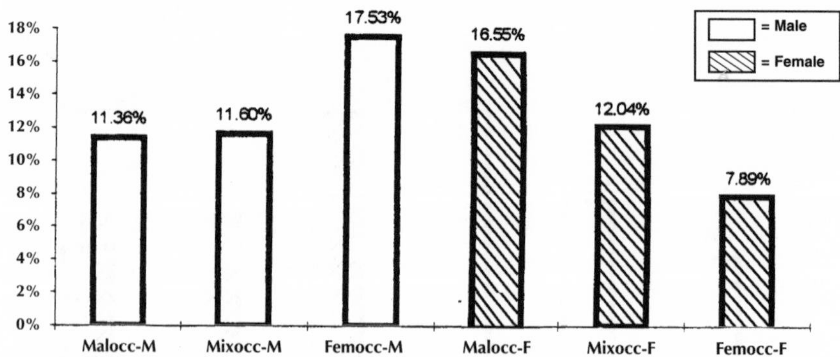


*Figure 2.* Percentage promoted after ten years by gender, and occupation type (white-collar-origin job only).

stepping-stone occupations, the effect of occupation type on promotion chances is more similar for men. On the other hand, women in white-collar jobs clearly fare better when they work with other men, and the gap in exit rates between male- and female-dominated origin jobs widens for women. Indeed, the lowest rates of promotion in Figure 2 are for women in female-typed occupations.

These results support the claim that for women, placement in a typically female job is to be consigned to a position with short or nonexistent career ladders resulting in women's stagnant career development. While there is ample evidence of discrimination against individual women as workers, these results suggest that employers discriminate against *jobs* held primarily by women. Such jobs are evaluated as having lower skills, offer fewer training opportunities, and do not link women to jobs higher up on the organizational pyramid (Baron et al. 1986; Kanter 1977; Steinberg 1990). Since women as a group are more likely to be viewed as unstable workers who are more committed to family than to their career (Bielby and Baron 1986), assignment to jobs that are held in lower esteem by the organization significantly handicaps women's career development.

But having female co-workers is advantageous to men's career development. Williams (1992) analyzed men who aspired to careers in typically female jobs and found that they suffered from discrimination, but of a different sort. Co-workers and clients alike viewed men in nontraditional occupations as deviants from cultural norms, which defined such jobs as proper places of employment for women, but not men. Thus, in order to improve workplace morale and customer relations, organizations promoted men in female-dominated occupations to managerial status (whose job requirements of showing initiative and giving orders are believed to be consistent with the skills that men possess). In Williams's (1992) words, the discomfort of co-workers and clients in dealing with men in typically female jobs produces a "glass escalator," which results in men's promotion to management. Some men recognize this, with many admitting that they opted for careers in female-dominated occupations because they provided a stepping stone to management status (see also Schreiber 1981).

Before concluding this discussion of results, it is necessary to take other perspectives into account in analyzing gender differences in promotion chances. For example, it is possible that educated women are more likely to work in male-dominated occupations, while women with fewer skills work in female-dominated occupations, which could explain the pattern of findings for women. To take this argument into account, those who had college diplomas were selected and the survival curves for promotion were examined.

Figure 3 shows that when college graduates are selected, men's promotion patterns differ little by occupation type. This is not true for women, how-

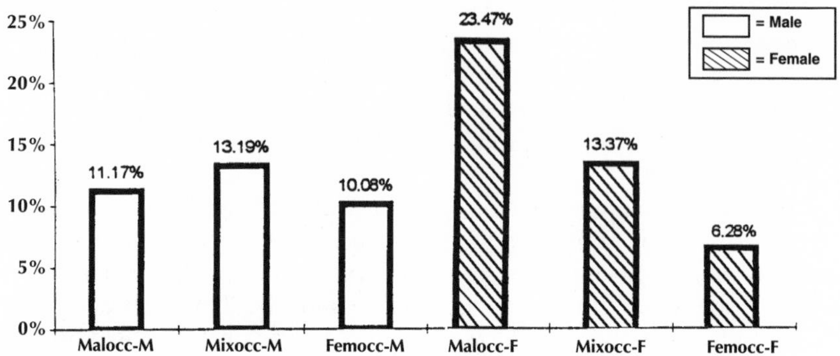


*Figure 3.* Percentage promoted after ten years by gender, and occupation type (college graduates only).

ever. College-educated women assigned to female-dominated occupations were *four* times less likely to receive a promotion than similarly credentialed women in male-dominated occupations. If occupation type had no effect on careers, then women's waiting times for a promotion should approximate those of men. Rather, it is clear that college-educated women must avoid working with other women if they desire managerial promotions, and the few women who do work with male colleagues have shorter waiting times for promotions.

The internal labor market perspective suggests that employment experiences differ when firms promote from within, rather than seeking to fill managerial positions from outside the firm. Government is often taken as an example of an internal labor market that benefits the careers of women and minorities because of its greater commitment to hire and promote with affirmative action guidelines in mind (Collins 1983). Figure 4 shows the promotion experiences of those whose origin jobs were in government.

For men, promotions are achieved more quickly in the private sector, while employment in government lowers the chances of receiving a promotion (compare the bar charts for men in Figures 1 and 4). Moreover, as in Figure 3, men's promotion chances in the public sector are less sensitive to the gender type of the origin job than is the case for women. Women who work in government receive more promotions when they work in male-dominated occupations (12.29 percent), and their ten-year rate of exit out of female-dominated jobs is extremely low (3.54 percent). These findings suggest that access to male-dominated jobs is as important in the public sector as it is in the private sector (Steinberg et al. 1990). More important, perhaps, is that the pattern of women's promotions in Figure 4 differs little from those shown in Figure 1, suggesting that employment in the public sector does not appreciably enhance women's careers.

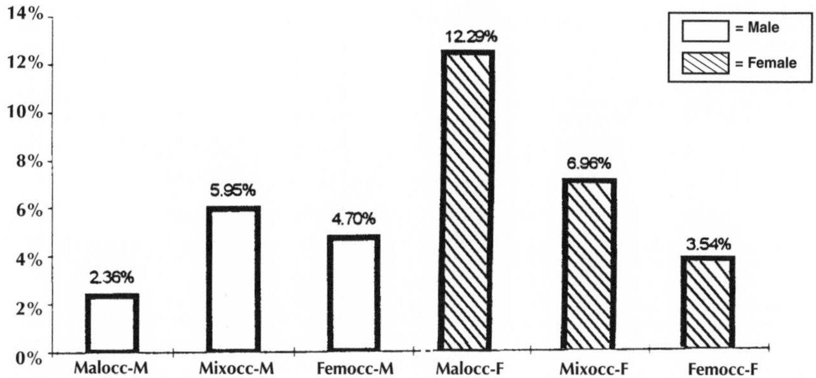


*Figure 4.* Percentage promoted after ten years by gender, and occupation type (government employees only).

## SUMMARY AND SUGGESTIONS FOR FUTURE RESEARCH

This chapter began by noting the increasing representation of women among the ranks of managers. It is estimated that women's entry into management accounts for one-fourth of the decline in occupational segregation since 1970 (Jacobs 1992). But is this progress real or illusory? Jacobs (1992) concludes that this progress is real, accompanied by rising salaries and increased job satisfaction. Skeptics contend that the increase in female managers may be due to two factors. First, pressure from Equal Employment Opportunity legislation forces organizations to retitle female clericals as managers with little authority (for example, by changing a woman's title from secretary to executive assistant; see Smith and Welch 1984). Second, men leave occupations with declining status, thereby opening up management opportunities for women (Reskin and Roos 1990).

For those who embrace the skeptical view of women's entry into management, the findings of this chapter add to an already gloomy picture. These data cannot determine whether or not women in this sample are advancing to positions of "glorified secretary" or into declining positions vacated by men. But, if they are, employment in a female-dominated occupation slows women's progress into even this vacuous form of equality. This finding is in stark contrast to the experiences of men who use female-dominated jobs as a springboard into supervisory positions. Moreover, women's careers do not appreciably benefit by employment in the public sector, and the importance of avoiding female-typed jobs is magnified when women hold a college diploma.

The skeptical view of women's entry into management can be examined with longitudinal data on authority relations in the workplace and control over the company's resources. If women are making real progress toward parity with men, they should be increasing their rate of movement into positions that have numerous subordinates, and controlling the firm's operations. Hachen (1990) examined authority mobility with retrospective data, but he did not explicitly include occupational segregation as a control. Steinberg et al. (1990) found that women were excluded from positions that led to supervisory positions in New York State government, but a similar study in the private sector has not yet appeared. Clearly, this is a topic in need of further research.

Whether one is skeptical of or heartened by the entry of women into management, further research is needed on whether women stay in managerial positions. Men's negative reactions to female co-workers range from sexual harassment to the silent treatment. Such resistance has resulted in some women leaving male-dominated jobs (Jacobs 1989). Studies that examine the impacts of occupational segregation, workplace dynamics, and corporate policies on women's "exit rate" from management are also needed to assess whether women's recent progress in entering management is real or illusory.

## REFERENCES

Acker, Joan. 1990. "Hierarchies, Jobs and Bodies: A Theory of Gendered Organizations." *Gender and Society* 4:139–58.

Acker, Joan and Donald R. Van Houten. 1974. "Differential Recruitment and Control: The Sex Structuring of Organizations." *Administrative Science Quarterly* 19: 152–64.

Allison, Paul D. 1984. *Event History Analysis: Regression for Longitudinal Event Data.* Newbury Park, CA: Sage.

Baron, James N., Allison Davis-Blake, and William T. Bielby. 1986. "The Structure of Opportunity: How Promotion Ladders Vary within and among Organizations." *Administrative Science Quarterly* 31:248–73.

Baron, James N., and Andrew E. Newman. 1990. "For What It's Worth: Organizations, Occupations and the Value of Work Done by Women and Nonwhites." *American Sociological Review* 55:155–75.

Beck, E. M., Patrick Haran, and Charles M. Tolbert III. 1978. "Stratification in a Dual Economy: A Sectoral Model of Earnings Determination." *American Sociological Review* 43:704–20.

Bielby, William T., and James N. Baron. 1986. "Men and Women at Work: Sex Segregation and Statistical Discrimination." *American Journal of Sociology* 91:759–99.

Bridges, William P. and Robert L. Nelson. 1989. "Markets in Hierarchies: Organizational and Market Influences on Gender Inequality in a State Pay System." *American Journal of Sociology* 95:616–59.

Cordtz, Dan. 1994. "The Glass Ceiling," *Financial World,* August 16, p. 64.

Chinoy, Eli. 1955. *Automobile Workers and the American Dream*. Garden City, NY: Doubleday.

Cockburn, Cynthia. 1991. *In the Way of Women: Men's Resistance to Sex Equality in Organizations*. Ithaca, NY: ILR.

Collins, Sharon. 1983. "The Making of the Black Middle Class." *Social Problems* 30:369–82.

DiPrete, Thomas A. and Whitman T. Soule. 1988. "Gender and Promotion in Segmented Job Ladder Systems." *American Sociological Review* 53:26–40.

Doeringer, Peter B. and Michael Piore. 1971. *Internal Labor Markets and Manpower Analysis*. Lexington, MA: Heath.

Edwards, Richard C. 1979. *Contested Terrain*. New York: Basic Books.

England, P., G. Farkas, B. S. Kilbourne, and T. Dou. 1988. "Explaining Occupational Sex Segregation and Wages: Findings from a Model with Fixed Effects." *American Sociological Review* 53:544–58.

Farkas, George and Paula England. 1988. *Industries, Firms and Jobs: Sociological and Economic Approaches*. New York: Plenum.

Fierman, J. 1990. "Why Women Still Don't Hit the Top." *Fortune*, July 30, 1992, p. 42.

Garland, S. B. 1991. "Throwing Stones at the Glass Ceiling." *Business Week*, August 19, p. 29.

Goldin, Claudia. 1990. *Understanding the Gender Gap: An Economic History of American Women*. New York: Oxford University Press.

Hachen, David S. 1990. "Three Models of Job Mobility in Labor Markets." *Work and Occupations* 17:320–54.

Halaby, Charles. 1979. "Job-Specific Sex Differences in Organizational Reward Attainment: Wage Discrimination vs. Rank Segregation." *Social Forces* 62: 467–87.

Hartmann, Heidi I. 1987. "Internal Labor Markets and Gender: A Case Study of Promotion." Pp. 59–92 in *Gender in the Workplace*, edited by Clair Brown and Joseph A. Pechman. Washington, DC: Brookings Institution.

Hill, Martha. 1980. "Authority at Work: How Men and Women Differ." Pp. 107–46 in *Five Thousand American Families*, Vol. 8, edited by Greg J. Duncan and James Morgan. Ann Arbor: University of Michigan Press.

———. 1992. *The Panel Study of Income Dynamics: A User's Guide*. Newbury Park, CA: Sage.

Institute for Survey Research. 1982. *Current Population Survey: Annual Demographic File, 1981* [MRDF]. ICPSR study #7863. Ann Arbor: Survey Research Center.

———. 1992. *A Panel Study of Income Dynamics: Procedures and Tape Codes* [MRDF] (various years). ICPSR study #7439. Ann Arbor: Survey Research Center.

Jacobs, Jerry A. 1989. *Revolving Doors: Sex Segregation and Women's Careers*. Stanford, CA: Stanford University Press.

———. 1992. "Women's Entry into Management: Trends in Earnings, Authority, and Values among Salaried Managers." *Administrative Science Quarterly* 372: 282–301.

Jacobs, Jerry A. and Ronnie Steinberg. 1990. "Compensating Differentials and the Male-Female Wage Gap: Evidence from the New York State Comparable Worth Study." *Social Forces* 69:439–68.

Kanter, Rosabeth Moss. 1977. *Men and Women of the Corporation.* New York: Basic Books.

Kilbourne, B. S., P. England, G. Farkas, K. Beron, and D. Weir. 1994. "Returns to Skill, Compensating Differentials, and Gender Bias: Effects of Occupational Characteristics on the Wages of White Women and Men." *American Journal of Sociology* 100:689–719.

Konrad, W. 1990. "Welcome to the Woman-Friendly Company." *Business Week.* August 6, pp. 48–55.

Olson, J. E., and I. H. Frieze. 1987. "Income Determinants for Women in Business." Pp. 173–206 in *Women and Work: An Annual Review,* Vol. 2, edited by A. H. Stromberg, L. Larwood, and B. A. Guteck. Beverly Hills, CA: Sage.

Reskin, Barbara. 1988. "Bringing the Men Back In: Sex Differentiation and the Devaluation of Women's Work." *Gender and Society* 2:58–81.

Reskin, Barbara and Catherine E. Ross. 1995. "Jobs, Authority and Earnings among Managers: The Continuing Significance of Sex." Pp. 127–51 in *Gender Inequality at Work,* edited by Jerry A. Jacobs. Thousand Oaks, CA: Sage.

Reskin, Barbara and Patricia Roos. 1990. *Job Queues, Gender Queues: Explaining Women's Inroads Into Male Occupations.* Philadelphia: Temple University Press.

Rosenbaum, James E. 1979. "Tournament Mobility: Career Patterns in a Corporation." *Administrative Science Quarterly* 24:220–41.

Rosenfeld, Rachel. 1980. "Race and Sex Differences in Career Dynamics." *American Sociological Review* 45:583–609.

———. 1983. "Sex Segregation and Sectors: An Analysis of Gender Differences in Returns from Employer Changes." *American Sociological Review* 48:637–55.

Rytina, N. F. 1982. "Earnings of Men and Women: A Look at Specific Occupations." *Monthly Labor Review* (April):25–31.

Sandefur, Gary D. 1981. "Organizational Boundaries and Upward Job Shifts." *Social Science Research* 10:67–82.

Schreiber, Carol T. 1981. *Changing Places: Men and Women in Transitional Occupations.* Cambridge, MA: MIT Press.

Smith, James P. and Finis T. Welch. 1984. "Affirmative Action and Labor Markets." *Journal of Labor Economics* 2:269–301.

Sorenson, Elaine. 1989. "Measuring the Effect of Occupational Sex and Race Composition on Earnings." Pp. 49–70 in *Pay Equity: Empirical Inquiries,* edited by R. T. Michael, H. I. Hamann, and B. O'Farrell. Washington, DC: National Academy Press.

Spaeth, Joe L. 1985. "Job Power and Earnings." *American Sociological Review* 50:603–17.

Srenson, Aage B. 1977. "The Structure of Inequality and the Process of Attainment." *American Sociological Review* 40:456–71.

Srenson, Aage B. and Nancy B. Tuma. 1981. "Labor Market Structures and Job Mobility." Pp. 67–94 in *Research in Social Stratification and Mobility,* Vol. 1, edited by D. J. Treiman and R. V. Robinson. Greenwich, CT: JAI.

Steinberg, Ronnie J. 1990. "The Social Construction of Skill." *Work and Occupations* 17:449–82.

Steinberg, Ronnie J., Lois Haignere, and Cynthia H. Chertos. 1990. "Managerial Promotions in the Public Sector." *Work and Occupations* 17:284–301.

Teachman, Jay D. 1983. "Analyzing Social Processes: Life Tables and Proportional Hazards Models." *Social Science Research* 12:263–301.

Tomaskovic-Devey, Donald. 1993a. *Gender and Racial Inequality at Work.* Ithaca, NY: ILR press.

———. 1993b. "The Gender and Race Composition of Jobs and the Male/Female, White/Black Pay Gaps." *Social Forces* 72:45–76.

Tuma, Nancy B. 1976. "Rewards, Resources and the Rate of Mobility." *American Sociological Review* 41:338–60.

Waite, Linda J. and Sue E. Berryman. 1986. "Job Stability among Young Women: A Comparison of Traditional and Nontraditional Occupations." *American Journal of Sociology* 92:568–95.

Walby, Sylvia. 1986. *Patriarchy at Work.* Minneapolis: University of Minnesota Press.

Williams, Christine L. 1992. "The Glass Escalator: Hidden Advantages for Men in the 'Female' Professions." *Social Problems* 39:253–67.

Wolf, Wendy and Neil D. Fligstein. 1979. "Sex and Authority in the Workplace: The Causes of Sexual Inequality." *American Sociological Review* 44:235–52.

# Employer-Based Health Insurance in a Changing Economy 13

Lisa A. Cubbins

## INTRODUCTION

Employer-based health insurance is one of the most important fringe benefits offered to workers. It affects not only workers' access to health care but their families' access as well. While employment is the primary source of health insurance coverage (Harrison, Tuchfarber, Smith, and Cubbins 1994; Piacentini and Foley 1992; Wiatrowski 1995), not all American workers are equally likely to receive employer-based health insurance. Both a worker's sociodemographic characteristics and his or her position in the labor market are related to receiving health insurance through an employer (Seccombe and Amey 1995; Swartz 1992; Wiatrowski 1995). Given the link between employment and health insurance, changes in the U.S. economy may affect the likelihood of receiving employer-based health insurance for some workers. Since the early 1980s, many U.S. industries have transformed the nature and organization of their productive activities. The decline of production industries and of union membership, the expansion of service and trade industries, the increase in part-time work, and other economic shifts may have worsened the chances of receiving employer-based health insurance for some groups.

In this study, I examine how women and nonwhites have fared given changes in labor market conditions that affect employer-based health insurance. I examine the following questions: First, between 1989 and 1995, did the probability of receiving employer-based health insurance change for women workers and nonwhite workers? Second, does variation in worker resources and labor market location explain gender and race differences in the receipt of employer-based health insurance among U.S. workers? I argue that the distribution of employer-based health insurance is a product of three types of influences: individual labor resources, such as human capital; institutionalized discrimination; and location in the labor market. Due to these three types of influences, women and nonwhites are expected to be less likely to receive employer-based health insurance than are other workers. In addition, economic changes since the early 1980s are expected to have reduced opportunities for women and nonwhite to receive employer-based health insurance.

## THE DISTRIBUTION OF HEALTH BENEFITS

Past studies have shown that both individual and labor market characteristics are related to whether or not a worker receives employer-based health insurance. Sociodemographic factors that are associated with the receipt of health benefits include gender, race, age, marital status, education, and poverty status. Women (Knoke 1994; Seccombe and Amey 1995; Seccombe and Beeghley 1992) and nonwhites (Seccombe and Amey 1995) tend to be less likely to receive health benefits than are men and whites, respectively. Workers who are younger, less educated, and not married do not receive health benefits from their employers as often as other workers (Bureau of Labor Statistics 1993; Seccombe and Amey 1995; Swartz 1992). Family economic status also plays a role, with workers in families just above the poverty line being less likely to receive employer-based health insurance than poorer workers or those with families at higher income levels (Seccombe and Amey 1995; Swartz 1992).

In addition to sociodemographic characteristics, an individual's employment behavior and labor market experience are critical elements in the determination of health benefits. Along with other factors, employers use the amount of time an individual works at their firm to determine whether or not job benefits will be rewarded. Individuals who work part-time are much less likely to receive health benefits than are full-time workers (Snider 1995; Wiatrowski 1995). For example, in a survey conducted between 1990 and 1991, 79 percent of full-time workers received health care benefits, compared to only 17 percent of part-time workers (Bureau of Labor Statistics 1993).

Labor market location has been found to be strongly related to health benefits (Root 1985; Perman and Stevens 1989; Seccombe and Amey 1995; Seccombe and Beeghley 1992; Solnick 1985). Past studies have pointed to key characteristics of labor market location as influencing health care coverage by employers. Smaller firms are consistently less likely to offer health benefits than larger firms (Alpert and Ozawa 1986; Knoke 1994; Nelson 1994; Seccombe and Amey 1995), though union representation tends to increase the chances of receiving health insurance from an employer (Alpert and Ozawa 1986; Freeman 1981; Seccombe and Amey 1995; Solnick 1985). Certain types of industries—service, trade, and agriculture, in particular—have lower levels of health insurance coverage than other sectors of the economy (Alpert and Ozawa 1986; Piacentini and Foley 1992; Wiatrowski 1995).

The relevance of labor market factors for health benefits is of special concern for workers, given recent changes in the U.S. economy. Four prominent trends have emerged in the U.S. economy in the past twenty years that are of special importance for employer-based health insurance: First is the increase of part-time jobs in the labor market (Conference Board 1996; Tilly 1991). In 1969, there were 10.8 million part-time workers, compared to 20.7 million in 1993. This resulted in a 91.7 percent increase in the number of part-time workers during the 15 year period, with 25 percent of new entrants to the labor market being part-time workers (Snider 1995). A second trend that has occurred since the early 1980s is the corporate reengineering that often entailed downsizing and changes in labor-management relations (Uchitelle and Kleinfield 1996). Business cost-cutting measures frequently involved reductions in employee benefits programs, including the level of health insurance coverage. The third trend is industrial restructuring, which occurred with the shift from manufacturing production and employment to expanding service production and employment (Levit, Olin, and Letsch 1992; Wiatrowski 1995). This trend has been most notable as it involves the expansion of certain industries that are less likely to offer health benefits, alongside the contraction of industries that have been more likely to offer health benefits. Finally, the long-term decline of union membership has continued into the 1990s (Curme, Hirsch, and MacPherson 1990; Renner and Navarro 1989; U.S. Bureau of the Census 1993). As discussed above, each of these labor market conditions—part-time work, firm size, type of industry, unionization—is related to receipt of employer-based health insurance.

Coinciding with these economic changes has been a decline in the receipt of employer-based health insurance among American workers (Levit et al. 1992; Piacentini and Foley 1992). For example, 75 percent of full-time workers received employer-based health insurance in 1990, which is down from 82 percent in 1979. Among the working poor, the decline in coverage has been even more dramatic: 57 percent of full-time poor workers received employer-based health insurance in 1979, compared to 34 percent in 1990.

## THEORETICAL FRAMEWORK

To explain the unequal distribution of employer-based health insurance I draw on theories of economic mobility and status attainment that have been used to account for patterns of income and job benefits. These explanatory models tend to focus on one of three primary sources of inequality: First, differences in job rewards such as health benefits are explained as the product of variation in worker resources, including education, training, and work experience (Granovetter 1981; Sørensen and Tuma 1981). Employers frequently treat job benefits, including health insurance, as critical incentives in attracting and keeping productive and highly skilled employees. Given this argument, variation in health benefits may be partly attributed to differences in accumulated labor market experience across the labor force. Workers who are more highly educated and/or have more labor market experience will receive higher rewards than other workers. Further, to the degree that human capital factors vary by gender, race, ethnicity, or poverty status, one would expect to see similar variation in job rewards, including employer-based health care coverage.

A second model of differences in job rewards points to unequal treatment of certain groups (particularly women and race and ethnic minorities) in the labor market that place them at a disadvantage in obtaining better jobs and in receiving equal compensation. Unequal treatment may take different forms, such as blatant discrimination (Becker 1971; Thurow 1969) or institutionalized distinctions (Baron and Bielby 1985), all of which use group status to define individual access to opportunities and rewards in the labor market. This model, then, predicts variation in health benefits along gender, race, and ethnic lines, in part due to unequal treatment in the labor market. As such, women and race and ethnic minorities are expected to receive lower earnings and less attractive benefits than other workers.

The third approach adopts a structural view of differences in employment outcomes, arguing that the location of workers in the labor market defines their opportunities to achieve certain employment rewards (Beck, Horan, and Tolbert 1978; Bibb and Form 1977). Systematic differences in employment outcomes have been observed across occupations, firms, industries, and economic segments. Differences within these labor market units in organization and resources produce variation in workers' opportunities and rewards. For example, workers employed in firms requiring high firm-specific training may be offered higher incentives (e.g., health benefits) in order to reduce turnover. The capacity of firms to offer their workers health benefits also may vary depending on such characteristics as firm size or the level of competition within the firm's industry (Doeringer and Piore 1971; Hodson 1986; Knoke 1994; Nelson 1994). Because of economies of scale, larger firms are more able to provide health coverage to their employees than are smaller firms. In addition, larger firms are better able to engage in long-term planning than are smaller firms (Galbraith 1973) and tend to have greater stability in product demand. As such, larger firms are better able to bear the costs of higher job rewards than smaller firms (Kalleberg, Wallace, and Althauser 1981). Firms operating in a highly competitive environment may restrict employee wages and benefits in order to keep costs down.

Another key aspect of labor market location is the collective power of workers in a firm or industry to press for higher job rewards. Workers employed in industries typified by high union representation will tend to have higher rewards than other workers (Cornfield 1991). In contrast, where the labor force composition includes higher concentrations of groups associated with lower rewards (e.g., women, nonwhites), individual workers will have lower pay and fewer benefits, regardless of group membership (Treiman and Hartmann 1981).

Following Hachen (1990), I draw on the three models described above in developing the hypotheses to be tested. In this, it is important to recognize that the three models are interrelated. Both worker resources and labor market location vary systematically by gender, race, and ethnicity. In turn, worker resources are an important predictor of labor market location. Thus, variation in health insurance benefits by gender, race, and ethnicity may be explained partly by gender, race, and ethnic differences in worker resources and labor market location.

I propose three hypotheses. First, I consider change in the probability that workers will receive employer-based health insurance. Due to broad-scale changes in the economy, I expect there has been a reduction in opportunities for receiving employer-based health insurance between 1989 and 1995. The combined forces of downsizing, deindustrialization, and reduced worker power will have eliminated many jobs with high rewards, including health coverage. Thus, I predict the following:

Hypothesis 1: *The probability of U.S. workers receiving employer-based health insurance declined between 1989 and 1995.*

The second hypothesis concerns group differences in health benefits. As a consequence of unequal worker resources and differential treatment in the labor market, women and nonwhites are expected to be less likely to receive employer-based health insurance than other workers. Further, because of changes in the labor market, it may be harder for women and nonwhite workers to find jobs in industries in which health benefits are offered. Increased competition for good jobs that offer high wages and generous job benefits, along with unequal treatment, may confound efforts by women and nonwhite workers to obtain employer-based health insurance. Ironically though, actual job opportunities for less skilled, lower paid workers may have increased, given the expansion of the service and trade industries. However, many new jobs in these industries are part-time and often lack health benefits (Snider 1995; Tilly 1991). Essentially the changing labor market is not expected to have provided women and nonwhite workers career paths to jobs offering health benefits. Further, I expect that worker resources and labor market location affect individual chances for job rewards, including employer-based health insurance, and may explain variation in health benefits by gender and race. For these reasons, I predict

Hypothesis 2: *Gender and race differences in the probability of receiving employer-based health insurance increased between 1989 and 1995.*

Hypothesis 3: *Worker resources and characteristics of labor market location account for gender and race differences in the receipt of employer-based health insurance among U.S. workers in 1989 and 1995.*

As change occurs in the labor market, the likelihood of receiving health insurance from an employer will also change. In addition, the relationship between labor market characteristics and health insurance may change differently for different groups. For example, there may be little effect of labor market changes for highly skilled workers (such as professionals) who receive health insurance coverage as part of a lucrative set of job rewards that are aimed at maintaining employer attachment and reducing turnover. However, employers who primarily employ less skilled workers may be less concerned about retaining any specific worker, and more concerned with reducing labor costs in general. Not offering or eliminating health insurance coverage may be one means to remain competitive in a changing economy.

## RESEARCH METHODS

### *Data*

To test the hypotheses, an individual-level analysis was conducted using data from the CPS Annual Demographic Files for 1989 and 1995. The Annual Demographic Files of the CPS are conducted each March by the Census Bureau in order to provide national estimates on the demographic and labor market characteristics of the U.S. population. The CPS annual series contain questions on sociodemographic characteristics, labor force participation, health insurance including coverage provided through an employer or union, as well as other employment-related characteristics. The CPS is based on a national probability sample of households. Approximately 56,000 housing units are contacted each March, with an additional sample of 2,500 Hispanic households. In the analyses, all data are weighted so as to represent the national population for the year in which the data were collected. The sample is restricted to respondents in the primary work years, ages eighteen to sixty-four.

### *Measures*

The dependent variable, receipt of employer-based health insurance, is measured based on the response to a CPS question on whether or not a worker's employer or union contributes to his or her health insurance costs. While this question addresses receipt of employer-based health insurance, the CPS does not ask whether an employer offers health insurance benefits. Given that a worker may choose to refuse employer contributions (perhaps to receive higher wages), the health insurance measure I use should not be interpreted as an indicator of the level of employer-based health insurance available in the labor market. Instead, I can only examine receipt of, rather than access to, employer-based health insurance.

In the analysis, I investigate two primary group differences—gender and race—in the receipt of employer-based health insurance. Gender is dummy coded, with women as the reference category. Race is measured with a three-category measure for whether the respondent is white (reference), black, or has another racial background.

Additional individual level measures are created to control for factors that have been found to affect receipt of employer-based health insurance. Two indicators of worker resources are created. A measure of age is included to capture the accumulation of job experience that can be translated into higher job rewards, including benefits. Since those more highly educated may have access to jobs with higher pay and more generous health benefits than those with less education, I include an indicator for completed years of education. Workers who are married may have alternative sources of health insurance through their spouses. Therefore, a measure for marital status is created, distinguishing those who are currently married from those who are previously married or never married.

Three indicators of labor market location are used. Since employer-based health insurance is associated with the amount of time employed, a dummy measure for part-time work is included in the analysis. I also measure for whether or not the respondent is a union member or is covered by a union contract. Finally, a fourteen-category measure is constructed showing the industry in which a respondent works.

### *Analysis*

The data analysis is carried out in two stages: First, descriptive univariate and bivariate statistics on the variables in the analysis are produced. Univariate statistics are calculated for the dependent and predictor variables for each year in the analysis. Bivariate analyses are conducted, showing the distribution of the receipt of employer-based health insurance across categories of the predictor variables.

The second stage of the analysis involves tests of the three hypotheses through bivariate and multivariate analysis. To test the first hypothesis, a difference of proportion test will be conducted comparing the proportion of workers receiving employer-based health insurance in 1989 to those receiving it in 1995. This will show whether or not there was a change the overall likelihood of receiving employer-based health insurance. The second hypothesis concerns changes in gender and race differences in the health insurance benefits between 1989 and 1995. This is evaluated by comparing the percentage distributions on the receipt of employer-based health insurance for 1989 and 1995 by gender and by race. The third hypothesis suggests that worker resources and labor market location account for gender and race differences in the receipt of health benefits. I test this hypothesis through a logistic regression analysis using measures for gender, race, worker resources, and labor market location to predict receipt of employer-based health insurance. Finally, I consider whether the effects of these predictor variables changed between 1989 and 1995.

## RESULTS

The first hypothesis on changes in health benefits between 1989 and 1995 is supported. For the total sample, receipt of health benefits declined from 65 percent in 1989 to 59 percent in 1995. These statistics are consistent with the long-term decline in employer-based benefits described in other studies.

Table 1 presents the descriptive statistics on the 1989 and 1995 CPS samples separately by gender. In 1989, 69 percent of employed men and 56 percent of employed women received employed-based health insurance. By 1995, receipt of health benefits had declined for both men and women (65 and 53 percent, respectively). While there continued to be significant gender differences in receipt of employer-based health insurance, the gender gap in health benefits had only a negligible increase during this period. A race difference in health benefits also was found in 1989 and 1995, though there was minimal change in the level of difference between groups. In 1989, 64 percent of whites, 58 percent of blacks, and 61 percent of other race groups received health benefits. These percentages had declined to 60, 56, and 52 percent, respectively, by 1995. Only the comparison of whites versus other race groups experienced an increase in the likelihood of receiving health benefits. Thus, based on the gender and race distributions, the second hypothesis is not supported.

As shown in Table 1, the sample is approximately 85 percent white in both years, with roughly two-thirds of the men and slightly more than half of the women being married. The statistics on educational attainment show increases for both men and women between 1989 and 1995. In 1989, 44 percent of the employed men and women had more than 12 years of education. This increased to 56 percent for men and 59 percent for women. As others have shown, the American labor force is becoming more educated, and notably employed women seem to be surpassing employed men in this form of human capital. It should be noted, however, that some of the apparent increase in educational attainment may be an artifact of CPS changes in the measurement of education between the survey years.

*Table 1.* Percentage Distributions on Socioeconomic Characteristics by Gender for 1989 and 1995

| | *1989* | | *1995* | |
|---|---|---|---|---|
| | *Men* | *Women* | *Men* | *Women* |
| Employer-based health insurance | | | | |
| Receives | 69.2 | 56.0 | 65.0 | 52.9 |
| Does not receive | 30.8 | 44.0 | 35.0 | 47.1 |
| Race | | | | |
| White | 86.5 | 84.5 | 85.1 | 83.1 |
| Black | 10.6 | 12.5 | 10.7 | 13.1 |
| Other | 2.9 | 3.0 | 4.2 | 3.8 |
| Education | | | | |
| Less than 12 years | 16.0 | 11.6 | 11.9 | 8.4 |
| 12 years | 39.7 | 44.2 | 32.2 | 32.8 |
| More than 12 years | 44.3 | 44.2 | 55.9 | 58.8 |
| Marital status | | | | |
| Currently married | 63.9 | 57.2 | 60.3 | 56.3 |
| Postmarried | 9.7 | 19.9 | 10.2 | 18.9 |
| Never married | 26.4 | 22.9 | 29.5 | 24.8 |
| Hours worked | | | | |
| Part-time | 7.1 | 20.2 | 10.6 | 26.8 |
| Full-time | 92.9 | 79.8 | 89.4 | 73.2 |
| Union member or union coverage | | | | |
| Yes | 23.1 | 15.3 | 20.0 | 14.2 |
| No | 76.9 | 84.7 | 80.0 | 85.8 |
| Industry of employment | | | | |
| Agriculture, forestry, & fisheries | 2.1 | 0.6 | 1.8 | 0.6 |
| Mining | 0.8 | 0.03 | 1.1 | 0.2 |
| Construction | 9.4 | 0.9 | 8.1 | 0.9 |
| Manufacturing of durable goods | 18.0 | 7.8 | 14.9 | 5.7 |
| Manufacturing of nondurable | 9.7 | 8.8 | 8.6 | 6.1 |
| Transportation, communications, & other public utilities | 9.7 | 4.9 | 10.5 | 5.0 |
| Wholesale trade | 4.9 | 2.1 | 5.0 | 2.3 |
| Retail trade | 13.3 | 15.7 | 15.2 | 16.9 |
| Finance, insurance, & real estate | 4.7 | 9.5 | 4.5 | 8.5 |
| Business & repair services | 6.7 | 5.1 | 6.4 | 4.1 |
| Personal services including private households | 1.9 | 4.6 | 1.6 | 4.5 |
| Entertainment & recreation services | 0.8 | 0.8 | 1.5 | 1.6 |
| Professional & related services | 12.1 | 34.0 | 15.0 | 38.1 |
| Public administration | 6.0 | 5.3 | 5.9 | 5.6 |

Table 1 also shows change in three measures of labor market location: hours worked, union membership or coverage, and industry of employment. Men experienced nearly a 4 percent increase in part-time work between 1989 and 1995, while the percentage of women working part-time increased from 20 to 27 percent. Union membership or coverage declined for both groups, though slightly more for men than for women. The percentage distributions of men and women employed across industries showed some change. Both durable and nondurable manufacturing experienced slight declines, while retail trade and professional and related services had the greatest proportional increases.

Given the short time span of only seven years covered by this study, it is not surprising to find relatively small shifts in where men and women are working. Yet the observed slight increases in part-time work, declines in union membership or coverage, and the contraction of manufacturing do follow longer term and similar patterns of change in these characteristics. As noted above, hours worked, union membership or coverage, and industry location are all related to receipt of health benefits. Changes in these factors may contribute to changes in the overall distribution of employer-based health insurance.

A further question on the effects of labor market location is how well these factors, e.g., union membership, have preserved the health benefits so desired by workers. The statistics in Table 2 address this issue, showing the percentage of part and full-time workers who received health benefits across union and industry statuses. It appears that between 1989 and 1995 union membership or coverage was important in maintaining health benefits but only for full-time workers. Among part-time unionized workers, 64 percent received health benefits in 1989, but this declined to 57 percent in 1995. Still, part-time workers who were union members or were covered by a union contract fared far better in receiving health benefits than their nonunionized counterparts. Among part-time workers unaffiliated with a union, only 24 percent received health benefits in 1989, and this declined to 22 percent by 1995.

Receipt of employer-based health insurance clearly varies across industry. The highest percentages of workers receiving health benefits are found for those in manufacturing (durable or nondurable), professional and related services, and mining. In contrast, retail trade, business and repair services, agriculture, and personal services all have lower levels regardless of the number of hours worked.

Looking at variation in receipt of health benefits across industry categories between the two years, there appear to be distinct changes for part-time versus full-time workers. In some industries (nondurable manufacturing, wholesale trade, and retail trade), there were declines in receipt of employer-based health insurance for both part-time and full-time workers. Other industries

*Table 2.* Percentage Distributions on Receiving Employee-Based Health Insurance across Union and Industry Statuses for 1989 and 1995

| | *1989* | | *1995* | |
|---|---|---|---|---|
| | *Part-Time* | *Full-Time* | *Part-Time* | *Full-Time* |
| Union member or union coverage | | | | |
| Yes | 63.7 | 83.6 | 56.7 | 83.9 |
| No | 23.7 | 64.4 | 21.5 | 62.9 |
| Industry of employment | | | | |
| Agriculture, forestry, & fisheries | 15.8 | 34.4 | 16.8 | 33.1 |
| Mining | 65.0 | 78.1 | 45.3 | 82.7 |
| Construction | 25.8 | 56.2 | 31.0 | 51.2 |
| Manufacturing of durable goods | 47.7 | 78.3 | 57.0 | 79.2 |
| Manufacturing of nondurable | 39.9 | 74.7 | 34.9 | 72.0 |
| Transportation, communications, & other public utilities | 59.2 | 77.2 | 39.5 | 78.3 |
| Wholesale trade | 49.6 | 75.4 | 33.7 | 71.3 |
| Retail trade | 20.6 | 52.1 | 15.8 | 48.4 |
| Finance, insurance, & real estate | 43.8 | 70.1 | 28.2 | 70.4 |
| Business & repair services | 11.7 | 55.2 | 18.6 | 51.7 |
| Personal services including private households | 9.5 | 45.4 | 15.5 | 41.0 |
| Entertainment & recreation services | 0.0 | 60.7 | 18.2 | 56.9 |
| Professional & related services | 49.8 | 80.12 | 27.3 | 82.4 |
| Public administration | 31.9 | 71.2 | 44.6 | 70.3 |

experienced mixed changes, with increases in one group, declines in the other. Only in durable goods manufacturing were there proportional increases in health benefits for both part-time and full-time workers, though the change was slight for the latter. These increases are notable as durable goods manufacturing also experienced proportional declines in the percentages of men and women working in the industry (see Table 1). Effectively, both part-time and full-time workers who entered or retained positions in durable goods manufacturing improved their chances of receiving health benefits between 1989 and 1995.

The multivariate analysis of receipt of health benefits is shown in Table 3. Since the dependent variable is a dichotomous outcome, I have used logistic regression in the multivariate analysis. The statistics shown in Table 3 include the logistic regression coefficient (log odds) $b$ and the predicated probability $p$. The predicted probabilities are calculated such that all other variables in the model are set at their mean values; only the variable of interest is allowable to vary.

Measures of demographic characteristics, workers resources, and labor market location have significant effects in both years. Women and nonwhites

*Table 3.* Results of Logistic Regression Analyses Predicting Receipt of Employer-Based Health Insurance in 1989 and 1995

| | *1989* | | *1995* | |
|---|---|---|---|---|
| | *b* | *P* | *b* | *P* |
| Gender | | | | |
| Men | .42* | .69 | .34* | .64 |
| Women | — | .60 | — | .56 |
| Race | | | | |
| White | — | .66 | — | .62 |
| Black | –.28* | .59 | –.24* | .56 |
| Other | –.11 | .63 | –.34* | .53 |
| Education | | | | |
| Less than 12 years | –1.11* | .47 | –1.09* | .39 |
| 12 years | –.49* | .62 | –.34* | .58 |
| More than 12 years | — | .73 | — | .66 |
| Marital Status | | | | |
| Currently married | — | .63 | — | .59 |
| Postmarried | .19 | .68 | .45* | .69 |
| Never married | .18 | .68 | .01 | .59 |
| Age | | | | |
| 18–25 years | –.69* | .51 | –.86* | .42 |
| 26–35 years | –.09 | .66 | –.05 | .62 |
| 36–50 years | — | .68 | — | .63 |
| 51–64 years | .26* | .73 | .31* | .70 |
| Hours worked | | | | |
| Part-time | –1.40* | .36 | –1.46* | .32 |
| Full-time | — | .69 | — | .67 |
| Union member or union coverage | | | | |
| Yes | .93* | .80 | .99* | .78 |
| No | — | .61 | — | .56 |
| Industry of employment | | | | |
| Agriculture, forestry, & fisheries | –1.02* | .39 | –1.05* | .35 |
| Mining | .49 | .74 | .92 | .79 |
| Construction | –.51* | .52 | –.62* | .45 |
| Manufacturing of durable goods | .56* | .76 | .68 * | .75 |
| Manufacturing of nondurable | .49* | .74 | .39 * | .69 |
| Transportation, communications, & other public utilities | .32* | .71 | .37 * | .69 |
| Wholesale trade | .46* | .74 | .23 | .66 |
| Retail trade | –.38* | .55 | –.53 * | .47 |
| Finance, insurance, & real estate | .29 | .70 | .23 | .66 |
| Business & repair services | –.51* | .52 | –.44 * | .49 |
| Personal services including private households | –.71* | .47 | –.78 * | .41 |
| Entertainment & recreation services | –.64 | .48 | –.39 | .51 |
| Professional & related services | — | .64 | — | .60 |
| Public administration | .39* | .73 | .58 * | .73 |
| Constant | .79* | | .65 * | |
| Model chi-square | 14,682.61* | | 15,070.08 * | |

*Note:* For each year, the logged odds (*b*) and the predicted probabilities (*P*) are shown. The predicted probabilities are calculated such that all other variables in the model are set at their mean values. For 1989, $N = 13{,}149$; for 1995, $N = 13{,}673$. * $p < .001$

are less likely to receive health benefits in both years than their respective counterparts, even after controlling for measures of worker resources and labor market location. In 1989, men have a 69 percent likelihood of receiving health benefits, while this is only 60 percent for women. By 1995, these percentages have declined for both groups but an 8 percentage point gender gap remained. Blacks also are consistently less likely than whites to receive employed-based health insurance, with roughly 6 percentage points separating the two groups in each year. The findings are less consistent for the other race group. While there is no difference between whites and the other race group in 1989, whites are significantly more likely to receive health benefits in 1995.

Hypothesis 3 states that worker resources and labor market location will account for gender and race differences in the receipt of employed-based health insurance. However, the multivariate results on gender and race differences provide little support for the hypothesis. Although the gender gap in health benefits declines once worker resources and labor market location are taken into account, the reduction is quite minimal. Comparing the percentage distributions for gender in Table 1 to the predicted probabilities for gender in Table 3, it is appears that controlling for the other factors in the model reduces the gender gap in health benefits by only 3 to 4 percent. In contrast, race differences in health benefits actually increase once other demographic measures, worker resources, and labor market location are controlled.

As measures of worker resources, age and education both have significant effects on the likelihood of receiving health benefits in both years. Older workers are more likely to have employer-based health insurance than younger workers. The likelihood of health benefits also increases with additional years of education. Notably, using predicted odds (the antilog of *b*), it appears that those with more than twelve years of education are three times more likely in 1989 and 1995 to have health benefits than those with less than twelve years of education. As with income, receipt of health benefits is closely linked to the human capital a worker has gained through education.

The remaining individual level predictor, marital status, has only a slight influence. In 1989, marital status makes no difference in the receipt of health benefits. In 1995, however, one significant group difference is observed, with those who were previously married being more likely to receive health benefits than those who are currently married. Since those currently married may have an alternative source of health insurance coverage through their spouses' employers, this may reduce the likelihood of their receiving (or accepting) health benefits compared to previously married workers. It is not clear, though, why a similar effect was not found in comparing the currently married to never-married workers.

All three measures of labor market location—hours worked, union status, industry of employment—are significantly related to the probability of receiving health benefits, even after controlling for worker resources. Part-time workers are much less likely to receive health benefits than full-time workers. Workers with union coverage, though, are more likely than other workers to receive health benefits. In 1989, union workers have a predicted 80 percent chance of receiving health benefits, compared to 61 percent for nonunion workers. For both groups, the likelihood of receiving health benefits declined by 1995, more substantially for nonunion workers than union workers.

The industry in which a worker is employed also significantly influences the receipt of health benefits. In 1989, the industries with the highest probabilities (.70 or higher) of receiving health benefits include mining, manufacturing of durable or nondurable goods, transportation and other public utilities, wholesale trade, finance, insurance, and real estate, and public administration. In 1995, mining, manufacturing of durable goods, and public administration were the only industries in which workers had a 70 percent chance or better of receiving health benefits. Industries with the lowest chances of receipt of health benefits include certain service industries (business and repair, personal services, and entertainment and recreation), construction, and retail trade. Workers in each of these industries have roughly a 50 percent or less chance of receiving health benefits in each year.

Industry differences in health benefits likely reflect variation across industries in average pay levels, firm size, demographic composition, as well as patterns of growth and decline (e.g., downsizing). For example, the significant difference observed between retail trade and the reference category, professional and related services, may be related to variation in the gender composition of each industry. Since industries with higher percentage female tend to have lower pay levels overall, the likelihood of receiving health benefits also may decline with increases in the proportion female. These findings argue for further research on the specific characteristics of industries that are related to receipt of health benefits.

In a final analysis, I tested to see whether the effects of the predictor variables changed between 1989 and 1995. This was done in a single model combining data for 1989 and 1995. In the analysis, I regressed the dependent variable, receipt of employer-based health insurance, on the predictor variables along with interactions between each predictor variable and a dummy variable for the year of the survey. By observing the significance of the interactions between each predictor with the year variable, I was able to evaluate whether or not the effects of the predictor variables changed between 1989 and 1995. However, none of the interaction terms were significant. This suggests that while sociodemographic factors, worker resources, and location in the labor market had significant effects on the likelihood of receiving health benefits in 1989 and 1995, the effects of these factors did not significantly change between the two years. Instead, these influences appear to be stable in their effects over this period.

## DISCUSSION AND CONCLUSION

This research has furthered knowledge about employer-based health insurance, its relationship to labor market characteristics, and how these factors may have special consequences for women and nonwhites. It was found that between 1989 and 1995, the percentage of workers receiving employer-based health insurance declined significantly. In addition, demographic characteristics, worker resources, and labor market location each played a role in determining whether or not a worker received health benefits in 1989 and 1995. However, the effects of these factors did not change between the two years; the positive or negative effects of demographic characteristics, worker resources, and labor market location remained stable from 1989 to 1995. This finding is striking given the major economic shifts, including recession and recovery, that occurred during the period.

The findings, as well as limitations, of this study suggest possible paths for future research. First, this study has a limited time frame of 1989 to 1995. Important shifts in the likelihood of receiving health benefits might better appear over a longer period of observation. However, such studies would be dependent on available data with consistent measures of health benefits. Second, alternative sources of health insurance might be considered in the analysis, such as receiving health benefits through a spouse's employer. Workers with viable alternatives for health coverage might forgo health benefits from their own employer. Finally, while worker resources and labor market location made little difference in reducing the gender and race gaps in health benefits, these factors may operate differently by gender and race in their effects on health benefits. For example, women and men in the service industry may have differing likelihoods of receiving health benefits because of gender-typed occupations they hold in those industries.

Understanding which labor market factors are related to employer-based health insurance will be important to policymakers as they consider changes in the health care system related to the heightened role of employers contributing to health care access through insurance benefits. Given the link between health insurance and access to quality health care, long-term trends in the receipt of employer-based health insurance may explain group differences in health care use and health status. Further, the pattern of recent economic changes that may alter the probability of receiving employer-based health insurance likely overlap with gender and race distinctions in the labor market. While this study identifies key differences in health coverage from employers, there is much yet to be explained about this important work outcome. Without additional research that focuses on these economic changes and their consequences for women and nonwhites, policymakers will be unable to anticipate and address significant gaps in the U.S. health care system.

## REFERENCES

Alpert, W. T. and M. N. Ozawa. 1986. "Fringe Benefits of Workers in Nonmanufacturing Industries: They Vary by Employee Income, the Marginal Tax Rate, Union Status, and Firm Size." *American Journal of Economics and Sociology* 45:173–88.

Baron, J. N. and W. T. Bielby. 1985. "Organizational Barriers to Gender Equality: Sex Segregation of Jobs and Opportunities." Pp. 233–51 in *Gender and the Life Course,* edited by A. S. Rossi. Hawthorne, NY: Aldine de Gruyter.

Beck, E. M., P. Horan, and C. Tolbert. 1978. "Stratification in a Dual Economy: A Sectoral Model of Earnings Determination." *American Sociological Review* 43:704–20.

Becker, G. 1971. *The Economics of Discrimination.* Chicago: University of Chicago Press.

Bibb, R. and W. F. Form. 1977. "The Effects of Industrial, Occupational, and Sex Stratification on Wages in Blue-Collar Markets." *Social Forces* 55:974–96.

Bureau of Labor Statistics, Department of Labor. 1993. "BLS Reports on Employee Benefits in the United States, 1990–91." *Bureau of Labor Statistics Report* 93(4, June).

Conference Board. 1996. "Part-Time Employment." *Work-Family Roundtable* 63(10).

Cornfield, D. 1991. "The U.S. Labor Movement: Its Development and Impact on Social Inequality and Politics." *Annual Review of Sociology* 17:27–49.

Curme, M. A., B. T. Hirsch, and D. A. MacPherson. 1990. "Union Membership and Contract Coverage in the United States, 1983–1988." *Industrial and Labor Relations Review* 4:45–29.

Doeringer, P. B. and M. J. Piore. 1971. *Internal Labor Markets and Manpower Analysis.* Lexington, MA: Heath.

Freeman, R. B. 1981. "The Effect of Unionism on Fringe Benefits." *Industrial and Labor Relations Review* 34:489–509.

Galbraith, J. K. 1973. *Economics and the Public Purpose.* Boston: Houghton-Mifflin.

Granovetter, M. 1981. "Toward a Sociology Theory of Income Differences." Pp. 11–47 in *Sociological Perspectives on Labor Markets,* edited by I. Berg. New York: Academic Press.

Hachen, D. S. 1990. "Three Models of Job Mobility in Labor Markets." *Work and Occupations* 17:320–54.

Harrison, D., A. J. Tuchfarber, A. E. Smith, and L. A. Cubbins. 1994. *National Health Survey, University of Cincinnati Medical Center Summary of Results.* Institute for Health Policy and Health Services and the Institute for Policy Research, University of Cincinnati.

Hodson, R. 1986. "Modeling the Effects of Industrial Structure on Wages and Benefits." *Work and Occupations* 13:488–510.

Kalleberg, A. L., M. Wallace, and R. P. Althauser. 1981. "Economic Segmentation, Worker Power, and Income Inequality." *American Journal of Sociology* 87: F651–83.

Knoke, D. 1994. "Cui Bono? Employee Benefit Packages." *American Behavioral Scientist* 37:963–78.

Levit, K. R., G. L. Olin, and S. W. Letsch. 1992. "Americans' Health Insurance Coverage, 1981–91." *Health Care Financing Review* 14:31–57.

Nelson, J. I. 1994. "Work and Benefits: The Multiple Problems of Service Sector Employment." *Social Problems* 41:240–56.

Perman, L. and B. Stevens. 1989. "Industrial Segregation and the Gender Distribution of Fringe Benefits." *Gender & Society* 3:388–404.

Piacentini, J. and J. D. Foley. 1992. *EBRI Data Book on Employee Benefits,* 2nd ed. Washington, DC: EBRI.

Renner, C. and V. Navarro. 1989. "Why Is Our Population of Uninsured and Underinsured Persons Growing? The Consequences of the 'Deindustrialization' of the United States." *International Journal of Health Services* 19:433–42.

Root, L. S. 1985. "Employee Benefits and Social Welfare: Complement and Conflict." *Annals of the American Academy of Political and Social Science* 479:101–18.

Seccombe, K. and C. Amey. 1995. "Playing by the Rules and Losing: Health Insurance and the Working Poor." *Journal of Health and Social Behavior* 36:168–81.

Seccombe, K. and L. Beeghley. 1992. "Gender and Medical Insurance: A Test of Human Capital Theory." *Gender & Society* 6:283–300.

Snider, S. 1995. "Characteristics of the Part-Time Work Force and Part-Time Employee Participation in Health and Pension Benefits." *Journal of Labor Research* 16: 239–48.

Solnick, L. M. 1985. "The Effect of Blue-Collar Unions on White-Collar Wages and Fringe Benefits." *Industrial and Labor Relations* 38:236–43.

Sørensen, A. B. and N. B. Tuma. 1981. "Labor Market Structures and Job Mobility." Pp. 67–94 in *Research in Social Stratification and Mobility,* Vol. 1, edited by D. J. Treiman and R. R. Robinson. Greenwich, CT: JAI.

Swartz, K. 1992. "A Research Note on the Characteristics of Workers without Employer-Group Health Insurance Based on the March 1988 Current Population Survey." Pp. 13–19 in *Health Benefits and the Workforce.* Washington, DC: Pension and Welfare Benefits Administration, U.S. Department of Labor.

Thurow, L. C. 1969. *Poverty and Discrimination.* Washington, DC: Brookings Institution.

Tilly, C. 1991. "Reasons for the Continuing Growth of Part-Time Employment." *Monthly Labor Review* 114(3):10–18.

Treiman, D. and H. Hartmann. 1981. *Women, Work, and Wages Equal Pay for Jobs of Equal Value.* Report of the Committee on Occupational Classification and Analysis. Washington, DC: National Academy Press.

U.S. Bureau of the Census. 1993. *Statistical Abstract of the United States 1993,* 113th ed. Washington, DC: USGPO.

Uchitelle, L. and N. R. Kleinfield. 1996. "The Downsizing of America." *New York Times,* March 3, p. 1.

Wiatrowski, W. J. 1995. "Who Really Has Access to Employer-Provided Health Benefits?" *Monthly Labor Review* 118(6):36–44.

# The Impact of Family Caregiving to the Elderly on the American Workplace: Who Is Affected and What Is Being Done? 14

Judy Singleton

Because many family caregivers are now also in the workplace, it is far less possible to sharply separate the work and family lives of employees. Helping employees balance both spheres of their lives has become a more pressing issue for businesses in the last decade. By providing resources and programs that acknowledge the lives of employees outside work, companies hope to increase the focus and concentration of employees while at work. According to a 1995 Hewitt Associates (1987) survey of 1,050 major U.S. companies between 1990 and 1995, the number of employers offering programs and policies that help employees balance their work and family lives increased significantly. Child care assistance was found to be offered by 85 percent of employers in the survey, up from 64 percent in 1990. Eldercare benefits, however, more than doubled, from 12 percent in 1990 to 26 percent in 1995. This chapter summarizes the state of eldercare support in the U.S.

## WHAT IS ELDERCARE?

Studies in the area of caregiving for the elderly focus on different aspects of caregiving, ranging from very specific skilled care services to a vast range of general assistance, such as providing companionship. In their review of eldercare research to date, Tennstedt and Gonyea (1994) report that definitions of caregiving usually fall into one of three categories:

1. caregiving in dyadic relationships—the caregiving spouse and offspring, other kin or friend;
2. age of the elderly care receiver as a variable; and
3. caregiving intensity or involvement—defined by minimum number of hours per week or certain types of help (i.e., personal care vs. laundry).

But what is caregiving? Caregiving can be defined as unpaid assistance for the physical and emotional needs of another person. Actual service provision can range from a few hours per week to twenty-four-hour care, with or without assistance outside the family (Clark and Weber 1996). This service provision generally can be categorized by helping with activities of daily living (ADLs) or instrumental activities of daily living (IADLs). ADLs include activities such as eating, getting in or out of bed or a chair, dressing, bathing, toileting, or controlling bladder or bowels. IADLs involve meal preparation, housekeeping, running errands, shopping, taking medications, using the telephone, transportation, and money management (Schneider, Galper, Gottesman, Kohn, Morrell, Staroschik, and Sterthous 1982). Providing companionship and home maintenance are significant IADLs as well (Anastas, Gibeau, and Larson 1990).

There is increasing use of the term "dependent care" to connote policies and benefits for employees needing to balance family responsibilities with work. Though there may be similarities in the day-to-day problems of caring for a child or an elderly parent, there are also distinct differences between the two situations. Like child rearing, meeting the dependency needs of a parent may be extremely demanding physically and psychologically. Unlike child rearing, in which the child's physical and emotional dependence gradually diminishes, parent-caring involves the caregiver in meeting the sustained or increasing physical and emotional needs of the older person (Archbold 1983). Some research has indicated that eldercare can be more stressful than child care (Wagner, Creedon, Sasala, and Neal 1989).

Variations obviously exist among eldercare recipients, yet there are some common characteristics. Typically, one finds that the eldercare recipient is a widowed mother or mother-in-law aged seventy-five years old or older (Anastas et al. 1990).

The income of the elderly person receiving care is often limited (ibid.). It is not surprising that women are more often care recipients, for men have higher death rates than women at every age. In 1994, elderly women outnumbered elderly men by a ratio of 3 to 2—20 million to 14 million (Economics and Statistics Administration, U.S. Department of Commerce 1995). Advancing age increases this ratio: at ages sixty-five to sixty-nine, the ration is 6 to 5; at age eighty-five and over, however, it reaches 5 to 2. Elderly men are also more likely than elderly women to be married. In 1993, 75 percent of noninstitutionalized elderly men were married and living with a spouse compared to 41 percent of women. For both sexes, increasing age increases the chances of living alone, but women are more likely to live alone than men (Economics and Statistics Administration, U.S. Department of Commerce 1995).

One percent of people aged sixty-five to seventy-four years old lived in a nursing home in 1990; almost one in four people aged eighty-five or older did. With advancing age, there is greater likelihood of chronic, limiting illnesses or conditions, such as arthritis, diabetes, osteoporosis, and senile dementia. Other people are needed to help one if such illnesses or conditions arise. In 1990–1991, 50 percent of those noninstitutionalized persons aged eighty-five or older needed some type of help with activities of daily living; 9 percent of those aged sixty-five to sixty-nine years old did (Economics and Statistics Administration, U.S. Department of Commerce 1995).

## STRAIN AND COSTS TO WORKING CAREGIVERS

The estimated dollar cost to caregiving employees is $4.8 billion for unpaid labor, lost wages, and missed opportunities (Spalter-Roth and Hartmann 1990). Brody, Kleban, Johnsen, Hoffman, and Schoonover (1987) found that 28 percent of caregiving daughters must quit their jobs, thus sacrificing earnings, employee benefits, retirement benefits, and a source of personal satisfaction (Rimmer 1983). Burdens working caregivers bear have effects in the workplace in the form of reduced attendance and concentration or poor job performance in general. The strains are also felt at home in aspects of family life, such as in relations with spouse or children or in such psychological symptoms as depression (Anastas et al. 1990). While studies indicate these "women in the middle" are accomplishing much in the realm of caregiving, albeit with costs, they also suggest that these women feel they are not doing enough (Brody 1985). Recent studies of caregiving have found that daughters who care for a parent continue to meet their caregiving responsibilities even though they are employed (Brody and Schoonover 1986; Cantor 1983).

Findings by the Families and Work Institute mirror Brody et al.'s (1987) research. A recent study of 305 employees caring for elderly relatives demonstrates that 25 percent had changed jobs due to their caregiving responsibilities, 39 percent reported being distracted at work, 22 percent had considered quitting, and 14 percent actually had quit work because of the caregiving responsibilities (Galinsky, Bond, and Freidman 1993).

## STUDIES ON ELDERCARE

As the phenomenon of eldercare is a relatively new occurrence, most studies and meta-analyses have been done in the past fifteen years.

According to Tennstedt and Gonyea (1994), the prevalence of the dual roles of caregiver and employee can be addressed from two perspectives, and the rates of employed caregivers viewed from each perspective will differ accordingly. That one-third of caregivers are employed has been found repeatedly in national and regional studies. By excluding spousal caregivers who are less likely to be employed because of advanced age, however,

Tennstedt and Gonyea found that employment rates among caregivers approach 50 percent.

Tennstedt and Gonyea report that the second perspective in looking at the dual roles of caregiver and employee reviews samples of employees recruited from specific corporations. There is less consistency among these studies, ranging from as little as 2 percent of the work force to one-third or more. Across the board, corporations estimate that about 20 percent of their employees are involved in caregiving.

Gorey, Rice, and Brice (1992) reviewed seventeen surveys on employment and caregiving and found that the different studies' achieved response rate as well as the chosen operational definition of caregiving were the two primary factors influencing the prevalence rates of caregiving in the workplace. When a broader definition of caregiving was used in conjunction with a lower response rate, Gorey et al. found a high prevalence rate of caregiving among employees. In studies in which the response rate was less than 60 percent, the mean prevalence rate was about 25.3 percent. In contrast, in studies with at least a 60 percent response rate, the mean prevalence rate was about 7.4 percent. Overall, Gorey et al. concluded that it was "reasonable to assume that at least 8 percent of the work force [had] some elder care responsibilities" (1992:414).

## DEMOGRAPHIC FORCES AFFECTING ELDERCARE

Within the family mosaic, women traditionally function in the caregiving role for parents in need of assistance (Brody 1990; Cantor 1983; Stone, Cafferata, and Sangl 1987). Yet unlike their mothers before them, modern-day women caring for elderly parents have more roles, and thus more role demands upon them. These "women in the middle" (Brody 1981:471) are generally in the middle from a generational standpoint, with aging parents as well as children at home, and in the middle in that the demands of various roles compete for their time and energy (ibid.). Traditional roles as wives, homemakers, and mothers are more often coupled with roles as paid workers and as caregiving daughters to dependent parents.

The woman in the middle is a prototype as there are many variations in the ages and stages of life at which one may become a woman in the middle (ibid.). However, what women in the middle share is a situation produced by major demographic shifts and changes in women's life-styles:

- Kin networks are become increasingly top-heavy, with more older family members than younger. For the first time in history, the average married couple has more parents than children (Preston 1984).
- Due to lengthening life expectancy and lower birth rates, shifts are occurring in the time spent in various family roles. For example, mid-

dle-generation women in the future will probably spend, on average, more years with parents over sixty-five years of age than with children under the age of eighteen (Watkins, Menken, and Bongaarts 1987).

- Declining birth rates will also lead to smaller sibling networks and therefore it will be more likely that women will be only children or the only daughter (Kola and Dunkle 1988).
- Women are marrying at a later age, increasing the likelihood of caring for younger children and parents at the same time (ibid.).
- The divorce rate may also affect the prevalence of eldercare. There will be fewer spouses to provide care, and adult children may be faced with caring for divorced parents living in separate locations (Clark and Weber 1996).

Demographic changes reflect not only the large numerical and proportionate increase in the older population but also the lengthening of the time people are elderly. The number of elderly persons has almost doubled since 1960, from nearly 17 million at that time to a projected 51.1 million by 2020 and 66.6 million by 2040. By 2040 people ages sixty-five and older will compose 23 percent of the total U.S. population (Siegel and Taeuber 1986). The most rapid growth will occur among people who are eighty-five plus. This age group will triple by 2020 and nearly double again by around 2040–2060, when the baby boom generation will join the ranks of the oldest old (Soldo and Manton 1985). Although most older people over sixty-five years of age are not in need of a personal caregiver, overall estimates of the proportion of elderly who need supportive services are roughly one-third of the sixty-five plus age group, or 10 million people (Schick and Schick 1994). Those oldest-old, aged eighty-five and older, are the most likely to require assistance (Scharlach 1987:627).

Occurring almost simultaneously with this growth of the aging population is the growth in numbers of women entering the work force in unprecedented numbers. There has been a fourfold jump in women in the labor force the past fifty years (ibid.). While young and single women used to predominate in the work force, now the largest category of working women is middle-aged, married women (Bengtson and DeTerre 1980). Within this decade, it is expected that women will continue to enter the labor force in substantial numbers; and by the year 2000, 48 percent of the work force will be women, and 61 percent of working age women will be employed (Johnston and Packer 1987).

## TRAITS OF COMPANIES THAT HAVE ELDERCARE

There are some common characteristics shared by companies that provide eldercare support. Liebig (1993) found that employers with eldercare programs are generally much larger corporations. They also have greater proportions of female employees. Close to two-fifths of these companies have a work force of 61–70 percent female compared to 53 percent for employers that do not have eldercare programs. In Liebig's study (1993), thirty-eight percent of the companies that had eldercare programs had large proportions of female managers, ranging from 31 to 50 percent. In contrast, 48 percent of the employers without eldercare programs had rather small proportions of women mangers, ranging from 10 to 20 percent.

Liebig also found that companies with eldercare programs reported "extreme awareness" of work-family conflicts on the part of individuals at a rate nearly double of that of companies without such programs (62 vs. 32 percent). Employers with eldercare programs also were more likely to have higher levels of awareness of work-family conflicts than employers without such programs.

Fifty-three percent of the individual respondents in Liebig's study of sixty-six employers in California indicated that they felt eldercare concerns were very to extremely important issues in their company while only 11 percent of individual respondents in companies without eldercare programs felt that eldercare concerns were very important issues in their companies.

Liebig found that 93 percent of companies with eldercare programs reported they established benefits to help their employees with their family concerns, whereas only 31 percent of companies without eldercare programs report this. Instead, these latter companies were more likely to view improving the lives of family caregivers as the responsibility of the government and employee, or solely an employee responsibility.

Liebig identified three barriers to developing eldercare programs in the companies she studied whether or not they had an eldercare program in place: high costs, low awareness of employee-caregiver needs, and a lack of information about program development. Lack of employee demand and lack of community resources were identified by both companies with and without eldercare as inhibiting eldercare program development. Top management support, cost effectiveness, and managers' experiences were influential factors for the companies that had eldercare programs.

What may be most important, however, for companies that have success with eldercare benefits is a conducive workplace culture. The norms and values that regulate behavior at work are important. Any company can have a multitude of benefits, but if managers place many stipulations upon using benefits, employees may never feel comfortable taking them. Real change depends not only on having the policies in writing, but also having an atmosphere in which people feel free to use them. It is necessary to have the commitment of senior managers for the workplace culture to accept support for work-family issues. More middle and senior managers may appreciate the demands that eldercare makes on employees, since they are usually at ages when eldercare is closer to their own current needs than child care (National Institute for Social Work 1995).

Some employers do not acknowledge that eldercare is an issue for their employees. Some assume basic benefit packages will meet the need. Others are just beginning to evaluate and possibly implement such programs in the future. Still others have full-scale eldercare programs in place. "Eldercare is where child care was 15 or 20 years ago," says Diane Piktialis, vice-president of Work/Family Directions, a Boston consulting firm that provides elder- and child-care resources to employers (Lawlor 1995:40).

Fran Rodgers, the founder of Work/Family Directions, is trying to promote eldercare programs in the corporate world. Her company, one of the nation's largest providers of work/family resource and referral services, has grown from serving one company covering two hundred thousand employees in 1988 to sixty clients representing over two million employees today (MacPherson 1995). In 1992, her company pulled together a landmark collaboration of over one hundred companies, called the American Business Collaboration for Quality Dependent Care, to fund work-family community services for employees (Gordon 1993; Lawlor 1995). The Collaboration, which is referred to as the largest private endeavor of its kind, devoted $25.4 million to creating three hundred new or improved care programs for babies, school children and the elderly in forty-four communities around the United States. The second phase of this collaborative effort began just recently. Twenty-one of the nation's largest employers will be giving up to $100 million to the American Business Collaborative for Quality Dependent Care. This second phase of the 1992 start-up now includes one thousand projects in thirty-one states and the District of Columbia (MacPherson 1995). Has it been successful? Of the $27 million invested as of June 1995, only about 6 percent ($1,620,000) has been for eldercare programs (Lawlor 1995). Though the majority has gone for child care, the over $1.5 million for eldercare demonstrates progress.

## ELDERCARE SUPPORT BEING PROVIDED

Some benefits are not actually defined as eldercare specific, but instead are part of a basic benefit package. Some employers may not even realize that these benefits are being used for eldercare purposes.

Caregivers use basic benefits such as vacation, personal leave, and sick leave extensively for eldercare purposes. One recent study (Liebig 1993) demonstrated that nearly two-thirds of all respondents from companies with specific eldercare programs as well as those from companies with no designated eldercare programs reported that they used vacation and personal leave for eldercare purposes. However, this same study found that employees working in companies in which no specific eldercare benefits are available use sick time much less (30 percent) than employees in companies in which specific eldercare programs are available.

Other benefits are available for eldercare assistance but are not necessarily designed for that purpose. Flexible spending accounts/dependent care assistance plans, made available by section 125 of the Internal Revenue Code, are a relatively new phenomenon with the regulations being in effect only since 1984 (Denton, Love, and Slate 1990). This tax credit benefit involves using pretax dollars for medical expenses and/or dependent care. Section 125 of the Internal Revenue Code allows the money deducted from the gross pay of each paycheck to be exempted from both income and Social Security taxes. After paying the expenses, the employee submits receipts to the employer for reimbursement. This option requires only administrative support from the employer, and it is fairly widely used for child care (Creedon 1987). However, because dependent care spending accounts used for eldercare are subject to stricter legal restrictions than those stipulations established for child care, these accounts are rarely used by employees for eldercare (Hewitt Associates 1995).

Flextime, another benefit, allows employees to work nonstandard hours. Companies differ in this benefit. Some allow flexible variability in alternative work schedules; others allow changes only with advance notice and difficulty (Denton et al. 1990). A University of Bridgeport survey of employee assistance programs (Creedon 1987) found that flextime was the most frequent response to employee's requests for help with eldercare assistance.

Information services likewise vary greatly among companies. Examples of this benefit include seminars, caregiver fairs, printed materials, and referral services. In their study of Chicago organizations, Denton et al. (1990) found that most companies disseminated some type of information, usually newsletters or interoffice memos that supervisors share with employees.

Employee assistance programs (EAPs) are now a popular benefit. Hewitt Associates' 1995 survey of 1,050 companies found that EAPs were offered by 84 percent of employers, up 11 percent from 1990. They were most commonly provided through a contract with an outside agency. These programs were developed in response to substance-abuse problems that interfered with employees' ability to work effectively (Denton et al. 1990). However, many EAPs now provide counseling and referral services for financial problems, spouse and child abuse, child care, eldercare, and other marital and family problems.

Flexplace, sometimes called telecommuting, allows employees to work at a location other than the primary workplace. Usually the location is the individual employee's home. With flexplace, a caregiver can have more time at home with a care receiver.

Subsidies or vouchers may also be provided to employees to use for employer-provided services (most commonly day care) or with employer-contracted agencies. Employees who use the services of such agencies are issued vouchers, which are given to the specific agency when a service is provided. The employer then reimburses the agency upon receipt of the voucher. However, Denton et al. (1990) found no employer who provided vouchers for eldercare.

Although health insurance is available for many employees, most plans cover only the employee, spouse, and children. There are plans, however, that do offer extended family member coverage. Long-term care benefits available to retirees have become more common. The Health Insurance Association of America (HIAA) reported large increases in recent years in the number of Americans purchasing long-term care protection through individual or employer-sponsored plans, or as riders to life insurance policies (Weldon 1996). Premium costs vary immensely, depending on the employee's age and level of coverage.

The Family and Medical Leave Act (FMLA) provides up to twelve work weeks of unpaid leave within any twelve-month period for one or more of the following reasons:

1. the birth of a child of the employee and to care for this child;
2. the adoption (or foster care) of a child by the employee;
3. caring for the spouse, child, or parent of the employee; if the spouse, child, or parent has a serious health condition;
4. a serious health condition that makes the employee unable to perform the functions of the position.

The FMLA does have limitations, however, namely that the leave is unpaid and that employers with less than fifty employees are exempt from it. Per Kittay (1995), the majority of workers are employed in companies with less than fifty employees. Moreover, the 1995 Hewitt Associates survey found that 72 percent of employers require unpaid leave to be offset with some or all paid leave provided.

## SERVICES OFFERED BY PUBLIC AGENCIES

The University of Bridgeport (Creedon 1987) indicates that some companies offer their own in-house employee assistance programs or contract out for such services to help employees with an array of issues. Other companies are investigating the services offered by the network of public agencies, national organizations, and local agencies all over the country.

The National Association of Area Agencies on Aging has conducted research exploring the prevalence and the impact of caregiving on full-time employees, and the findings of this research are being used nationwide to promote employer awareness of caregiving by employees and to then develop creative responses tailored for each community. The American Association of Retire Persons (AARP) serves approximately three hundred corporate clients each year with technical assistance developing responses to eldercare issues and information resources for employee caregivers. Similarly, the American Society on Aging also serves corporate clients primarily in the area of training and education rather than direct employee service.

The Travelers Companies implemented their own caregiving survey in 1985. Based on the result of this survey, they initiated the following programs to assist employees and retirees caring for older relatives and friends: caregiving information fairs, lunchtime educational seminars, weekly support groups, video programs on monitors, caregiving books in the corporate library, and articles on caregiving topics in the company's newspapers.

In addition to eldercare services provided to their own employees, The Travelers Companies serve numerous corporations nationwide with a long-term care insurance product for employees, their spouses, and parents. The product includes home care and adult care, and does not require hospitalization prior to nursing home care. The Travelers Companies also offer consultation to companies considering employee caregiving programs.

Across the country, family service agencies are active in providing employee assistance programs. Although not specifically geared to eldercare benefits, Alperin (1993) found a nearly 70 percent increase in the number of family service agencies offering eldercare/supportive services to aging from 1980 to 1990. Overall, this same study found that agency directors reported a nearly 55 percent increase in the demand for eldercare services during this same time period. And, while family service agencies increased their provision of services in almost all areas, the most growth (283.3 percent) occurred in services to businesses and industry.

## COSTS OF ELDERCARE FOR EMPLOYERS

There is much discussion regarding the employer costs for working caregivers; however, few studies have analyzed actual dollar amounts. One that has is The MetLife Study of Employer Costs for Working Caregivers (Washington Business Group on Health 1995). This study of a major manufacturer with a salaried population of 86,952 persons found that 2 percent, or 1,739 individual employees, were providing personal eldercare to older spouses, parents, parents-in-law, and grandparents at a total cost of $5.5 million dollars per year. These costs represent solely those associated with ADLs such as eating, bathing, dressing, and toileting. Costs associated with long-distance caregivers and others who are unavailable to provide day-to-day personal care or work—providing only IADLs, managing or supervising finances, medications, transportation, errand-running, cooking, etc.—were not included in this study (ibid.).

The MetLife Study of Employer costs for Working Caregivers calculated costs associated with salaried employees providing personal care to older adults by using estimates in three areas: employee productivity, management/administration, and health/mental health care. One limitation of this study is that it focused only on personal care, which may be understandable in that the study was done for an insurance company; almost all long-term care insurance plans provide coverage only for skilled services, and not for custodial services such as running errands, housekeeping, and cooking. The researchers for the study did note that there appears to be a large gap between the services that caregivers spend the most time providing (IADLs) and those services for which coverage is provided under long-term care insurance plans, that is, skilled and personal care. The most time spent by employees on caregiving activities fell into the IADLs, not the personal care activities.

Similarly, Scharlach (1994) estimated that eldercare responsibilities costs employers, on average, $2,500 per caregiving employee per year, or roughly about $17 billion dollars. He also estimates that companies recover only about one-third of every dollar spent on eldercare benefits. In contrast, Diane Piktialis, vice-president of Work/Family Directions, reports that resource-and-referral services save companies $2 to $3 for every dollar spent on them for caregiving programs (Lawlor 1995).

Some employers, however, insist that dependent care benefits are costly, rather than beneficial, to their companies. In particular, some employers argue that the FMLA has created higher costs to companies by requiring that health insurance coverage be maintained for employees on leave while simultaneously the company incurs the costs for recruitment and training of replacement workers for these employees (Tennstedt and Gonyea 1994).

## CONCLUSIONS

There are programs and services available to assist individuals in caring for their elderly parents or loved ones. However, with more care being transferred to families from hospitals, the medical professions, and the government (Glazer 1993), it is unlikely the current sources will provide individuals with enough help in the future. Additional research is needed to assess the costs to employers for eldercare programs as well as to weigh the benefits of community partnerships in the provision of such benefits. Work-family benefits from employers can allow employees to care for elderly persons; however, without adequate community service programs to assist workers in providing eldercare, workers who care for elderly relatives will have to take time from work to help them. With the rise in the proportion of elderly people in the United States and the steady growth of women in the work force, work-family conflicts experienced by adults of working age seem likely to increase unless private and public action is taken that will help to reduce them. The availability, cost, and quality of care for elderly persons are important concerns that cannot be ignored in today's workplace.

## REFERENCES

Alperin, D. 1993. "Family Service Agencies: Responding to Need in the 1980s." *Social Work* 38(5):597–602.

Anastas, J., J. Gibeau, and P. Larson. 1990. "Working Families and Eldercare: A National Perspective in an Aging America." *Social Work* Vol. 35(5):405–11.

Archbold, P. G. 1983. "Impact of Parent-Caring on Women." *Family Relations* 32:39–45.

Bengtson, L. and M. DeTerre. 1980. "Aging and Family Relations." *Marriage and Family Review* 3:51–76.

Brody, E. M. 1981. "Women in the Middle and Family Help to Older People." *The Gerontologist* 21:471–80.

———. 1985. "Parent Care as a Normative Family Stress." *Gerontologist* 25:19–29.

———. 1990. *Women in the Middle: Their Parent-Care Years.* New York: Springer.

Brody, E. M., M. H. Kleban, P. T. Johnsen, C. Hoffman, and O. B. Schoonover. 1987. "Work Status and Parent Care: A Comparison of Four Groups of Women." *Gerontologist* 27:201–8.

Brody, E. M. and C. B. Schoonover. 1986. "Patterns of Parent-Care When Adult Daughters Work and When They Do Not." *Gerontologist* 26:372–80.

Cantor, M. H. 1983. "Strain among Caregivers: A Study of Experience in the United States." *Gerontologist* 23:597–604.

Clark, J. and K. Weber. 1996. "Family Relationships—Elderly Caregiving." *Human Environmental Sciences,* publication GH6657 [on-line]. Available at http://muextension.missouri.edu/xplor/hesquide/humanrel/gn6657.htm (March 15).

Creedon, M. (Ed.). 1987. *Issues for an Aging America: Employees & Eldercare: A Briefing Book.* Southport, CT: Creative Services, Inc.

Denton, K., L. Love, and R. Slate. 1990. "Eldercare in the '90s: Employee Responsibility, Employer Challenge." *Families in Society* 71(June):349–59.

Economics and Statistics Administration, U.S. Department of Commerce. 1995. "Sixty-Five Plus in the United States." In *U.S. Census Bureau Statistical Brief* [online]. Available at http://www.census.gov/ftp/pub/socdemo/www/agebrief.html.

Galinsky, E., J. T. Bond, and D. Freidman. 1993. *The Changing Workforce: Highlights of the National Study.* New York: Families and Work Institute.

Glazer, N. 1993. *Women's Paid and Unpaid Labor: The Work Transfer in Health Care and Retailing.* Philadelphia: Temple University Press.

Gordon, S. 1993. "Helping Corporations Care." *Working Woman* 18(1):30–32.

Gorey, K. M., R. W. Rice, and G. C. Brice. 1992. "The Prevalence of Elder Care Responsibilities among the Work Force Population." *Research on Aging* 14:399–417.

Hewitt Associates. 1995. *Work and Family Benefits Provided by Major U.S. Employers in 1995.* Lincolnshire, IL: Author.

Johnston, W. and A. Packer. 1987. *Workforce 2000: Work and Workers for the Twenty-First Century.* Indianapolis, IN: Hudson Institute.

Kittay, E. 1995. "Taking Dependency Seriously: The Family and Medical Leave Act Considered in Light of the Social Organization of Dependency Work and Gender Equality." *Hypatia* 10(1):8–29.

Kola, L. and R. Dunkle. 1988. "Eldercare in the Workplace." *Social Casework* 69(November):569–74.

Lawlor, J. 1995. "Parental Guidance." *Working Woman* 20(6):37–41, 70, 73.

Liebig, P. 1993. "Factors Affecting the Development of Employer-Sponsored Eldercare Programs: Implications for Employed Caregivers." *Journal of Women & Aging* 5(1):59–78.

MacPherson, D. 1995. "It's a Family Affair." *Relocation Journal & Real Estate News* [on-line]. Available at http://www.relojournal.com/dec95/family/htm (December).

National Institute for Social Work. 1995. "Work and Family Life." In *National Institute of Social Work Policy Briefings, No. 8* [on-line]. Available at http://www.nisw.org.uk/polb/fulltext/niswpl8.html (January).

Preston, S. 1984. "Children and the Elderly: Divergent Paths for American Dependents." *Demography* 19:549–65.

Rimmer, L. 1983. "The Economics of Work and Caring." Pp. 131–47 in *A Labour of Love: Women, Work, and Caring,* edited by J. Finch and D. Groves. Boston: Routledge and Kegan Paul.

Scharlach, A. E. 1987. "Role Strain in Mother-Daughter Relationships in Later Life." *Gerontologist* 27:627–31.

———. 1994. "Caregiving and Employment: Competing or Complementary Roles?" *Gerontologist* 34:378–85.

Schick, F. L. and R. Schick (Eds.). 1994. *Statistical Handbook on Aging Americans.* Phoenix, Arizona: Oryx.

Schneider, B., M. Galper, L. Gottesman, P. Kohn, B. Morrell, L. Staroschik, and L. Sterthous. 1982. *The Channeling Case Management Manual.* Philadelphia: Temple University Press.

Siegel, J. and C. M. Taeuber. 1986. "Demographic Dimensions of An Aging Population." In *Our Aging Society: Paradox and Promise,* edited by A. Pafer and D. L. Bronte. New York: Norton.

Soldo, B. J. and K. G. Manton. 1985. "Health Status and Service Needs of the Oldest Old: Current Patterns and Future Trends." *Milbank Quarterly* 63:286–319.

Spalter-Roth, R. and H. Hartmann. 1990. *Unnecessary Losses: Cost to Americans of the Lack of a Family and Medical Leave.* Washington, DC: Institute for Women's Policy Research.

Stone, R., G. L. Cafferata, and J. Sangl. 1987. "Caregivers of the Frail Elderly: A National Profile." *Gerontologist* 27:616–26.

Tennstedt, S. and J. Gonyea. 1994. "An Agenda for Work and Eldercare Research." *Research on Aging* 16(1):85–108.

Wagner, D. C., M. A. Creedon, J. M. Sasala, and M. B. Neal. 1989. *Eldercare: Designing Effective Responses for the Workplace.* Bridgeport, CT: University of Bridgeport, Center for the Study of Aging.

Washington Business Group on Health. 1995. *The MetLife Study of Employer Costs for Working Caregivers.* Washington, DC: Author.

Watkins, S. C., J. A. Menken, and J. Bongaarts. 1987. "Demographic Foundations of Family Change." *American Sociological Review* 52:346–58.

Weldon, J. 1996. "Locals Slow to Offer Long-Term Care Insurance." *Cincinnati Business Courier,* August 12, p. 3C.

# V

# Summary and Conclusions

# Problems and Prospects for More Effective Integration of Work and Family in the Twenty-First Century 15

Dana Vannoy

Most of the chapters in this collection were originally generated for the conference, *Agenda for the 21st Century Labor Force: Implications of Changing Family Structure, Diversity, and Jobs*, speak to a specific issue of the importance of integrating work and family more thoroughly in our thinking, in our theoretical and practical approaches to innovative social structures, and in our behavior as individuals. The interdependence of economy and family has been the dominant theme in the academic journals focusing on family over the last decade (see Bowen and Pittman 1995:1). Both the conference and this collection have unashamedly had the goal of raising the consciousness of scholars, managers, and community leaders about the need to think of work organizations and families as institutions more thoroughly integrated with one another. Only with this approach can people in the twenty-first century be whole people free from feelings of being divided into work and family selves. This approach can contribute to homes becoming healthier environments in which to live and raise children and work organizations becoming more productive and less wasteful of human resources.

We began this conference project with the idea of addressing five issues highly relevant to social and corporate policy for the next century. These issues include: (1) the need for more families to function well (in response to family instability and its effects for children); (2) the need for new structures of work allowing parents to be employed and raise children (in response to the prevalence of and trend toward dual-earner families); (3) the need for healthy work environments for all (in response to the inevitable, increasing diversity and diminishing civility in some arenas of work); (4) the need for reasonable security or adequate pay for citizens (in response to the developing dual economy and growing poverty); and (5) the need for work for more persons to do in postindustrial society (in response to technological change). Each of these goals depends upon the next in a hierarchical order that suggests the interdependence of institutions. We wanted to recognize and emphasize the ways social structure influences individual orientations, choices, and behaviors—in this case, the way the economic system shapes our lives within families and communities as well as within workplaces.

Public discourse often refers to the need for "balancing" work and family, and scholars of family and the economy often refer to the work/family "interface." Neither word sufficiently conveys the reality of lives in postindustrial society, where most men and women are employed in work organizations outside the home. The two realms are integrated in so many ways that they are better thought of as one systemic whole rather than two competing places for individuals to exist (Friedlander and Delbecq 1996). Because of the economic importance of work for family well-being and the emotional "spill-over" from one setting to the other for individuals (Bowen 1991), the split between the two environments is an artificial one, a legacy of early industrialization when workers for the first time left the home to earn a living. Today human beings, both managers and workers, both men and women, spend much of their lives in work organizations and the remainder of their waking hours tending to the needs of family, home, and community. More often than not, they experience competition occurring between the demands of these two essential realms.

The organization of the modern industrial system has not "caught up" with the reality of most people's lives, nor acknowledged or honored its own potential for creating more reasonable life-styles for most people rather than the extremes of wealth and poverty. The business community seems increasingly driven solely by the profit motive. The demands placed on all levels of workers in capitalist, economic organization are making it more and more difficult for both managers and workers to survive, let alone to have full lives and thrive. Finally, the elimination of many working people may eventually curtail the capacity of the population to consume the goods produced. As technological and social change race on at an ever more rapid pace, it will be up to corporate and community leaders to redirect the priorities of work organizations to benefit the workers as well as to generate profit and capital.

In this summary, I wish to draw attention to two changes that pull together the concerns being reflected in the personal problems of individuals today. They are: (1) *the inclusion of women in the work force and the predominance of dual-earner families,* and (2) *the shift from the predominance of the industrial sector to the predominance of the information sector in the economy.* This second trend is responsible for extensive job loss and what has lately been termed "downsizing." Finally, I want tie these trends to the thoughts of Jeremy Rifkin (1995) about "the end of work." It seems to me that we will soon need to think differently about the significance of paid work, especially as a central criterion for personal worth in the overall scheme of life.

## WOMEN AND DUAL EARNER FAMILIES

As Kathleen Gerson notes in the first chapter of this collection, deeply anchored economic and social changes ensure that both the incorporation of women into the labor force and diversity in family forms are here to stay. In 1995 men accounted for 54 percent of U.S. labor force participants and women for 46 percent. Women are projected to comprise 48 percent in the year 2005. Nearly 60 percent of all women over age sixteen were in the labor force in 1995 (U.S. Department of Labor 1996). Women are still concentrated in low-paying jobs. Nearly three-fourths of employed women are in nonprofessional occupations, and two-thirds of minimum wage workers are adult women. While women have made great strides in becoming entrepreneurs, in 1992 only 6.6 percent of all working women were employed in occupations in which 75 percent or more employed in those jobs were men (National Commission on Working Women 1993).

While women are increasingly employed because of their own need for livelihood and that of their children, as a whole, women have not made great strides toward employment opportunities as rewarding as men's employment opportunities. Families maintained by women had a median income of $17,443 in 1993, while families maintained by men with no wife present had a median income of $26,467. The median income of married couple families was $43,005 (U.S. Department of Labor 1995). In addition, mother-only families have increased dramatically since the 1960s, and now the majority of children can expect to live part of their lives in such a family (McLanahan and Booth 1989). These data underscore the need to open more training and education opportunities to women as well as men.

Because of men's traditional attachments to roles and identities shaped by paid work outside the home and women's attachments to unpaid work inside the home since early industrialization, there have been more mechanisms to help routinize the multiple status obligations of work and family for men (Coser and Rokoff 1974). One of those mechanisms has been the support services of wives. Clearly, a different reality exists today for both men and women, but society has been slow to organize work in ways that recognize the participation of women and men in the labor force at near equal levels. Researches are accumulating to indicate that women's employment has positive outcomes for them, such as delaying marriage and childbirth, greater life satisfaction, and better health (Spitze 1988), and is also a stabilizing force for families (Greenstein 1990). However, research conducted by O'Neill and Greenberger (1994) indicates that only the privileged can comfortably "balance" the commitments of work and family roles. They conclude conditions in which multiple roles enhance each other are not ones to which most people can reasonably aspire today.

Class structure and the varied human capital resources of family members set the stage for how well a family may fare. Then the state of the economy determines the extent to which adequate employment and income are available to people. Finally, employers vary in the extent to which they provide policies and programs that enhance the ability of families to coordinate their work and family demands.

Programs and policies such as family leave, child care, part-time opportunities, and flexible work schedules are significant ways to create a culture of family support. Corporate culture and philosophy powerfully influence the work environment, which in turn affects outcomes at work and at home. For example, Guelzow, Bird, and Koball (1991) found among dual-career couples that men who have flexible work schedules indicate significantly lower marital, parental, and professional stress as well as fewer distress symptoms. Orthner and Pittman (1986) found that perceived organizational support is related both to job commitment and to family support for job commitment. Family support also is directly related to job commitment. Such results suggest that organizational and family support work together to influence job commitment, and, ideally, productivity.

In this volume Singleton has ably spelled out the challenge of being employed and caring for elderly family members, and how flexibility within work organizations may help. This challenge will gain more recognition as the large population of baby-boomers reaches older ages. Raabe describes a study exploring the practicalities of part-time employment in management. Experiments with these kinds of arrangements will be essential as we are to create realistic possibility of carrying out both the necessary caring work and the economically productive work of the society.

## SHIFT TO THE INFORMATION SECTOR

The second social change from the predominance of the industrial sector to that of the service and information sector in the American labor force is directly or indirectly responsible for the more widespread unemployment and growing poverty for some parts of the population. Structural changes in the economy such as the shift from manufacturing to services, declining *real* wages, and increasing inequality create economic distress in the form of employment instability. It is clear that these shifts have negative impact upon marital and family relations and the adjustment and health of children (Voydanoff 1992).

Juliet Schor (1991) reports that American productivity has more than doubled since 1948, meaning that we can produce our 1948 standard of living in less than half the time it took then. However, Americans are working longer hours today than forty years ago. More than 25% of full-time workers are working more than forty-nine hours per week, and the amount of paid vacation time and sick leave has declined over the past two decades.

While many people are out of work, those still holding jobs are working more to compensate for reduced wages and benefits. Companies have eliminated many workers, employing a smaller work force at longer hours thereby saving the costs of additional health and pension benefits. In this collection Wallace has described the pervasiveness of downsizing since 1980, and Perrin has described how this trend has affected community well-being and attitude, even in a city dominated by industrial high-technology such as Rochester, New York. Wallace also provided some analysis of the demand for specific skills in some areas of the economy. This discussion highlights the mismatch between the nature of jobs available and the lack of training and skills of those people without work.

Forty to 50 percent of the unemployed in the United States are functionally illiterate. About a third of job applicants are rejected for lack of basic reading and writing skills, and yet more than half of all new jobs created between 1984 and the year 2000 will require an education beyond high school. The U.S. economy suffers an estimated $140 to $300 billion annual productivity loss traced directly to adult worker illiteracy (Michigan Literacy, Inc., 1994).

Jobs available to women with poor reading and writing skills are the lowest paying jobs in the economy—for example, cafeteria workers, housekeepers, health aids, sewing machine operators. And of the 3.8 million mothers on AFDC, 44 percent have less than a high school education. Thirty-eight percent have completed high school, and 19 percent have had some college (Census Release 1995).

These kinds of data underscore the importance of basic skills education. The Farkas et al. chapter in this volume describes a concrete approach to preparing future generations for the highly skilled labor force that will be required. More work will need to be done with those who have already reached adult ages. Companies are likely to train employees in job-specific skills, but not basic skills. Yet, we know that adult student reading scores improve one grade level with thirty-five hours of tutoring (Kerka 1989), and basic skills provide the essential base for further training.

If this challenge is not embraced we face greater social problems as more and more individuals find themselves economically irrelevant with no way to earn a legitimate income to support their own survival. Increasing unemployment is leading to a rise in crime and violence, and we know there is also a correlation between growing wage inequality and increased criminal activity (Merva and Fowles 1992). It is not surprising that rising unemployment and loss of hope for a better future turn youth to a life of crime and violence.

On the one hand we have some people working much more and for less—dual-earner families struggling to maintain jobs and a home life. On the other hand, we have some people not working at all—eliminated as players in the economy. According to Jeremy Rifkin (1995:216) the third industrial revolution throws into question some cherished ideas about the meaning of progress. For those with power in the economic system progress may mean unlimited production, rising consumption, faster breakthroughs in technology, integrated markets, and more instant gratification. For others the triumph of technology has made them redundant, and there is a sense of the world passing them by. They are outcasts in the new global village.

The very concept of work is at issue. Much formal work has passed from people to machines. Our social agreements have been based on human beings selling their labor as a commodity in the open marketplace. We are fast approaching a different reality. I suggest that the sooner we come to grips with the new future, the better. It seems to me that the same kind of solutions that address the second issue I have addressed (the shift from industrial to information sectors) will be solutions for the problems posed by the first issue (the participation of both men and women in the workplace and the resultant concerns about time for family life) and vice versa.

Rifkin (1995:217) suggests two actions as important. The first is that productivity gains resulting from new labor-saving technologies be shared with the millions of working people, not only those in command. This must involve increases in salaries and wages in order to ensure an equitable distribution of the fruits of economic progress and a public able to purchase. It must also involve reductions in the number of hours worked as a means of sharing work. The four day work week and the curtailment of overtime are simple measures to help provide decent wages and benefits to more people.

The second action is focusing greater attention on "the third sector"—the nonmarket economy or the social economy of the nation. The shrinking of mass employment in the formal market economy and the reduction of government spending in the public sector will necessitate greater attention to the social economy to address personal and societal needs no longer addressed by the market or the government. This will involve partial transfer of personal loyalties and commitments on the part of individuals away from the first two sectors to the informal, social economy; however, these activities can provide a much needed alternative source of identity and personal worth for individuals. The choice might be described as *unemployment* (idleness and feelings of irrelevancy) or *leisure activity* (voluntary participation in social activities with a sense of personal worth).

Rifkin (1995:240) believes opportunity exists to harness the unused labor of millions to constructive tasks outside both the private and public sectors. These activities can create a third force that flourishes independently. They may be directed toward rebuilding local communities, social services, health care, education, research, the arts, home building, religion, advocacy, community service, assisting the elderly, assisting the handicapped, or serving as foster parents. Interestingly, the assets of the third sector now equal nearly half of those of the federal government (O'Neill 1989). The government might consider providing a "social wage" as an alternative to welfare and benefits for those permanently unemployed. Such work in the nonprofit sector would help not only the recipients but also the communities in which their labor is used (Rifkin 1995:258).

It is terribly important that we as social scientists and community and corporate leaders do not reify social structure in our hearts, minds or actions. Although social forces often have a life of their own, as individuals we are not passive agents totally at the mercy of the influences of broader social milieu. As men and women, as parents, workers, and managers, we have the capacity to change the structures in which we live and to create mechanisms that better serve our human needs and provide for a just society.

## REFERENCES


Bowen, G. L. 1991. *Navigating the Marital Journey. MAP: A Corporate Support Program for Couples.* New York: Praeger.

Bowen, G. L. and J. F. Pittman. 1995. *The Work & Family Interface: Toward a Contextual Effects Perspective.* Minneapolis, MN: National Council of Family Relations.

*Census Release AFDC Recipients Report.* 1995. Washington, DC: U.S. Census Bureau (on-line). Available at Pio@census.gov (March 3)

Coser, R. L. and G. Rokoff. 1974. "Women in the Occupational World: Social Disruption and Conflict." Pp. 490–511 in *The family: Its structures and functions,* edited by R. L. Coser. New York: St. Martin's.

Friedlander, F. and A. Delbecq. 1996. "The Reciprocity of Work Life and Home Life." Paper presented at the *Agenda for the 21st Century Labor Force Conference,* Cincinnati, OH.

Greenstein, T. N. 1990. "Marital Disruption and the Employment of Married Women." *Journal of Marriage and the Family* 52:657–76.

Guelzow, M. G., G. W. Bird, and E. H. Koball. 1991. "An Exploratory Path Analysis of the Stress Process for Dual-Career Men and Women." *Journal of Marriage and the Family* 53:151–64.

Kerka, S. 1989. *Women, Work and Literacy.* Columbus OH: ERIC Clearinghouse on Adult, Career, and Vocational Education.

McLanahan, S. and Booth, K. 1989. "Mother-Only Families: Problems, Prospects, and Politics." *Journal of Marriage and the Family* 51:557–80.

Merva, M. and R. Fowles. 1992. *Effects of Diminished Economic Opportunities on Social Stress: Heart Attacks, Strokes and Crime.* Washington, DC: Economic Policy Institute.

Michigan Literacy, Inc. 1994. *Literacy in the United States: 50 Facts.* Lansing: Library of Michigan.

National Commission on Working Women of Wider Opportunities for Women. 1993. *Women and Nontraditional Work.* Washington, DC: Author.

O'Neill, M. 1989. *The Third America: The Emergence of the Nonprofit Sector in the United States.* San Francisco: Jossey-Bass.

O'Neill, R. and E. Greenberger. 1994. "Patterns of Commitment to Work and Parenting: Implications for Role Strain." *Journal of Marriage and the Family* 56:101–12.

Orthner, D. K. and J. F. Pittman. 1986. "Family Contributions to Work Commitment." *Journal of Marriage and the Family* 48:573–81.

Rifkin, Jeremy. 1995. *The End of Work.* New York: G.P. Putnam's Sons.

Schor, J. 1991. *The Overworked American: The Unexpected Decline of Leisure.* New York: Basic Books.

Spitze, G. 1988. "Women's Employment and Family Relations." *Journal of Marriage and the Family* 50:595–618.

U.S. Department of Labor, Women's Bureau. 1995. *Twenty Facts on Working Women,* No. 95-1. Washington, DC: Author.

———. 1996. *Twenty Facts on Working Women,* No. 96-2. Washington, DC: Author.

Voydanoff, P. 1992. "Economic Distress and Family Relations: A Review of the Eighties." *Journal of Marriage and the Family* 52:1099–1115.

# Index